MW01224957

1969
and
Then Some

A MEMOIR OF ROMANCE, MOTORCYCLES, AND LINGERING FLASHBACKS OF A GOLDEN AGE

BY ROBERT WINTNER

YUCCA

Copyright © 2014 by Robert Wintner

All rights reserved. No part of this book may be reproduced in any manner without the express written consent of the publisher, except in the case of brief excerpts in critical reviews or articles. All inquiries should be addressed to Yucca Publishing, 307 West 36th Street, 11th Floor, New York, NY 10018.

Yucca Publishing books may be purchased in bulk at special discounts for sales promotion, corporate gifts, fund-raising, or educational purposes. Special editions can also be created to specifications. For details, contact the Special Sales Department, Yucca Publishing, 307 West 36th Street, 11th Floor, New York, NY 10018 or yucca@skyhorsepublishing.com.

Yucca Publishing® is an imprint of Skyhorse Publishing, Inc.®, a Delaware corporation.

Parts of the chapter entitled "Over the Mountains and Into the Sea" first appeared in *Sports Illustrated Magazine*.

Visit our website at www.yuccapub.com.

10 9 8 7 6 5 4 3 2 1

Library of Congress Cataloging-in-Publication Data is available on file.

Cover design by Yucca Publishing

Print ISBN: 978-1-63158-019-2
Ebook ISBN: 978-1-63158-021-5

Printed in the United States of America

For Paul Kohman, who has been experienced.

Were You There?
Sir, Really?

HAPPINESS RUNS IN *a circular motion*; Donovan sang that, and I believe it. Good times come and go and change in nature over the years. We age and season and enjoy life as we can.

But if we isolate the old, golden glow of endless horizons and eternal youth, we may more easily recall Sly Stone's assurance at a hundred ten decibels that

> *I want to*
> *I want to*
> *I want to take you haaah-yer,*

On that note we may hark to an era more unique than your average once-in-a-lifetime. Who knows when so much fun will happen again?

The warmth lingers. Sounds echo down the decades. Single frames of it clarify concepts like doubtlessness, wanderlust and a sense of well-being. They seem so indefinite now, after so many laps around the track and so much happiness come and gone and come again and gone again. Life was full and fuller then, with good vibrations seeming involuntary as breath or pulse. Never before and not since then have a handful of seasons so exquisitely defined the difference between right and wrong. With the gift of vision we saw, sensed and savored the laughably clear distinction between the profit motive and greed, between truth and propaganda, between national interest and defense contractors, between democracy and a war of attrition, between a lovely cloud of smoke and smoke up the collective ass, between a lovely cloud of smoke and napalm, between a lovely cloud of smoke and the phantoms of security, complacency and atrophy. Sustained on smoke—stoned to the gills and then some—we saw, we felt, we knew, some of us. Others observed, apart, sticking a left foot in, pulling a left foot out, but not quite jumping to the full Hokey Pokey. From those same sidelines they still observe, some with superiority, confirmed by success.

Tom Brokaw, a cultural clarion claiming that the WWII years framed the best generation, regretted "the 60s" as a lost opportunity. He dismissed the idealism of "the 60s" as a failed promise, a fantasy unrealized and unworkable in the world at large. Tom Brokaw aired a TV special called "The 60s" with personal recollection of "what it was like." He'd been alive at the time, and he recalled sanguinely his young adulthood in "the 60s," when his hair touched his ears, and bell-bottom pants and a turtleneck were typical for a walk down to the park with his young kids. At the park others tended their kids in bell-bottoms and period accoutrement. Tom Brokaw from Indiana, grounded by heartland values from a bastion of Republican virtue, delivered the news nightly for years with competent credibility, so his opinion would be hard to refute. But I hail from Hoosierville too, and I'm here to tell you: both Tom and his kids missed the best part of it—missed the part best defined by no definition, an anarchy of intent and a mission to more fully penetrate the mystical meaning of fun as we knew it. Fun wasn't part of life; fun was all of life.

Of course WWII was about as great a war to fight as ever could be. Could an enemy rouse any more fervor than the Nazis?

Yet hardly a generation after "the best generation" came another mass fervor against another enemy as formidable and sinister as the Nazis, and that enemy was war itself. For the first time in the history of man and women a generation sang out in harmony for harmony. *Hell no, we won't go.*

War had changed. We had no Nazis. We had Johnson, Nixon, Westmoreland and Dow Chemical urging war to protect a way of life. The nation changed, because it wasn't our way of life and *we don't want your dirty war*. Maybe Old Mom, a bona fide best generation gal with pinpoint recall on those years of denial in Western Europe, on the Wehrmacht backing into Poland like the butt-end recoil of a 12-guage shotgun, on the sneak-attack bombing of Pearl Harbor, on the Viche Government and the resistance, the struggles from England to North Africa, D-Day and the Beach at Normandy, the Manhattan Project, Enola Gay and oh, my God, the songs, said it best of her sons on the subject of military service in Vietnam: "Oh, you're going to Viet Nam. Over my dead body you're going."

Old Mom, patriotic as anyone from her generation, also knew a thing or two about fleecing a flatlander, which is what the Johnson, Nixon, Westmoreland juggernaut felt like to her in the heart of the heartland. The 60s legacy was that war is over. That legacy has since been lost, because the military/industrial complex realized that the Selective Service Draft beat them—beat them in the streets, beat them on the airwaves, in the schools, the homes and watering holes around the nation. The m/i complex cannot force peaceable, over-educated people to fight a war of resource allocation with no share of the dividends. Volunteers must do the fighting for the sheer love of battle and for national fervor. And we as a culture must praise those volunteers as heroes, or, short of praising our soldiers, we must stay mum when cultural leaders praise them. And so they do, and we do too. War wages on with fewer complaints.

Meanwhile, Tom Brokaw, a homespun fellow in a turtleneck and bell-bottoms, walked his kids to the park in "the 60s," hardly oblivious to the world at large. But by making personal selections in his perceptive life, he missed the 60s. No shame there, with a dynamic career in broadcast news to consider.

Sly Stone was another homespun fellow but from the other side of town. Sly woke the crowd with the cutting edge of revolutionary good taste. Sly got down and let it rip. He said it all, on his game with an irrepressible downbeat on a funky lyric for the ages. Sly Stone never shared billing with John Denver, who stood on a stage in a mop-top to yell, "Far out!" Sly Stone felt connected to the central nervous system while John Denver probed and Tom Brokaw watched. Everything was everything, but how could such disparate parts cohere? Ah, yes: and the doobie's red glare, the thoughts bursting in air, gave goofs through the night, and we needed more beer. Paradox prevailed in chaotic times.

Tom Brokaw seemed outside the action, yet Dick Nixon was in it. Tom Brokaw wore a turtleneck as seen on Bobby Kennedy in a radical fashion statement, indicating Brokaw's willingness to dabble in daring—adding bell-bottoms didn't mean shit, because department stores overflowed with 60s ornamentation once marijuana hit the suburbs; once TV was rife with reefer wry humor and everybody wanted to be hip. Pat Boone doused *Tutti Frutti* with corn syrup, turning Little Richard's original classic from funk and soul to shit with sugar on top. Self-respecting white kids knew little Richard and resented the theft. Dick Nixon loved Pat Boone and lunched alone on cottage cheese and ketchup, transcending the munchies with perversion.

Riptides made for differences and cultural rift both general and personal, delineating sides. Tom Brokaw hit the park in timely style, reflecting awareness or hip taste. At another park down the street or cross-town, others gathered in ragtag consensus, smoking joints, commiserating on strategy and taking solace in the music, wondering along with one lyric or another where America as a concept had gone to, asking if it still cared for its sons and daughters, asking if it could sense the monster. Or had the monster already prevailed?

The Monster voiced the harsh sentiment and growing divide. No candidate could easily embrace a lyric that questions the continuing legitimacy of the government, and the cultural rift still festers. Now down to septic level and festering worse than a faulty drain field, the two-party system is stymied. Problems persist through power grabs and shit slinging until one party fails. Self-righteous buttholes still spew dogma that you will accept or be damned. Christian standards will determine family values or you will be deemed subversive and damned again. They did it in the 60s—and the 50s too.

The good news is that no other culture in history was ever more ready to self-efface, to find truth in humor than in the U.S.A. *The Monster* touched a nerve for poignancy. Creedence Clearwater Revival touched a different nerve on a rockabilly downbeat for equal effect by poking fun at the culprits.

Who was the silver-spooned draft dodger that inspired *Fortunate Son*? Just look: two ranking political families with draft age sons qualified, both sons fortunate, silver-spooned, as it were. Both sons would in time be candidates for the Presidency of the United States of America. Both would dodge military service in Vietnam by sleight-of-hand maneuvers, with Daddy on the phone for some well-placed calls to gatekeepers with needs of their own.

The guys hungry for battle along with the poor dumb fucks who got snookered fought that war. Meanwhile, Al Gore and George W. Bush were getting drunk and snorting cocaine…

Wait a minute. Al Gore was never a lush and didn't snort cocaine and served in the military, and his father, Senator Al Gore, Sr., was a leading critic of that war. Well, hell…

What was the take away? It seemed obvious: you needed some Steppenwolf to balance your Creedence according to the mood of the hour. Because the mood could change from dead serious to rock out—to acid blues—Ooh! Get some Moody Blues too, because the cosmic truth was so simply stated in a lyric revealing that Timothy Leary was not dead but merely outside—outside conventional behavior, society and reality, like we could be, should be, would be—looking in.

Because getting the music right could affirm faith that the correct park had been found.

The 60s and the Universe turned in on themselves to reveal the inner core in layered patterns. Frank Zappa, Janis, Jimi—hell, Captain Beefheart, Country Joe, Joe Cocker, the Stones, Beatles, Buffalo Springfield, America, Steely Dan, Quicksilver and on and on gave voice to the insurrection, affirming the common view. Buddy Miles and Mike Bloomfield banged drums and steel guitars like blacksmiths on anvils, pounding things back to the truth. *The Killing Floor* came out in '65 as a Howlin' Wolf blues ballad set in the meat-packing district of Chicago, meant as analogy to Howlin' Wolf's love predicament. He was the meat, and romance kept butchering him no matter what he did.

When reality got inappropriately touched by grown men who should have known better, it was up to voices in the wilderness of the 60s to cry out, even though the grown men had warned that this little event should not be mentioned to anyone. The United States of America waged a war of massive attrition for the benefit of certain people who did not fight that war.

Electric Flag covered *The Killing Floor* in '68, beginning the cut with Lyndon Johnson:

> *"I speak tonight for the dignity of man,*
> *and the (heavy guitar down stroke) destiny of mankind..."*

Next came audience laughter—Lyndon Johnson had just carpet-bombed Hanoi to prove a point and shorten the war with a knockout punch. Next came Bloomfield's guitar hard charging a different kind of cavalry with Buddy Miles on drums. The slaughterhouse was ambient. We were in line for a killing down on the floor.

Revolutions in Iran, Tunisia, Egypt, Yemen, Libya and Syria over forty years later rose against other despots with social networking as the great unifier. People hit the streets to stand up, shout out and fight for change.

In the 60s it was smoke and music lifting spirits, building momentum and rising to life as it's rarely been lived. Talk about Ethernet; we were on the airwaves, wireless, tuned in.

A turtleneck and bell-bottoms? Are you for real?

We Have Ignition and…

IT DID NOT begin on New Year's Eve of '69. By then we were well into the essence of the thing, confident of scratch in all four gears, even as traction became metaphysical, an esoteric concept to ponder in still life. But that night shines with everlasting light.

A dozen of us, give or take a few comers and goers through the evening, had gathered at Marcia Sacks' and Betty Boop's place to celebrate the new decade with spaghetti and LSD. Marcia, our hostess for the evening, was old hat on the psychedelic scene, tripping with moderate frequency over the previous few years. She'd prepared a great, hardy sauce. A dozen hits of acid wasn't so easy to come by in one fell swoop in mid-Missouri, but we began a few days out, so by sundown on the 31st we had enough to go around—purple microdots, pink barrels, Owsleys, orange sunshine and blotters—with a single electric neon Jesus and a few odd extras in case of late arrivals or acid malfunction.

Betty was gone, off to Boston to visit her fiancée. That was a certain tender subject for me, since she'd been my main squeeze since Halloween, and sixty days was a stretch of many moons in college time, in the heart of the sexual revolution. Bona fide beautiful and acutely intelligent in her personal, parochial way, Betty seemed less than stable on the emotional front, even skittish at times. She wanted acceptance as something other than a spectacular beauty. She craved recognition for her wit, insight and clever quips instead of her perfect figure. Physical self-consciousness was compounded for her in those days of wild hair and hippy clothes. Betty was perfect and couldn't help it. Worse yet was her impending marriage to a dolt she did not love but would marry anyway because he profiled so suitably. Her parents approved of the beau, and so she went along. Going along with the parental program, she did not fit in and could not find the words to rationalize such a wrong path. Oh, she tried. She got stuck on self-incrimination every time. The phrase still in its germinal phase was *copping out*—trading the adventurous prospects before us for the same sameness smothering our parents in the life-stifling suburbs. Maybe her last ditch bid for redemption was telling me matter-of-factly that she would cancel her holiday visit to Boston and cancel her engagement too, if I'd only say the word. She batted her big brown eyes and licked her lips to show how much she liked me, and I think she did like me and would have liked me without inclusion at last in a greater whole that she sorely wanted to call her own. Betty craved the outside but just couldn't fit in.

Of course her name wasn't really Betty Boop; I called her that because she stole my heart on a single beat, just like her namesake did when I was eight. I don't remember which Betty Boop cartoon crushed me in a love embrace, whether it was Betty running for President or merely saying *booby dooby dooby doop, boo boo be doop!* I learned why love leads to marriage in that moment, falling hopelessly head over heels in love with Betty Boop. I planned to marry a cartoon character. I was only eight but it didn't matter, because she was everything. I recall with relish that George Coleman's little brother experienced similar pangs and announced *his* intention of marrying Betty Boop. George's little brother wasn't even seven but was smart enough to back off when I told him, "Forget it, you little shit. She's mine. *I'm* marrying Betty Boop." How did I know such foul language at that tender age? Easy: *you little shit* was my sister's nickname for me; without being entirely hateful it conveyed thorough revulsion.

Betty Boop the cartoon character had an oversized head surrounded by spit curls and a quaint body that was usually encased in a one-piece swimsuit. Betty Boop my unlikely squeeze who was engaged to be married to an egghead Ivy-Leaguer, wore her auburn hair long and silky smooth, flowing to her shoulders and down her back, which, like her front, bottom and sides, was as quaint as Betty Boop's. To say I was smitten would be an understatement. Events occurred too quickly for thorough assessment, but that would have been crazy anyway.

My college Betty was a profile in cameo femininity, an intellect with limited common sense, and a generally nice person yearning to fit in with a crowd in synchronous convergence, in high times as a defense against the real times. In our Never Never Land, reality took a holiday. Youth was not then wasted on the young; it was met with an old spirit of political conviction—of love, trust, understanding and lust.

I helped her with the sensible part too. But nah, I did not take her up on her suggestion of making her a better offer, or even saying the word, or offering encouragement for herself and me as an item in any way. For starters, I had nothing to offer—no money, no prospects, no nothing but youth and the wits, so far, to survive. These were impressive assets in the neighborhood but hardly of value in an Ivy League world. Even as we spoke or engaged in any exchange, her soon-to-be husband was establishing friendships and contacts that would form a network to secure his place in the financial, intellectual, social hierarchy of America. We could only speculate on prospects for my ilk. The future shaped up like an extended Halloween, with buccaneers, cowboys, Indians, Vikings and artists. My non-Ivy future could be evaluated by the contents of my pockets, which in those days barely cleared the grocery store and the landlord.

Of course that's a simplification. The youth and wits to survive so far were no small or casual assets. We lived with a forced military draft into an undeclared jungle war halfway around the world. Survival assets were applied more often and specifically than the college degree would ever be brought to bear on the be-all challenge of those days: avoiding that draft. It was a full-time job, no less consequential than looking both ways before crossing the street or not stepping off the path that ran along the cliff edge. The student deferment was good for four years, if you made grades.

Besides those practical considerations, Betty was engaged to a goof and was willing to marry him despite his deficiencies of soul, humor and spirit. Why? Because he profiled "correct" in her parents' view of the world. Because he aspired to a few more years of grad school and then a few decades on a campus, where he would teach something soft. Betty would be happy on a campus, thinking, sharing her thoughts with others, reading books and continuing to develop new thoughts.

Besides all that, I was short on words in those days. I didn't need as many words in those days, and in this case my verbal efficiency went to 100%; I said nothing.

Besides that, I kept two sets of books on the personal value issue. In one set, I was broke. In the other set I had a whole world in front of me with its exotic potential, foreign shores and years of adventures. This seemed painfully obvious to our friends and to me. I loved Betty, loved her sparkling eyes, her infrequent but incisive wit, her generosity in what counts most to a young man and every square centimeter of her perfect physical self. I feared my own arrogance, casually dismissing such beauty, but I frankly anticipated a juicy population of incredible women in the coming years. Besides that, Betty Boop would be back from Boston in a week and wouldn't leave again to be married until June. Plenty of time.

Call me egregiously practical, but everyone tacitly agreed that it was for the best, that Betty was not a good candidate for spaghetti and acid. Too flighty, skittish, vulnerable and inexperienced, unlike us seasoned veterans, she was far better off discussing things in Boston. I tried to put her out of my mind.

At that age in those golden years we didn't ponder too much for too long. We rather watched a gray, dim dusk dip to near freezing and turn dark—never mind; we had gathered in a huge, old house, Marcia's house, with great good friends and spaghetti on hand, with a sumptuous sauce, abundant wine and reefer to get us started. The perfect repast filled us up and helped quell the giddy anticipation that verged on anxiety. On that new frontier, we were the modern pioneers. Failure to grasp that imagery indicates absence from that moment in time. Full of laughter, good cheer, optimism and blithe spirit, we were poised to embark on a journey to the cosmos in mere minutes, like our brethren who'd landed on the moon only five months prior. They required a space ship and years of planning and a million details boiled down to perfection with technical formality that allowed no error, none. We, on the other hand needed only spaghetti, wine, reefer, good friends, LSD and a whole new decade to usher in with flourish, with unbelievable insight and fun. Just as ground control instructed Major Tom to take his protein pills and put his helmet on, we donned our game faces and popped our little space pills. Man, David Bowie was a gas, in the groove and right on. Who couldn't feel it?

The easy buzz and dulled edge of the reefer and wine and a hot meal soon gave way to ignition and liftoff in variable succession. The group gained orbital speed, one after another or sometimes in twos and threes. Started on the journey is what we got, most of us, in forty-five or ninety minutes. Yet I remained sated and stoned on the launch pad. I thought I'd eaten too much spaghetti, smothering the drug in pasta. The snow began falling, little, wet granules plunking along the windowsills like lunar modules plunking into the sea.

After two hours, I thought I'd drawn a dud.

Marcia suggested another hit, underscoring her most admirable strength, which wasn't her moderation in all things but rather her coherence and ability to speak clearly while tripping madly.

I declined; what if it came on along with the first hit?

Marcia giggled, "So? You took two hits."

But no. I wasn't willing to risk Mach V. I'd seen those who took multiple hits. Some of them handled it well.

After three hours I decided to go home. So I got up from the sofa and went to the door to wrap myself in my rig. In those days it was a full-length overcoat and top hat from Goodwill along with a seven-foot muffler knitted by Old Mom, though she couldn't see the need for seven feet of it. I explained that I needed to dress for success. Ah, success: now that she understood. Under the coat were bell-bottom jeans, a ruffled tuxedo shirt and a brown vest with keyhole piping above and below the buttonholes in gold brocade to match the epaulet fringe and needlepoint arabesques. I'd bought most of those things at Goodwill, which wasn't hip in those days, unless you were avant-funk and knew what to look for. I got the vest the previous summer at a London flea market. I got the boots in Amsterdam for eight bucks, unbelievably cool boots with round toes instead of club toes like everyone else's Dingos, which set me apart and helped immensely with identity, because the boots reflected the soul and more, what in later decades would be called image, and then values. How could a young man walk the earth without the right boots?

I opened the door to see that the snowflakes had swelled to dreamy proportion—big, fluffy flakes plummeting softly as paratroopers, and a blanket already a few inches thick covered the yard, the street and the trees. The flakes zigzagged earthward on no breeze, infusing the stillness with a metronomic yet overlapping pulse that strained, nay, insisted on life, even as snow was a harbinger of Death in D.H. Lawrence's *The Fox*, read only recently for personal edification; school was such a waste of time.

But wait.

This was life such as a hatchling might sense on its first stirring within the shell. The air felt less chilled than at sundown. It looked like the right time for a stroll, given the brisk stillness and solitary brilliance of the night. I opened the door and felt refreshed, stepping from the boisterous indoor atmosphere of friends tripping on rock and roll into a night of luminous darkness...

But then Marcia, the perfect hostess for altered realities, touched me sweetly. I turned to her smile and could plainly see an original spark of love in her lovely smiling eyes as she asked where I was off to. I shrugged. She could see that I hadn't achieved ignition, much less blast off. So she advised that I come back in and sit on the sofa and relax, because it was New Year's Eve, and love was all around us, and because she had a special surprise, and besides all that, Ray Haney would arrive in no time with a baggy full of acid, uncapped. Ray had called to ask if we could help him cap his acid—to put the loose powder into the empty gelatin capsules, by hand, four hundred hits of it, give or take. And to think how we'd scrambled to round up a measly baker's dozen.

It just goes to show you. Anyway, Ray was offering samples, in case anyone needed a sample, in case anyone might want to check out '71, '72 or '99 while we were at it. What a laugh. What a goof. Yet we took his meaning.

So I went back in, de-rigged and sat back on the sofa, resigned to a New Year's Eve of love all around us, though for me it would be squeezeless and tripless. Maybe it was a first lesson in letting go of that which is desired most and that which is desired second most. In a minute or two I noticed an odd quirk in the reality/cosmic interface.

Marcia's surprise was Led Zeppelin II, which she laid into place and carefully lowered the needle to the groove—

Led Zeppelin II?

You got Led Zeppelin II? Never mind that it was fifteen bucks, which was nearly half my share of the rent back then. It was brand new, out only a month or two and plain unavailable in the heartland till Marcia batted her baby blues at just the right dude who worked for this amazing radio station—FM—where they played real music and had hardly any commercials and none of that Top 40 pop crap. This dude scored advance copies all the time, including Led Zeppelin II! And he gave it to Marcia! Sure, he wanted to ball her. We were okay with that, considering the offer. Most of us had only heard about Led Zeppelin's second album and that it was even better than the first.

Even better?

Oh, right. But the Chosen Few who actually heard it had soberly confirmed.

A righteous moment of silence ensued as the record spun under the needle's sibilance that bolted into prayer, such as it was:

You need toolin',
Baby I'm not foolin'.
I'm gonna send you…back to schoolin'…

Bedom bedom Bomp! On first blush, first gasp, first absorption of first sound waves we knew it was a groove for the ages, not to mention the moment, which would linger in history forever as a moment eternal, and so it was, perfectly synchronizing time and place and mood and love and, yes, the feeling. The words floated out of the box and across the room at eye level, visibly readable in their own talk bubble, and I read along as I clearly heard them—but it wasn't really hearing; it was absorbing, assimilating into all as all accepted as everything—this was the osmosis I'd declined to pay attention to in biology but at that moment comprehended as if…as if sound waves were nice but not necessary, because this was meaning conjoining with being and yes, I was off.

And so it is, as few moments achieve.

Before you could say downward spiraling vortex, I was way off, then more off and offer and offer, till Kenny Visser offered a cross check from a far corner of the room, the town, the Universe, giggling and calling out from his perch on the edge of the double helix of that eternal moment. Nose pressed to Marcia's goldfish bowl, he grinned. Our viewpoints intersected much as two trekkers pass on wilderness trails on either side of an abyss high in the Himalayas. Eight feet and eons away, on his knees, he called across the canyon, "What ho?"

"Ho?"

In mellifluous inquiry he asked, "Is life so short that you have no time to snuggle with a snail?"

It hadn't seemed so short, and he wasn't actually snuggling with a snail. He was wiping nose grease on the fishbowl, and this exchange seemed longer than life to date, what with third stage boosters kicking in, just as those big fucking canisters from the second stage fizzled out and fell away slo-mo with the fundamental stabilizers fibrillating on all seams.

Oh, things were cracking up.

I lay back on the sofa to fasten the figurative seatbelt, because seasoned acidnauts knew that blasting through the nowheresphere will test a system's integrity every time, and that gyroscopic fortitude requires the vortex to spiral upward and not downward at all costs—or nearly all costs. I mean, be real. If you compound the challenges of quantum physics with the fundamental absence of a viable steering mechanism in deep space and no viable coordinates, like left, right, up and down, then navigation will default to spirit, to mood, to raw outlook, which must not look down. Not down. But up. Up, up, up.

Wait a minute. You said no up or down.

Yes! I didn't mean *that* up and down, you simp! I meant the ultimate up or down, the one emanating from the core.

Well, the core seemed accessible enough…

Fuck me! She suggested two hits!

But then the sofa needed nailing to the floor and the last fucking thing in the world I was up for was finding a hammer and nails. And straps, because we'd need some fucking straps, me and the sofa.

And the hammer. And nails. Kenny Visser called over his shoulder, "You gotta try this, man."

But I couldn't very well try anything with everything trying me—at once. In two shakes I was miraculously back up at the door and re-rigged. Did I say two? Make that one, or maybe a half, or a quarter. Eighth, sixteenth, thirty-second, sixty-fourth, one-twenty-eighth.

Chh. Chhhh. We interrupt this reality to revisit a specific moment from some years prior, in which Mr. Grayson asks an eighth grade science class: if a frog sits in the center of your desk and jumps halfway to the edge, how long will it take the frog to jump off. Some kids wave their hands madly, wanting to know the desk dimensions, as if it's a trick question.

But I know that it's no trick. The frog will never go over.

Mr. Grayson sees me staring obliquely at the self-satisfying answer, and he grants me an equally sublime smile before turning to the blackboard.

Drawing a square with equal sides, he labels each side as two units in length. He then connects two opposite corners with a diagonal line and turns back to the class with the easy task: write down the square root of two.

Doreen Gaunch was an anxious, straight-A girl with zits and thick, black glasses who would one day snatch an exotic beetle making the rounds for show and tell and eat it in one fell pop and crunch and then burst into tears. But that was later. In the moment she blurted that the square root of two is an infinite number and cannot be written.

I smiled again on the right side of knowing and assured Mr. Grayson that he had written the square root of two in its obvious entirety by connecting the two opposite corners of a square measuring two equal units on all sides.

Mr. Grayson nodded slowly. The rest of the class faded to green with envy, and like a punk not satisfied with a clear victory, I informed my dumbfounded audience that the frog would eventually fall asleep and teeter off the desk. An isolated laugh or two rounded my comedic moment as Mr. Grayson gazed at a plane of opposing logic. He seemed pleased with company at the summit with whom to enjoy the view. Mr. Pride, a dull, gray man obsessed with precision, gave me a C in Algebra and counseled that such a failure to give a shit, I mean care, could only predict the rest of life. Grayson was good for an A and a nod.

What?

Did I think something? I couldn't be sure, though the next frame arrived on fast forward to a few frames up in full stride—what we called trucking—headed into town in the snow, tripping way too hard but fairly fending the heebie jeebies with physical movement that felt like the antidote for mental movement, which was over the top. No, not an antidote but a compensation. That was it, the balance of the thing, in which success was easily measured in a left, right, left as necessary, which might be forever or the rest of this night or life, whichever came first.

I blinked to the inside lane as coming up alongside trucked Kenny Visser, his grin undiminished, pumping energy into his step with no as-if about it. He summed up the evening, the spaghetti and wine, the love all around us, the snails and snuggles, the snow and varying planes of reality in a word: "Man."

"Yeah."

Monosyllabic dialogue often indicates slang or pidgin, limited brainpower, an under-funded educational system or inbreeding. This was none of those; we were university students, a state university best known for animal husbandry, but still. Our communication was not minimal but vast, encompassing reality from molecular outward in layers with ready access to the original electrical synapse at the source of all life. What arced between us was not a short circuit but a pulse we shared with everything. Once stabilized at orbital altitude and velocity, we saw, we felt, we understood.

Many people seek meaning in middle age, as perspective changes between the beginning and the end, asking what might survive. Some people meditate and in time can empty the vessel, still the pond's surface, watch thoughts fly away like birds. These images help free the mind, opening it to essence. Essence is common in nature; say in a cat absorbing sunbeams, or a dog with his head out the window, or a bird singing. Sweet being can arrive, with no thoughts to disturb it.

The 60s were a struggle defined by war and a nation divided—and by essence. Drugs are easily discounted, but they took us within, to see what might be.

Kenny and I made it into town and ducked into a pizza parlor to warm up and maybe get something to eat. But we left in short order when a large pepperoni purple and flowing yellow pizza went to extra large and then jumbo and on to industrial megalith and finally *Godzilla!* The monster pizza rose up on dinosaur feet and roared. We gasped and ran as it chased us out and down the street. A hallucination? Maybe. But I saw it. Kenny saw it, and the converse of universal light is the other. A friend on a trip can help keep things light; we laughed like hyenas comparing details down to its curly eyelashes and nose pustules and the snot flecks dangling from the corners of its mouth. And what must have been a painful cavity in its third incisor that likely caused the bad breath too.

We needed more wine or beer or something to take the edge off, but we dasn't go back indoors in public—back among those who hadn't learned that love is all around us. So we came up with the perfect solution, to head back to Marcia's house for a joint.

Hardly two miles out, Marcia's house would have been a walk in the basil, had not a GTO pulled over just ahead and waited on the snow-drifted shoulder, its throaty 389 ca-chug, ca-chugging in baritone exhalation. Kenny mimed the super car as one more element to conjoin. The door swung open on two women heavily clad and introducing themselves as Janis Joplin and Grace Slick.

"Get in," Grace said. So we did. We didn't really think they were rock stars, but then we couldn't be too sure. Mid-Missouri was full of surprises in those days. They drove us twenty miles down the road to a trailer park in Kingdom City, where their roommate Queenie, another female in XXXL, lay sprawled impatiently on her massive threadbare sofa, awaiting her pizza and beer. Grace and Janis set the box on Queenie's belly. Queenie raised the lid to reveal the glop, no longer steaming.

Kenny gasped, "You caught it!"

It lay there on Queenie, congealing in its death throes. He and I glanced at each other and giggled at prospects of the pizza queen devouring the pizza. We feared another hyena round that would render us helpless among big, trailer-park women.

Queenie caught us snickering and cried out, "Balls, cried the queen! If I had 'um I'd be king!" The trailer wasn't at all like Marcia's place. Both places were tattered, but the trailer was brightly lit and slovenly, an example of the emerging phrase, *trailer trash*. It reflected none of the Age of Aquarius. It was a dump. I suspected Queenie's cry of balls and kingship was regular and predictable, and sure enough.

We entertained the three females briefly, answering their questions on how it felt to be college students and never having to work but then facing death in Vietnam as soon as we were done but then being able to finally die for our country, which should make anybody feel better about being a worthless piece o' shit for four years straight. "God, I hate those chickenshit fuckers!" Queenie cried out before leveling her gaze for the follow up. "Are you guys chickenshit?"

We pledged our sincere hope that we were not chickenshit and said we needed to get back. To our amazement, Janis and Grace were up and out and taking us back to Marcia's. We picked up a hitchhiker with a backpack on the way whose name was Clem or Zeke or Luke, who said he wasn't too sure where he was headed, except for into the future, unless we were going backward, and nobody could be sure we weren't. Clem was a hayseed who'd been to town and gone home but couldn't stay home, because of what he'd seen in town. Oh, those were the days, my friend. He too seemed uncertain on the plains of reality awaiting discovery. So his backpack preceded him into the backseat, where it and the three of us got squeezed like sardines as Janis showed us what that li'l sumbitch could do. It was her turn for a hyena chorus, spinning snow brodies between the ditches.

Clem got out with Kenny and me practically bonded by peril. We trooped into Marcia's where the gang had leveled at ninety thousand feet. Seated around the big dining room table, everyone listened to Ray Haney's instructions for capping his acid. "It ain't nothing to it. You just scoop a little fucker in a powder 'n 'en you scoop a other half 'n 'en you press 'um together. Like so. Don't lick your fingers. It gums everthang. 'N don't worry. You'll git off on account of what soaks in. I mean this shit's a McCoy."

Clem wanted to try this intriguing task, capping the magic and absorbing the dust on his fingertips. He broke into high-speed hayseed with Ray Haney like it was old home week for a couple cuzzins from the liberated side of Podunk Holler, and soon enough he reckoned Ray had a thing or two coh-rect. Then he too climbed to orbital altitude. Or maybe he only remembered what it had been like or how he imagined it to be. He glanced toward the kitchen at the sound of tiny clattering—a sound we'd long ignored, because it was only the mice playing hide and seek among the dinner dishes and pots and pans. Lindsay explained that they made more noise at first because they had to get a salad bowl moved over in the sink right under the faucet, so they could fill it with water and then dive off the faucet. Sometimes they liked to put a coffee cup right next to the salad bowl, you know, for the smaller mice who might need shallower water and a rim they could grasp more easily.

Clem looked serious, taking Lindsay at face value and holding the thought, like he needed a minute to actually paint this picture on his brainpan. He finally got up and walked over to his pack, where he retrieved a collapsible fishing rod with a small reel, a block of cheese and a knife. He stretched the rod out and strung the line through the eyelets and cut a cheese cube to bait his hook, and he cast it into the kitchen. We laughed, welcoming Clem to our world of commitment to anything that might goof on reality. We were soon humbled by Clem's commitment; he was dead serious on the vermin issue. So Marcia offered him a glass of wine and a joint, which he stared at for a long moment and then accepted as if accepting the future as Marcia explained to him the difference between varmints and critters, and the sameness of critters to creatures, of whom the mice and we were one, demonstrating yet again that love was all around us.

I remember the moment as microcosm of the age, an ideal verging on naiveté, yet given the context it was an ideal that glowed in the dark or the light. Viewing the mice as social contemporaries was a wild step beyond Disney, a giant, blessed step that we embraced, and in so doing became present in the 60s.

I don't wonder where Clem is now. I think often of Marcia and Kenny and that long, lovely night as a rare interlude. The world lit up in wonder and amazement with magic at every turn of every moment. The magic had been right there all along, waiting on the interface for a catalyst to set it free.

Six Months Earlier

IN JUNE OF 1969 Old Mom drove me to the airport more anxious than usual. I'd always seemed hell bent on self-destruction, but this outing was, to her, more focused. She had no doubts that this time I was out to kill myself. She just knew it, though she repressed her anxiety admirably, telling herself out loud that I was only fitting in with the other kids.

That is, a few would-be entrepreneurs across the land had discovered how to charter commercial jets and actually make money selling round trip flights, New York/London, by the seat at two hundred forty dollars each. This was long, long ago, way before the world got terrorized and then got protected by security, and adventures got shut down or rendered tediously humiliating.

Meanwhile, what did you say? Round trip New York/London for two forty? Well, so it wasn't a jet. It was a Scottish Airlines plane that went north to Nova Scotia to minimize over-ocean time and took sixteen hours. No frills? We didn't even know what a frill was. We napped on the floor. So what? And you still had to get to New York. So? You got ninety days of the whole wide world in the bargain, which was as different as Paris, Illinois from its namesake in France.

Anyway, Old Mom was only about fifty then, and though prone to nervous energy, she mostly had her emotions under control. But then she cried, broke down and sobbed, driving and reaching into her purse for five big ones folded neatly into a wad. Five hundred dollars was another world unto itself in those days. She handed it over boo hoo hooing, admonishing me to be safe and have a wonderful, safe time, and to get this…this…this thing out of my system and come home safely. "This is not to spend. It's for emergency. Keep it in a safe place."

Credit cards were for rich kids, kids who got new cars for a sixteenth birthday or a half-decent report card. Cell phones were still three decades away, even for rich kids. I guess Old Mom could have bought some traveler's checks if she thought I might lose the money, but she didn't think of that, or maybe she didn't want to pay those bastards the five or ten bucks for their fake money. Mom had lived through the Depression and knew what five or ten bucks could buy. Never mind. I spent the cash on day three, all of it, quick and neat, straight up.

You bounce back easily at twenty from sixteen hours of engine noise, stale air and seats as unforgiving as church pews. Halfway into the tortuous crossing most kids lay on the floor to get some Zs, and a lasting image of the times was an old Scottish turbo-prop droning across the Atlantic with its engine cowlings streaming fine rivulets of oil, its seats empty and its floor covered with youthful adventurers in fetal positions, hugging knapsacks and stuff. It could never happen again for practical reasons, with a world so much more aware of what might go wrong. But back then it was all right.

I traveled with a fellow student, a poet and adventurer, David Rayall, though David was more attuned to verse than horizons. A wanton intellect and surly thinker, David already shaved twice a day at twenty and was good and goddamn ready for a liberal dash of worldly spice in his cadence and meter. He envisioned pubs abuzz with lively discourse, literary annotation and Joycean ambience. From within the din he would find meaning and transpose it to lyric and round it out with artistry.

We found a pension in Russell Square—actually found it in *Europe on $5 a Day*, the student adventure bible of those days. Everyone read it religiously, because if you got careless for a blink, you were on your way to purgatory at $10, $12, even $20 on a single day with eighty-nine days to go. Fuck that.

On a lark, without a care, out in the world, on our own with nowhere and everywhere to go, we cruised London at random for the next few days. By chance we happened onto *Pride & Clark, Dealers of Fine Motors*, including four-wheeled motors and a vast array of two-wheeled motors. The motorcycling scene then was three-tiered and simple. Hondas weren't exactly for pussies, not like they would become later, with massive plastic engine covers and Winnebago travel trunks, the pinstripes, stuffed toys, reverse gear and the ultimate insult to the road gods: trailers. In fact, many high-mile riders over the years first felt the magic of motorcycling on a Honda. My first taste was a Super 90, soon followed by a dose of 160 Superhawk—it seemed like a major machine at the time, especially with a name of Superhawk. Both those Hondas belonged to a friend, one of the first kids at our high school to discover pot, so he didn't mind sharing his motorcycles. I probably had fifty or a hundred miles on those rides, enough to want back into that dimension soon and often. It was a feeling, systemic, in the bloodstream straight away for some of us. Wanting in became a craving, which, in youth, became the objective of life. Honda came out with a big, clunky 400cc model about then, but it had none of the pizzazz, color or flair of the British bikes.

Harley Davidson was still decades away from the mass market—not yet glommed on to the vast underbelly of suburbia. In the years ahead Harley Davidson would capture key market segments, beginning with young, urban professionals with oodles of leverage. Then came the overweight, hen-pecked crowd craving identity other than the one that befell them. Unavoidably, a tawdry disjunction emerged between appearance and reality, as the byways got crowded with suburban desperados—stable, secure guys with a hundred fifty bucks down and permission from the wife. Motorcycle traffic would get thick with non-riders—poseurs with props. Men seeking meaning would cast cash to the wind, to suit up for "the lifestyle;" live to ride, ride to live, with leathers and fringe, conchos and triple chrome bolts and cover plates, the patches and pins proclaiming Genuine Harley Davidson. Do you really need nine hundred pounds and 1600 cc for the short trip to the fern bar, to back in for the admiration of pedestrians? No, you don't, but then staying in town makes the lame swing arm more acceptable, since it won't likely fold up on a left turn yield into Whole Foods.

But I digress; back then Harley Davidson was for greasers. Even then they cost twice as much and were out of our range.

The motorcycle of choice for first-wave baby boomers on the tail end of adolescence and wanting to cross nations on two wheels was British. Royal Enfield was old, obscure and demanding but not demanded. Norton was very fast, nimble, exotic, dependable and in demand but not as popular or readily available as Triumph and BSA. Triumph was on top, first with a single carb Tiger but ultimately with the twin-carb Bonneville. Looking back, they seem simple, small and quaintly classic. Then they looked perfectly big. BSA followed suit with a single carb Thunderbolt and a twin-carb Lightning Rocket. These models all went 650 cubic centimeters and ran eight hundred fifty bucks brand new for the twin carb. Seasoned veterans of all ages recall that generation of British bikes for speed—one sixty to one seventy-five mph was attainable right out of the box for the truly crazy. Those were the days of fanciful engineering. The Triumph had double downtubes in front of the engine, while the Beezer had a single down-tube. Both frames were hollow and were rumored to be part of the oil circulation system in an early, primitive approach to oil cooling as a means of reducing engine heat. I don't know if that was true. I saw a wreck once with a frame mangled in pooling oil but didn't have the nerve to go in close, to see if it was oozing out the bones.

The Beezer was renowned for vibration, and a day of cruising at sixty could shake your brains looser still. But it could get up and go faster than anyone should go. Back then, BSA made a one cylinder model, the 441 Victor, with a panache all its own. No motorcycles had electric starters; all required a kick-start. And the 441 Victor's one big jug could catch on the compression stroke and not only kick you back; it could throw the unwary over the handlebars. Then again, taking the handlebar vault on a 441 kickback was the mark of experience. I took the dive and came up laughing about it and still laugh at the utter hazard and unnecessary risk of the thing. But then unnecessary risk was the risk most valued. The 441 Victor came only in yellow, and actually owning a 441 was a yellow badge of machismo—a pogo stick with incredible low-end torque.

We rode long hours with no windshields in those days, camping out and waking up in dew soaked bags on the stone cold ground, mustering the umph to rise to the frigid morning for a whiz, then firing up the camp burner for coffee, stoking a chunk of hash, blending into the mists and knowing the day ahead for what it would be worth, which was everything it could be. But I get ahead.

As if serendipitously parked in my path there on our walk of discovery into *Pride & Clark, Dealers of Fine Motors* gleamed a BSA Lightning Rocket hardly two years old—used but looking brand new. And what did the price tag say? Five big ones on the button. That kind of money would have seemed as insurmountable as a twenty-foot wall with barbwire on top, yet the bills lay neatly folded in my pocket as if ordained, or at least given by Old Mom, which was kind of the same thing. And yes, the elegant paper price tag dangling from the handlebar was in dollars; such was the rush of American boomers in rebellion, taking to the roads of Europe on two wheels—taking over those roads to show the locals how truly liberated anarchists could take the money their parents had given them and tear up the countryside as only free-wheeling Yanks could do. We were loved, because we had the credentials, the money and a war in Vietnam as the basis for Revolution.

I did take a minute or two for practical calculation on the savings available with a motorcycle. It was mostly on transportation, doing away with the need for train tickets or wasting time hitchhiking. I also factored a rare chance in life: before me sat a dream come true, so I woke up and lived it.

That Lightning Rocket was a glowing opportunity easily realized. I would ride it five thousand miles and know it intimately. Plagued with vibration, it could go as fast as I could imagine with a half inch of throttle remaining. Two carburetors, chrome fenders and a bulbous tank that was chrome on top and red on the sides identified the Lightning Rocket. Gold starbursts on red backfields on either side of the tank shot lightning bolts forward and back. Gold flames blew out the pipes, or so it seemed. I would drive it one-forty once, somewhere near seven grand—that's miles per hour at seven thousand rpm—before a curve came on quick as Earth in freefall at maximum velocity plus twenty. Increasing G-forces measured the sensation of speed and limitless acceleration to ninety or a hundred. Urgency to reach top end was driven by fear of running out of straightaway. Near a hundred came certainty that helmets would be incidental to starbursts and flesh melted over bent steel. The lumpy fondue imagery was satisfying, a notch up for an aspiring young daredevil.

Rising rpm whines to inaudible ranges over five grand in fourth gear, where things go perversely quieter. Back then, fourth gear was it. Over a hundred miles per hour the word becomes Om in a searing vibration around six thousand rpm, and the din becomes eerily calm. A rider must crouch into the tank or become a scoop for an instant before the wind scoops him off. Cheeks and wattles flop like crazy at seventy, but over a hundred the breeze can take your face off, so you stay low.

At one-twenty the air tingles. God speaks at one-forty with a question: *You wanna die, boy?* Deceleration takes as much focus as getting top end—on the way down one-ten seemed eminently controllable, except that one-ten is holy screaming Jesus fast enough to end in a blink.

So the future began at *Pride & Clark* in a similar blink, in hardly the time it took for a wild boy to forget everything his poor mother ever taught him about horse-trading. I counted out the five big ones and never looked back. I scanned the horizon out front and felt the urgency to catch up with the motorcycle wave breaking over Europe. David and I rode back to Russell Square, wobbly here and there but keeping things rolling. I parked and stared at my new meaning in life until David insisted that we celebrate my breakthrough by heading down to an area known for clubs. The world made such easy sense, and on a lovely stroll we found a fish and chips vendor for newspaper cones of greasy, salty cod. At 50p each, we were feeling more efficient all the time.

Making our way to the lively block where the music lived, we met a fellow about nightfall offering a small bag of opium for six pounds—about twelve bucks, or fifteen. That amount represented two and a half to three days of Europe, but we bought it, because this was the world.

Did we really want to meet it on opium?

Are you kidding?

We walked down the alley past a few bars and stopped at a place with a band playing *One is the Loneliest Number*. David had that album and out of his daze exclaimed, "It's them!" He meant Three Dog Night. That's how it was back then, in a world where reality was real and accessible, even on opium, or maybe especially on opium. I remember nothing after that but loud music, a long walk back to the pension and great relief at finding my new motorcycle where I left it.

We cruised a few days more and soon felt the itch to get out of town. So I lashed my backpack on back. David wore his. We got coffee and rolls and headed out with David riding bitch, though we didn't call it bitch then; we called it on back. He tried to keep the map from flopping out of control while I tried to keep us from dying as we wended our way through London, veering east-southeast for Dover and the bonnie cliffs and the ferry to the continent.

In a densely populated area on the outskirts of London we drove up a wooded road on David's insistence, arriving at a heavily wooded cul-de-sac, where he demanded that we stop immediately because he had to take a dump right now, because he ate too many crumpets, or trollops, or treacle, or buns, or rashers or any of those strange things the English eat. Squatting indelicately under a tree, just as a strange white man would plant a flag on the moon only a month hence, David laid claim for America. He draped his handkerchief over the top of it like a flag, sort of, though it lay limp, hardly discouraging the fly swarm or constraining the stink.

"I know I should be proud of you," I said, "but that's disgusting."

David was in no laughing mood, coming so close to a breach as I had caused him to do, and he assured me that it wasn't nearly as disgusting as some of the stuff I did.

"We could look at it. Poetically, I mean. We could call it the waste of wasted youth left behind for distant lands and a more brilliant wasting yet to come. Or some shit."

He didn't think that was funny either. The exchange was a symptom, a first friction between friends traveling together.

The road to Dover passed the castle at Canterbury, white-cliffed and seagull screaming, then it curved easy to the terminal for the Ostende Ferry. The channel rolled and sloshed, misty damp and dismal gray—I mean grey—churning the sea to frothy lumps of white cap and gruel as most passengers heaved over the rail. We watched like students and learned another lesson. Most passengers had hurriedly ordered sandwiches and coffee and gobbled and swilled quickly to beat the rough ride. We had watched them with envy, hours since breakfast but constrained by $5 a day. When the puking started hardly a mile out, the dining area emptied as most passengers moved swiftly to the lee rail. Some tables remained served but untouched. David had three half sandwiches. I sat down to a brand new platter of French toast. We dined on the house, picking out two untouched coffees and asking the galley for a reheat, *s'il vous plait*. We felt fairly satisfied and seasoned and ready for France. Out on deck, the sea and snacks rose, but an eye on the horizon got us to the French coast with the French toast held down.

Rolling off at Ostende we headed for Paris feeling purposeful and bound for deep penetration of left bank reality. Dead ahead was the truth that would change us from Midwestern children of the suburbs to worldly men. Maybe we would get black berets and wear them by necessity. Giant eucalyptus trees lined the French country roads on either side in perfect order, twenty or thirty to a cluster every few miles. Air pockets between each pair of sentries buffeted like giant kids swinging pillows, perhaps to humble our worldly insight with a beating as introduction to French hospitality.

Paris is not a biker's town. I remember feeling sort of okay, wending through the arrondissements in six lanes of traffic doing sixty, shifting lanes bumper to bumper, thinking it was crazy but I was good, very good, good enough for this action any day—when a screamer shot past doing a hundred ten, weaving like a wounded comet. I could never do that, and seeing another guy do it made me wonder if those skills were necessary to survive there. That guy looked like a high-miler.

More importantly, I didn't want to do that. I wanted out as quickly as we rode in. Paris was dirty, unfriendly and expensive. Call me philistine or too young to appreciate the arts, but I found a day at an art museum to be so uplifting and rewarding that I wouldn't need another day like that for a long time, maybe not for the rest of this lifetime. David swore that he loved it, maybe more than anything ever in his life—fairly challenging me to deny that *this* was why we had come. He demonstrated his point by scrutinizing a painting of some people on horseback on a woodsy road with everything in black or brown or dark green. He soaked it up like a true intellect and art appreciator for five minutes, ten minutes and fifteen. I left and came back and left again as he wallowed in artistic delight, imagining the very thoughts and sensitivities of the masters, his forbears in art.

He attributed my restlessness to chronic attitude. I couldn't argue. Attitude had been a problem enumerated on report cards for the first twelve grades, and though the revolution of the 60's justified my "attitude," anyone more willing to accept the conventional social norm could still build a case against me.

We walked along the Seine, maybe waiting for art to imitate life or vice versa, or maybe for a radical intellectual demonstration to break out on the occasion of our presence at the Sorbonne. David soon agreed, however, that Paris could not be met on $5 a day. He too would travel west-southwest to Biarritz, but not on back, no offense. He just couldn't take it. He would take the train since he'd budgeted that part of it in his $5 a day. And he liked the train, always had, after all.

And that was that. We parted company the next morning with a handshake and an agreement to meet up again, somewhere, maybe. I still marvel at the image of myself, alone on a BSA Lightning Rocket, maneuvering Paris. My motorcycle experience to date was the ride from London, plus a few miles on borrowed Hondas, plus about two hundred more miles on a Honda Dream.

I would have gone farther on the Dream, but it kept breaking down. I bought that one, my first motorcycle, in '67 in Memphis. It was a 305cc parallel twin, its pistons not sequentially timed but moving together, like a single jug split into two that for some reason never worked for Honda. I bought mine chopped with megaphone pipes; it looked so cool to a teenager, and I was still in a flush from my Superhawk experience. My Dream had probably run a few laps around the moon with some side trips across the Sea of Tranquility. But when the guy fired it up it went *WOMMMAAA!* I was smitten then too, and for the few miles it ran I got more exposed to the fundamentals of motorcycling. For starters, you can't steer one even if you want to. On my first curve (in town) I had to pull over to see why the handlebars were frozen. It was the self-preservation instinct overpowering the triple tree and preventing me from "turning" the handlebars. You have to lean a motorcycle to get it to turn. Now I know, kind of.

Mechanical thoughts and solitude filled in through the thinning refuse of urban Paris south and west toward Bordeaux, through a series of small towns till I got tired late in the afternoon and stopped. I used my high school French well enough to find a *chambre* to *louer* for the *nuit*. I remember that room as small and wood paneled up the sides and along the roofline too, on the second floor overlooking some narrow streets and other houses. It would have been unusable space in America, the United States of, but a typical frog family squeezed a few francs out of it.

The stuffy confinement and loneliness became oppressive and overwhelming, as if the French didn't care. Maybe they didn't, but they weren't the cause of my pain. It was a night of molting, of coming into the world, as everyone must leave the world, alone. Sleep came early, like a blessing.

The morning was better, warmer and livelier after coffee and a pastry. I mounted up for Biarritz.

The road to Bordeaux was also solitary, but with a pastoral backdrop and movement it was old home week. Maybe a night was all I needed; the route felt right, peopled with farmers and truckers and bartenders who know about coming off the road for a smoke and a wine to ease the neck knots. Just south of Bordeaux, I spotted two guys resting under a tree near a parked motorcycle, so I pulled over. "Assistance?"

"Yeah," the younger one said. "Got a light?" The bike was his, a '50s vintage Triumph 650 Thunderbird, the only touring motorcycle Triumph had ever built. Never exported to the U.S., its fender cowlings curled into running boards, and its English saddlebags and no chromium roll bar made it look lean and hungry for long miles. "Picked him up hitching," the younger one said, abrupt as urban adolescence.

John Levy from LA sat on the ground holding a 35mm camera, fondling and shifting it in his hands. He explained that he was a photographer. The pivotal points of his identification, LA and photography, pegged John as a purebred Californian and natural star. I would know him and Bruno for many miles but never saw him take a picture. Those were the days of film and thirty-six shots, so maybe he didn't have any, or many he waited for the perfect place to spend a roll.

John was only nineteen but could handle his Triumph Thunderbird like the road pro he bought it from, who assured him the high-mileage didn't matter, because it was broken in right and then maintained on steady cruising speeds. John's bullshit factor was soon evident, but he seemed like a good guy with a soulful motorcycle. He'd picked up Bruno hitching out of Paris—Bruno had to flee France because he had no money, not $5 or five liras a day. At twenty-two, Bruno was old man out, seeing the world on a shoestring budget just like we were, kind of, except that he was from Rome, the lower eastside of it, and he had holes in his shoes and makeshift strings. He loved the big motos, even riding on back. And a chance to sit up front would be heaven sent. John and Bruno agreed that Paris was a rip-off, and so was all of France, so they were headed to Spain, where a nickel could get you lunch.

Bruno said. "I hitch," holding up one thumb with a smile.

"He no speaka too gooda de English," John said. "Isn't that right, dumb shit?"

Bruno said, "Ey. Watcha you a call me."

John laughed. "He's got French and Spanish wired."

Bruno smiled again and pumped his head, affirming the resource he would contribute. "*Si. Et oui.* Wis me, you no a getting a fucked."

"Yeah, right. We're hauling ass out of France," John said. "It's too rich around here. Fuck these frogs." I nodded—a dollar made five francs then, and five francs got you half a cheese sandwich, except you couldn't get half. Roadside wine ran two francs a glass, and your average American kid had to go all summer on a few hundred bucks. Everyone knew we could call home for more, but that was throwing in the towel on pride and independence. I added a pinch of opium to the hash speck they were trying to light, and soon the pipe was stoked, signifying victory. And unity. With the bond sealed and the revolution intact, we dreamed south-southwest for Spain.

Bruno scanned the horizon before mounting up, and then nodded, "Spain. More cheaper everything."

We rode fast long hours, Bruno driving both bikes to spell John and me, because it was the age of brotherhood, and he said he knew how. He hadn't eaten in two days except for milk and bread, but crouching over the handlebars his energy was that of a child meeting Santa, face-to-face. He made no secret of his belief in American magic. Americans were rich in any man's country even if poor in their own. We laughed when Bruno complained of *moskweetos*. John asked him if he thought he would ever stop being a dumb shit. Bruno smiled yet again and sent a fine stream of wine between his two front teeth, dousing the arrogant boy. He stammered when I asked him which moto he liked best. He fidgeted and promised to decide. He said he could go two weeks on his current diet of bread and milk and had done it often and was comfortable with prospects of doing it again— it kept him young and strong. But he rubbed his belly at the other prospect of *sandweeches* in Spain, thick with meat.

He spoke sparse English and had little to say otherwise, but not from shyness. He came alive in negotiation with others in French or Spanish, waving his hands, laughing and scowling before walking away from a deal. He would walk to John and me to tell us how we'd fared, what the price would be for food, wine or a place to sleep. When it came time to pay, he stood back, head down with humility. Average cash out was around two dollars. He had not one cent, so he earned his keep and gave John at nineteen and me at twenty a look at another form of humanity we'd never known, a man of resource. I wondered how far I could make it on empty pockets. John wanted him to call us Bwana. Bruno puffed his cheeks with wine until John begged off.

In the south of France sit the little sisters astride the border, Biarritz on the French side, San Sebastian on the Spanish. After two days hard riding and little eating, we rode harder and ate less, bearing down on the promise of herring in oil, beefy sardines, horsemeat sandwiches, goat cheese and cheap wine waiting across the border. Light-headed we cat-and-moused, throttled down and sped up, weaving figure eights until ten miles from Biarritz, when we learned that even a Lightning Rocket is mortal. Its clutch cable broke near the lever. I squeezed nothingness and wondered what.

Coasting and kicking into neutral, the little party stopped. We sat and breathed and looked stupid, grinning as the hot metal ticked.

A motorcycle can be driven clutchless if the driver is sensitive to rpm and can hear the right time to shift. Even so, shifting isn't smooth but must be muscled up and down with unavoidable gear crunching. The cable had to be fixed. So we limped into Biarritz with John driving the bum Lightning Rocket, since he was the far more experienced driver and had driven hundreds of clutchless miles, no shit. I knew he was a punk and a liar and itching to ride my rocket, but he was good, better than I was, maybe. I was curious anyway to see if the Thunderbird was smooth as it looked, and I was tired, so we switched.

Inside the city limits of Biarritz we found no word that translates to motorcycle—moto covers it all, anything with two wheels and a putt, from mopeds to Lightning Rockets. After an hour or two of Bruno's genuflections with the peasantry, each exchange taking us a few blocks deeper into the bowels of Biarritz, we found a small street, more of an alley, since a car would never fit on it—not a real car. A real moto was iffy. But local motos were thick there, with the shop double doors open wide and mopeds and mobilets spewed onto the street like hatchling insects. 35 and 50cc models were everywhere with just as many rug rats swarming among the motos buzzing high rpm French voices, amazed at the Americans on their giant machines. Tired and hungry, we felt little optimism.

An old man came to the double doors like a hound to a scent, to see what was the matter, nose up to the sound of big motorcycles. Over six feet tall with yellow-white hair and an old jump suit to match but for the holes and grease spots, he thrust his flushed face out, leading with his French and whiskey nose. His hand grasping a door looked like a row of cypress knees, weatherworn and gnarled from wrench failure and age. The children followed his movement with their own, inching closer as he did, daring finally to touch the big motos, which got them tittering and chirping over the engine thunder, until the old man said, "*Alors...*"

Bruno dismounted as he spoke. We shut the engines down as he proceeded, showing the old man the broken cable. The old man furrowed and scratched and then spoke back. The word London came to the surface, followed by a big, helpless shrug. Bruno turned around with the news: The clutch cable assembly was a one-piece part, from the lever to the clutch. The little mobilets had no parts anything at all like the one required. If the old man called that day to London, a new one would arrive in a week or three weeks.

We hung our heads, mumbled and walked in circles. The old man watched, puffing his lower lip and throwing his hands in the air, which is French for *All of life is bullshit*, or *What are you going to do?* In intricate charade, he shooed us off, go, all but the broken Lightning Rocket. We should go and find a place, find a place and sleep because we looked very tired. *La moto malade c'est bonne ici, avec moi.*

He patted our sleeping bags, rounded us up and pointed in a long arc, spewing French directions to a bluff off a secondary road that overlooked a beach and was partially sheltered by bushes and trees. "*Allez!*" the old man clapped like a Sultan. "*Vite! Vite!*" And all the children yelped and shrieked as we three mounted the old Thunderbird with our gear under our arms, weighing her shocks down springless.

Around the corner at a shop just closing we bought a number ten can labeled SAUERKRAUT in block letters under a picture of some fairly good looking sauerkraut and sausage. Yum and grunt, we said, and got some mustard, bread and wine, two bottles. We drank one bottle on the curb for fortitude and acceptance of reality, which was an issue those days. Then we mounted up again.

We made camp while Bruno explained as best he could that the old man was the only human being in France who could give good directions, so maybe something good would happen. I said, "Yeah, like a miracle."

John opened the can and found only sauerkraut, no sausage. "Fuckers. They couldn't do this in America." But sauerkraut and mustard sandwiches weren't too bad, and the dream got better with another bottle of wine. Cocktails got better on Gauloises and a touch of opium. We escaped then, free at last of long hours in the saddle, broken cables and the high cost of France. The stars in the sky looked just like home.

We woke up in rolling fog at dawn with all the snails in France sliming over our bags like drunk cartographers. More sandwiches for breakfast, since we had plenty of the ingredients, led to more smokes and a last pull on the wine bottle, then into town for coffee.

We reached the shop early, all the mobilets and children still tucked in, asleep. The Lightning Rocket sat out front exactly as it had been left. The old man looked alive with the energy of those who don't sleep because something more important waits in the world. He pushed the double doors open and came out, hands up, as if greeting old friends, reunited at last. He and Bruno spoke and moved slowly together toward the Lightning Rocket, hands dancing in questions and answers and yes, buts, until a big paw moved quickly to the clutch lever and squeezed it—it resisted, fixed.

I walked over and squeezed it and saw what he'd done. Each thread of the cable, maybe twenty strands, had been welded back onto the metal plug they'd shorn from. Then he'd sculpted the mass down to diameter, allowing a smooth slide through the cable guide. John examined it and said, "holy fuckin'ay."

The old man nodded and smiled but would not look again at his work. He walked back into his shop with Bruno, who called us to follow, way back and then back farther, through the garage behind the shop and farther back to the quiet rooms where he lived, where the walls were strewn with photos of a man over six feet with dark hair and a big nose, wearing a jump suit and standing in front of one motorcycle or another with a different trophy in his hands for each photo. A hundred motorcycles in a hundred pictures looked like they covered a decade or two or three. Then the old man showed us his trophies, or the few he had left, bent, dinged and tarnished.

We scanned the wall in silence, touching the trophies.

Out front again I asked to settle up. "*Combien?*"

"*Cinq francs,*" he said.

"*Cinq francs?*"

"*Oui oui oui oui oui. Cinq francs.*" A dollar.

I paid it. "*Merci. Merci beaucoup, Monsieur...*"

"*Rien!*" It is nothing, he said, hands flying up. We lashed our gear then. He watched. I mounted the Lightning Rocket, turned the key and kicked it over. As the engine revved, the old man tilted an ear down as though to hear what it had to tell him.

Head cocked then like a curious pup's, the old man's eyes opened big when I revved again, dismounted and held a hand up, an invitation. He would not move. I nodded and said, "*Oui.*" He nodded too but stood still, listening.

"*Oui oui,*" he said at last, moving smoothly, one leg over, two hands on, settling in, revving and feeling the time between himself and the machine.

He squeezed the clutch lever without looking at it, found first gear and eased into it, accelerating up the street, slowly at first. When the engine roared the old man did not hesitate but slipped into second easy as two follows one, wound it out and double clutched to third. Doing nearly sixty approaching the corner, he double clutched back to second and leaned into the corner till the foot peg shot sparks off the pavement. We couldn't see him then but heard him come out of the turn winding up, shifting, winding up, shifting, winding up and away.

How could we not love Biarritz? It was a love meant to last. With warm hearts we meandered through town to the border and into Spain, San Sebastian, where *tapas* were invented, where we stopped at the first bar to find the counter lined with big, fat sardines, little cups of olives, fried squids, salamis, crackers, peppers, the works, for a penny a round. I was set, but John didn't like that weird shit, and Bruno was itching for something a bit more third world, where less money could generate more volume.

So we rode down to the beach promenade, because Bruno knew San Sebastian. He told us to park and wait. Then he waited while we found our money and gave him some, not too much, about three dollars. John looked wary. I felt the same, but Bruno shrugged and shook his head, like we were fucked up for thinking that, but if we wanted to choose an outlook on the negative side of potential rather than on a friendship secured, that would be our doing, not his, and he left.

He came back in ten minutes with four baguettes, a pound of cheese, a few bottles of wine—at seven cents (7¢) each—another can of sauerkraut and a few pounds of lunch meat. Oh, and some sugar sprinkled donut holes for dessert. He still had last night's jar of mustard in his pack, hardly half empty. Oh, and he had a guy in tow who he met at the market—not to worry; the guy had chipped in a dollar. The guy was David Rayall, my college classmate, the friend I'd left home with long ago. It was like that back then.

Bruno spread the stuff out on a bench, on the wrapping paper it came in, and then dove in, building a sandwich that could gag a horse. As we came to learn, the horse comprising the lunchmeat may have gagged on just such a sandwich. But while we with $5 a day and whatever else we might need in case of emergency hung back, he of the caput fortunes ate with a vengeance. Bruno drank wine from the bottle like it was milk, glug, glug, glug, and in mere minutes he was more satisfied and happier than he'd been in the two days I'd known him. We got a big room in a cheap hotel and lay around drinking wine and smoking opium.

We left the next morning for Madrid, dropping David at the train station and heading into the Pyrenees foothills, low-rolling scrub mostly, arid and empty but startling and beautiful too, except for the Guardia Seville—the Spanish police—who were equally arid and empty, low-rolling scrubs on their one-cylinder scooters that couldn't begin to keep up, resulting in a bunch of gun-toting fascists even more pissed off than usual with the Yankee boys on faster bikes. We got pulled over for a document check and explained to them, "No speaka too gooda de Espagñol. Parlez vous humma humma?" Then we turned it over to Bruno, who nodded obsequiously many times on cue and got us out of there in a few minutes, assuring us later that we were on our way to a solid fucking without him. Then he asked if it was his turn to drive yet.

We'd already smoked most of the opium and ditched the rest after meeting the Guardia Seville. Those were the last years of Franco, and nobody called him Uncle Franco. The difference between him and Stalin was the political spectrum between them—they butted heads at opposite ends, making them more similar than different. They both ruled by oppression with a heavy hand. Madrid was all new and old, an exotic city with open markets and strange things to eat for pennies. We enjoyed it for a day and headed out, because adventurers yearn for the open road, where things are more likely to happen. Besides, John Levy was from LA, where the latest, hippest, grooviest stuff broke first, and he had it on good sources that the real happening was only a week away in Pamplona, where the bulls would run for seven days, beginning at seven a.m. on the seventh day of the seventh month.

David had acquiesced to take the train to Madrid and join us for that tour but then announced that he would head to Florence, because he came for art, not cows, and we would meet up bye and bye, maybe. Bruno murmured that he loved art and could show David the best art museums and the best Italian home cooking from his mother too, if only David would lend him the paltry few lira for a ticket to Rome, where they should surely stop on the way to Florence. Bruno hadn't been home for a year and felt that it was time. David agreed, sensing intuitively that Bruno was an artistic person with a big heart and a giving nature, after all.

A unique characteristic of those days, or maybe of any days for people of a certain age, was our range of emotion. On one extreme was the overwhelming loneliness of my first night in the world with no friends or family. I remember the crushing sensation of cold potential, of death with nobody knowing or caring. The potential for life with no meaning, for that matter, seemed as frightening. Those feelings seem unfounded but may have been necessary to a wild boy raised softly in the suburbs.

On the other hand, parting ways with David and Bruno was casual as another slice of toast. We didn't review the good times, the high miles, the horsemeat sandwiches quelling our starvation, the big hotel room on the top floor where we smoked opium and drank another ninety-eight cents worth of Spanish wine, the random meetings, the adventure and youth that would be long gone all too soon.

Sharing those golden memories would have required perspective in the moment. We had none, whether from smoking too much dope or drinking too much wine, or amping too much youth like no tomorrow or remaining blind to all but tomorrow's potential. It was over and out, so long, farewell, *auf Wiedersehen*, good-bye.

See you on the corner, maybe, or maybe never.

Deep Penetration

SO YOUNG, SO open and alive, so free of regret and inured to loss. Ah, well, it was down to John Levy, LA photog, and me, back out on the rolling foothills of the Pyrenees Mountains, born to the saddle and bound for horizons. From side roads and on-ramps like tributaries to the greater flow, the boomer brotherhood rounding Europe on two wheels joined our cavalcade for a few miles or many. Most headed to Pamplona, some just up from Marrakech, a hotspot that summer where three bucks could buy a matchbox of kief—a blond, loose, fiber derived from cannabis but not marijuana and not hash. *It's really the best* was the word on the road, but then anything new or different gets to be really the best for a while. Rolling into Pamplona ten or fifteen motorcycles pulled over as if organized to share a few bowls and compare coordinates on who'd been where and seen what, while comparing kief from East Marrakech to kief from farther south.

This was the height of it, when all men were brothers and women too. We knew each other immediately by the bell-bottoms, beads, headbands, vests, tie-die, peace symbols, stoner halos and hair. The hair was straight, curly, kinky or ratty and all long. We didn't wear helmets. Hats weren't popular for another ten years or so, and long hair gets windswept into wings. We pointed and laughed: what a goof. We passed pipes with universal understanding and no explanation required, because we were in it together, loving the common adventure. Word was out, that it was happening at the campground four miles farther from the far side of town.

John and I stopped at a roadside café for breakfast. *Huevos con tomates* sounded disgusting but tasted delectable, as the waitress assured it would. A black-haired, dark-eyed beauty of eighteen, she didn't hide her favor for the stick-thin Americano in tight pants on a thundering moto with wanderlust in his eyes. She was Marisol and agreed in broken Spanish and English to meet by the creek at five. What creek? The one by the campground. *A cinco horas.* "Fife. Hat fife ho'clock."

So the world unfolded, its lovely petals and scents, colors and textures revealing wanton youth with no plan, no duty, no schedule, no rule, no reverence except to the gods of fun and high times—*nada* but a future of lusty potential, freedom in movement, beauty and *motorcycles.* Just look around and see what you like, then try as you might to use it up. You could go all night and have a lifetime left at sunrise. So what should you do? Pace yourself?

This imagery may suggest heavy action, but it more accurately recalls a period of rough transition for a boy who had yet to learn what is expected of a man.

The campground outside Pamplona was another rolling pastureland, grassy with shade trees and a *baño.* The tent campers were sectioned over there, just beyond the van campers. The motorcycles were backed to a hogwire fence so we could roll out our sleeping bags right beside our scooters—our salvation—and sleep the restful, soulful sleep of youth fulfilled, which we did till eleven or noon, not to worry; we could cop a couple hours more at siesta. If you picture a perfect setting in a faraway place and a long lost time with campers of every stripe and color convening in a single spirit of life and light, then that was it. The bulls wouldn't run for six more days, glorious days of idling away the hours, trading adventures and road yarns, smoking kief and drinking wine—oh, and meeting a certain señorita by the creek.

Dark and mysteriously lovely as an exotic woman could be, Marisol taught the universal language with unforeseen fluency, yet it remained ethereal, on the breeze, understood as a love everlasting but without real-world consummation. Yes, it had the scent, touch and potential of romance. We held hands. She murmured sweet nothings. She may have referenced love or eternity or maybe humility in requesting assistance and guidance as only a man can provide on this sensitive issue.

I watched her. She watched me back. I averted my glance while imagining her naked so that I would neither frighten nor offend.

She seemed perplexed. I smiled. We held hands. We kissed. She tasted of paella and eggs but remained very nearly perfect.

The campground filled with adventurers seeking bulls. Two high-spirited women pulled right in front of the motorcycles in a VW camper—the place was packed by then, and new arrivals pitched or parked in any space available. Jane, the driver, soon demonstrated that her revolutionary spirit had in no way been dampened by a multi-million dollar trust fund. John introduced himself as a photographer from LA. Small world—Jane was from LA too. Then they compared impressions of the European landscape, certain segments of which resembled those hallowed grounds of the California coast, like Mendocino, Big Sur, Pismo, and on down the Pacific Coast to Ventura Highway, where a Californian could hook a thumb in any direction and catch a ride, including up to the Cosmos and as far out as you cared to go. John and Jane got it on. Why wouldn't they? Two carefree souls in a carefree time that valued freedom and anarchy over all else—mix that with vigor, stamina, peak hormonal output and five more days till the bulls would run, and what do you get? Boom shacka lacka, to put it mildly. John and Jane seemed made for each other, a perfect match with all variables optimally met.

Jane's travel companion Rianne was less gregarious, which is not to say circumspect or reserved or even reflective. She seemed merely more self-contained, observant and cautious, perhaps driven inward or even made defensive by so many bulging eyeballs scanning her perfectly curved torso and svelte Levis to boot. Rianne hailed from Oregon, which may have factored in her softer demeanor, though Billy and Chas also hailed from Oregon, arriving soon after and camping nearby, where they whooped and hollered all night long, allowing a sleepless camper time to reflect on a little Spanish nightingale.

Maybe Marisol tired of the vibration with sparse verbal support and no physical backup, or she had to work double shifts, or she got grounded or a better offer. Maybe she resented our tedious whiles by the creek, with its rocky bed and none of the high times the Yankees were known for. I could only speculate. The only thing worse than making a move too soon was making no move at all. She stopped coming by.

Cold turkey is tough on young blood. As a draft-dodging campus refugee who could maintain a C- average by showing up for the first day of class and again for the final exam I felt qualified to be President of the United States of America—or would feel so qualified in another forty years.

Short of all things to all people in the 60s, I was just clever enough to survive on recreational drugs and crummy jobs, like picking apples or black walnuts, washing dishes and prepping pizzas, shingling roofs or any manner of minimum wage drudgery to pay the rent and buy groceries. A draft beer was 25¢. My share of the rent was $35. Reefer came in lids for $8, though the best Mexican reefer was $15, because it let you laugh for no good reason. Could I have excelled as an A-student if I'd applied myself? No. I could not. A-students are satisfied with sedentary pursuits, like studying.

I got a D in Español. I remembered a few nouns and transitive verbs, along with a profile of rightwing/Catholic propriety in a severely constrained culture preoccupied with chaperones to safeguard its young and presumably virgin beauties. Maybe my dark-eyed chiquita had murmured about rearranging the furniture in her parents' house once we were married. Maybe she'd asked for my preference on sexual favors. I told myself to regret nothing, even as hope faded. Yet I feared the fault was in me. I'd held back.

Next in the stepping-stones to insight came Rianne, who asked for a ride on my motorcycle with only four days till the bulls would run. "Okay," I shrugged, thinking immediately that a ride would give us a great opportunity to find a bathroom or at least a place to go peepee or even take a dump in a pinch—I could not think of Rianne in that way, possibly doubting that she actually took dumps or did anything outside the realm of perfection. At any rate the campground toilets had clogged and overflowed, illustrating the ultimate case against anarchy. World population in 1969 was right at half of what it would be forty years later, so clogged campground toilets also illustrated the ultimate case for family planning—a case that obviously failed. But nature didn't begin to die in earnest for another decade or two, so the seeping sewage swelling from a rivulet to a creek to step over was a joke, a bad one worth remembering. Should I take a roll of toilet paper? Nah. She'd bring that if she needed too, and at that point I wondered if she saw me only as a convenient means to a convenient place to take a dump, which of course she must do, even if I had trouble picturing it.

One toilet still functioned, but it had a waiting line that did not shorten till way after dark, and the area smelled like shit all the time. Rianne wanted to go to a yonder hill. She pointed just there, where she could see a building. She wanted to check it out. It sounded perfect; buildings have bathrooms. Maybe she thought I was checking her out as I scanned her fore and aft for a roll discreetly tucked.

Never mind. Many girls wanted to go for a motorcycle ride. Not all of them could, but Rianne could. We roamed the countryside looking for the right road to the hillside yonder and finally cruised along the base. The building turned out to be an abandoned church sitting near the hilltop that was otherwise plush green with grass billowing in the breeze. After exploring the old church she said, "This is nice" her first words since arriving. Then she found a place in the soft undulation to lie down with a sigh, arms and legs spread in an attitude of release with no inhibition. Rianne was so beautiful I couldn't speak, and hailing from Oregon, which is right on top of California, she was cool. She knew about cool things and places. What could a Hoosier possibly say to a cool beauty? Corn looks good this year? How 'bout them soybeans? Nah. She didn't care about Midwestern stuff. So I played it cool, saying nothing, trying not to stare and failing, wondering if I would ever find the elusive, mysterious key to understanding females.

She unbuttoned her shirt to take in more rays. I watched, *chewing on a piece of grass in the sun...shine.* I pondered the move but realized her shrewd defense—saw it clearly to my own disadvantage. The only move was to crawl over on all fours, and a guy couldn't very well do that, I thought; it would be so...so obvious and deliberate and... and... And it didn't make much sense to talk about current events or music or school or anything.

When she sat up to peel her blouse for even better rays, I gave up on trying not to stare. I knew that direct confrontation with the holy countenance would trigger regrettable behavior, and I was stuck, never having spoken to a woman with bare breasts on a grassy hill in daylight. I hadn't spoken to that many bare breasts at all.

With decades of hindsight, all fours or a belly crawl would have done to a T. Or a whistle or a blink. Or a how-do-you-do or a cock-a-doodle-do or a pulse, any pulse. Talk about nothing to lose. Maybe she'd have had nothing to say. Or maybe she was the one, as in one and only, which seems doubtful, but a boy feared rejection and accusation in the presence of a woman. Fuck, man, what were you thinking? What if she wound up with a round house right to the chin and knocked your fucking lights out? So what? How many hundreds of regrets could have been avoided on that lovely punch? But a young man didn't want to step over the line, even then with love all around us.

After a long while I said it was time to go. Actually, I had to go. She said yeah, maybe it is, sitting up and turning away more discreetly to put her blouse back on, behaving like the young deb I'd required her to be. I'd blown it. We stopped on the way back at a gas station with a bathroom. What a relief and my only consolation.

That night Rianne howled from the back of Jane's van as Chas pumped the jam for old Oregon.

The next morning at sunrise Billy said, "Man, Chas never got so fucked in his life. Man, I never seen a woman so horny. I think I might get some of that tonight myself."

"Yeah. Well." Call it a long jump from one stepping-stone to the next. At least more stepping-stones seemed likely, though the señorita and Oregon were among the sorriest missteps in life to date. I thought I'd learned my lesson, and that night went for a walk with a nurse from Canada, a uniquely shaped person with slight swayback leading to a big, firm ass that would have tilted her back except for the admirable counterbalance of her front. Frilly spit curls in sandy brown surrounded her round face and round features, rounding out her easy laughter and great good cheer for the times we lived in. Enjoying life and her summer trip, she was having fun and feeling grateful for the world around as it was, even with its ups and downs and roundabouts, because it stretched before us with so much lovely potential and so many wonderful adventures. Simply spherically happy, she took my hand and held it to connect us in the joy we shared. The night was so beautiful, she said, and we were so young and alive. She turned to face me and took my other hand as if to complete the circuit. She asked me if I had any idea of how rare, unique and unbelievably rich was the time we shared.

What could I say, yes? I thought of asking her if she had any idea what her luscious curvature meant to a young male with raging hormones. But I knew she knew. I could have shared the Moody Blues paradox, that thinking is the best way to travel, but most people would rather take the bus. But witticism seemed the better part of not getting any.

And what would the point be? Having learned my lesson on what women really want, I puckered up and leaned halfway in—too fast in closing the gap, maybe, but never mind; she made up her half the distance, and we stood in starlight smooching sweetly on the campground in Pamplona. It was easy, so thorough in its relief—not as thorough as it could be, but still, the gates opened. I reached up to squeeze a melon, because I knew that a woman would appreciate some foreplay before we found some relatively level ground on which to join the sexual revolution.

She shuddered. She swatted me away, stepping back and asking the ultimate stupid question, "What are you doing?"

"What do you mean, what am I doing?"

"You touched my breast."

"Well. Yeah. I can't really, you know, feel you…up. If I don't… touch…your breast."

It was like a different kind of joke, a bad one, hardly funny if you have to explain the punch line.

"I don't appreciate that at all."

"Sorry."

"Don't worry about it." And that was that; another hundred yards of small talk, over and out, giving me a long night ahead to ponder what I'd learned or hadn't learned or might never learn or maybe should seek special tutoring to learn…

Never mind; the sun rose on a day that will bring Americans together from here to eternity. Well, that might be a stretch, but it was

July fucking fourth, motherfucker, and we were feeling headstrong on a binge of kief and wine for four days straight—make that five. Wait a minute… Like magic, or maybe it was only collective addiction, the pipes came out and fired up in the dawn's early light. No matter how old you get to be or how young you were, no time shines like first light on a day of reckoning. Primed for the rocket's red glare, a day of days shaped up as an event, a happening, a… a…

Out of the hubbub a skinny hippy with all the trimmings pulled a four by eight American flag from his pack—the size of a sheet of plywood. The guy was not original but was uniquely complete, a page out of ZAP Comix with long hair, a hand-embroidered headband highlighting the psychedelic spectrum, tie-die guinea T, beads, embroidered patches covering holes, fringe, ribbons, fruit boots and bell-bottom jeans. Running on retreads he showed one-owner confidence. The flag was in deluxe deep hues with gold fringe. A felled sapling made a flagstaff that got lashed to a motorcycle—my motorcycle. Digger or Dirt or Sisyphus or whatever the skinny guy's name was sat on back, backwards to hold the flagstaff and orchestrate the parade and tell me what was up. Everyone agreed it would be perfect with fifteen motorcycles in the campground lining up two by two with me and Skinny up front. "It's one of my specialties, man."

"What's that?"

"Fuckin' orchestration, man. I'm really good."

Well, you got to love a parade, even one that sets you up in the crosshairs of the Guardia Seville. We cruised into Pamplona honking horns and revving engines. Skinny played the flagstaff like a fishing rod, heaving back to reel in the slack and really make the fabric billow dramatically. The local folk lounged on their balconies and terraces, gearing up for the Festival of San Fermin—they knew who we were and what day it was—and they cheered! It was a day of love for America and everyone, for Nixon and Franco and us, the ragtag revolutionaries who declined the jungle war and demanded its end, the anarchists who would rather get drunk and stoned than get a job or take a bath. Most of those we passed cheered for our side. Anyone could see what was going down.

Oh, Buffalo Springfield sang and we believed, and so the Spaniards sensed our commitment and sincerity. In cross-cultural communion we cruised the antiquated homes of Pamplona celebrating independence and freedom with the families who lived there, who cheered us in the universal language, and love was all around us. Something changed on that resonant reverberation, as two peoples, two cultures, two spirits conjoined in happiness and goodwill, until things changed, as anything good or bad will change.

Then came the Guardia Seville, who felt like a man with a gun over there many times over—like the Republican Party, even then. They chased us—I shitchu not—which was perhaps the challenge we both feared and fantasized. What could they do? Catch us?

Well, yes, they could catch anyone on a motorcycle with a backwards hippy on back holding onto a flag as big a quilt lashed to a small tree. Quicker witted in the survival realm than I was in romance, I had two or three turns before the jig would be up, so I took a narrow street into a narrow alley and told Skinny to get off.

Naturally, he resisted, pleading that I could not just leave him there, assuring me that it would not be cool, no way, man, no fucking way. I kicked out the side stand, pulled my knife and cut the bindings between the tree and the motorcycle and the tree and the flag and told him to hang on, which he gladly did, ditching the tree and stuffing as much of the flag as would fit under his shirt.

We hightailed it around the back way with Skinny facing front, calling directions. I followed his directions, knowing he could be no worse than me at navigating. Sure enough, we popped from the density onto a familiar road and made the campground in minutes. The others drifted in over the next hour, and another day of jubilation officially began with another adventure notched—a patriotic one. So fire the fucking pipes and man the wine bottles. Oh, say, can you see?

That afternoon the motorcycle campers had to move. The last toilet had clogged and backed. The showers were cut off. All bathing was constricted to the creek, and the creek was getting funky to a hundred yards down. The only part of camp life not deteriorating was John and Jane, who seemed like a settled couple so intimately joined that a glance told the tale. They looked calm and content as old married folk with one big difference: riding the wild rooster nightly with abandon, at first light to help them start a brand new day and casually in mid-afternoon to sustain their humility and gratitude. It was like they'd met only days ago.

The next two days blurred on toxic sludge and sunburn, sweat and dust and victory fatigue. The night of the sixth shaped up as a barnburner—or a brain burner. All those decades ago we were still a decade or two prior to the massive death of nature worldwide. Yet even then we saw symptoms of the end. I suspected that nobody in a half-mile radius had actually read *The Sun Also Rises*, in which a sadly wounded war veteran seeks redemption in Pamplona. But most of the campers had heard something about the book, like Ernest Hemingway wrote it, and it was cool. The end. The night before the running of the bulls was a debauchery, a binge-drunk by thousands of people clamoring madly to be something other than themselves. The festival had been debauched by then, and it's way more fucked now, nothing at all like the festival of the soul it once was. Maybe the *Fiesta de San Fermin* was destined to degrade, given the abuse of the bulls and the spread of humanity.

By sunrise on the seventh, I felt shot at and missed and shit at and hit. Up by six to get ready for the big doings in town, we could only get up, walk a few paces and take a whiz. No showers. No coffee. No breakfast—no worries, because nobody was ready for solid food anyway. We had nothing to do, really, but throw a leg over and ride the few miles into town and park and shuffle down to where we could watch.

Run?

No way. We could barely walk. I frankly felt part and parcel of the death of nature and culture even then and couldn't have given a flat flying fuck about running anywhere, much less down the middle of a street chased by a gang of abused bulls who knew they had nothing to lose.

So we jockeyed for a vantage and finally found a space that for some reason the crowd avoided. Oh, wait, that line painted right there on the street is the runner's line. We needed to be on the outside. But no sooner did I step back outside the line than a fascist billy club came down on my shoulder. The Guardia Seville yelled that nobody crossed back out. Maybe they recognized me. I shook my head. They shook their clubs, itching to brain me. I didn't think I'd puke for another few minutes but really couldn't lift my shoes from the sorry ass shuffle of the downtrodden. So I shuffled down the street, thinking I'd go ahead and shuffle into the arena before the bulls were released. After all, it was still two minutes to seven.

But someone shrieked in another universal language, and it was on. Bulls weren't actually necessary for the few ounces of adrenaline squirting into the heart. A few Spaniards in traditional white pants and shirts with red neckerchiefs ran past at full speed and jumpstarted me to the coronary redline on the very next beat. A quick glance back at the thundering tonnage of hooves confirmed the onslaught. Death was imminent. Way too big to dodge or duck under, the trampling wave pounded things senseless.

The first few bulls were fast, much faster than me, so I took a lead from a Spaniard and found a doorway to duck into. It allowed only a foot or so of recess, but that seemed better than sticking out from the wall. Many bulls remained, so I ran with the crowd toward the tunnel. The tunnel was mayhem if you got caught in there with the bulls. I slowed, glanced back and then downshifted for a balls-out sprint through the darkness that kept stretching, stretching, even as the turf pounded closer from the rear. Life would end in a pounding—but then shooting into daylight I ran for the perimeter of the arena, where fans cheered and beckoned me to run faster.

Andale! They urged with gaining urgency. Pop eyes and sweat-beaded faces reflected the reaper one step back.

With a hot snort on my neck I thrust both arms up just at the wall. In a blink the hands of God grasped my forearms and sprung me up and over to safety. Eager fans patted my back and head briefly then returned to the fray and another runner to save. Here too was rare evidence in the case for humanity. I loved them in a dazed hangover, panting and feeling existence just over the line.

Well, it was a beautiful time of survival, all things considered, but Pamplona felt ready for an exit, what with the shit and toilet paper running downhill and the binge going way past the limits of a binge.

Somewhere else seemed in order. Anywhere would do. The loosely spoken plan was for John and me to ride along with Jane and Rianne. Chas and Billy would ride in the van too, since they'd hitchhiked to Pamplona anyway, and Billy was still banging Rianne, though she'd cut him back to once daily, or maybe twice if it was a long day. I went along with the plan, grateful for friends who seemed to know the road and California, our spiritual base and the original Mecca of Revolution and Freedom.

Everyone was done with Pamplona after a week of watching the campground become a disaster area—like Earth in time-lapse. We would leave the following morning and gladly forego six more days of bull running because, frankly, we'd been there, done that. And by leaving early, we could beat the rush.

But another disaster occurred that changed everything. Near the summit of a sundown sexual interlude—a favorite time for John and Jane; the light was so soft, the campground so peaceful at that hour with everyone prepping dinner on their fires, and a nice fuck relaxed them so well—Jane found out or John let slip, that he was nineteen.

Jane was twenty-two.

It was over. She'd bargained on a man, not a kid on summer break. Not a…a…a fucking teenager! Fuck! Man! Packed and gone in mere minutes flat between dusk and dark, she gave him what for with a drop dead, motherfucker on the way out. She hit another wall besides the bingeing and the shit-smell walls and the crowded, dirty, nasty walls. Jane got clogged like the clogged up *baño* and had no choice but to overflow. Now where the fuck is that? At.

Beans and wine for dinner? Again? Just like that, Jane and Rianne were gone. So were Chas and Billy, and in spite of the difficulty before us, the outflow relieved many things that felt clogged. It would have been nice riding along with a van, but convenience seemed similar to baggage. For starters, Chas and Billy wouldn't shut up. Billy rambled over the incredible, amazing, unbelievably best fuck in his whole, entire life. "I'm dead motherfucking serious, man. Her pussy smells like gumdrops, or lightning oughta strike me fucking dead! Lemme tell you what she likes…" This, with Rianne paces away, as if brothers and sisters were meant to share natural truths naturally. It wasn't natural. In those first awkward phases of realizing that we were not in fact brothers and sisters, it was harsh.

Rianne and I blushed through those interludes. I wanted to comfort her but could not. Then she was gone.

John and I had a bowl of kief like men coming to terms with a milestone in life, looking ahead to what men must do. We would cross the Pyrenees into Andorra, a good ride for the morning, then head down to the coast and follow the coast road toward Monaco. We wanted to see the Riviera and the topless women there. I felt experienced and wanted to engage one in conversation. Then we'd head into Italy for what could well be a whole new phase of fun.

As our planning reverie finished, the nurse from Canada walked over to ask for a minute, please. I sensed a scolding for feeling her tit last night—or was it night before last? But she got me aside to say she'd been thinking, you know, and wanted to come along, you know, on back and be my, you know, date—not date, really, but you know, kind of a travel companion, you know...

I didn't know but heard the offer to ride both on and off the motorcycle. Her rack and glow and pretty face were compelling, but along with blowing sure shots on two beauties that week, I'd blown my reason and patience, too. I said, "No. I need to ride alone now."

She hung her head to murmur, "I understand." I'm not sure what she understood. Maybe she thought she shouldn't have complained about a tit squeeze. Maybe she sensed a rare chance to hang out with a free spirit on a motorcycle. Maybe she was twenty-five already, or twenty-eight. I wonder where she went. On a few common coordinates she was willing to ride on back across Europe, because we were young and could resolve the hormonal challenge of the times we lived in.

I walked toward the motorcycle bivouac through the disheveled, half-struck campground and campers cooking last meals before departure to fresher places. From the thick of it I turned to see her walking away among the campfires. Should I go get her? Is fate so fickle on a moment's indecision? I took a step in her direction—what the hell. When you got nothing you got... But from the dwindling motorcycle line-up near the fence came another chaos.

"Fuck!" John vented over love lost and more: Jane had split with his passport. Fuming and pacing he figured we could catch them if we left now, because failure would leave us stuck.

He wasn't worried about Andorra, because it's a principality, not a country, no need for passports there, and we could enter Monaco the same way. But Italy's border would be the end of the road with no passport. But shit, we had the Pyrenees Mountains and the entire south coast of France to catch them, which was good. And bad. Fuck. Who needs a mountain pass at midnight? Fuck that.

So we stoked another bowl and popped the last of the vino to ease into a night of reckoning and steel us for long, winding miles at breakneck speed.

What the fuck?

I thought about seeing if the nurse from Canada wanted to, you know, hang out for a while, to further examine prospects for traveling together, but the dope and potential rejection on a test grind, I mean a little quiet time together, undermined motivation, or rather burned it down to embers and ashes.

I drifted to dreamland on compound regret; events of the week had led to insight on the romance/love/sexual situation relating to women. Things were not yet clear, but a little light shone. That is, the Golden Fleece must not be pursued or resisted but sincerely observed. She would indicate what to do and when. Marisol and Rianne had shown the threshold, and I'd failed to carry them over. Unless I was wrong, and they too would have stopped cold on assault with attempt to grope. Unless, maybe...

At daybreak John cooked cowboy coffee on a camp stove, ready to go. Other campers were waking to the noise of campers leaving. The American contingent had shot its wad in the build-up; no way did this crowd want another six days. It was black coffee and a pipe for John and me. He passed a wine bottle. I declined—a growth moment. We mounted up on sparse talk and rolled across the campground berms ready to ride but fearing indefinite ignorance on the ways of women and their illogical wants for many miles. The Canada nurse would likely pull an Oregon on the next male encountered, if he could show a pulse, keep his mouth shut and do as instructed, whether she instructed it or not. Damn.

I glanced over the hillock where she would be waking up. She's sixty-five or seventy now with a nursing career behind her and many grateful recipients of her care. Does she remember the randy thin boy who got away in Pamplona? More aware than most of what was upon us, she called it *the times we live in and the world around us and the wonderful adventure ahead.* Simply stating the obvious truth, she recognized *the joy we shared.* She'd called the night beautiful and affirmed our youth and life.

Simon & Garfunkel sang of *Old Friends* with a perfect ballad for melancholy moments back then and forever more, its innocence and confidences flickering softly as candlelight at the shrine of the love all around us.

More reflective lyrics never were, but John made the pavement and throttled with a vengeance, leaving no choice but a power twist to follow suit. Then again, we strove for the nitty-gritty, for getting down and getting it on. Paring fat, ditching baggage, down to two guys on motorcycles felt free and easy as open road. And leaving a place never felt better. What a dump—we made it that way, with the drinking and doping, the sexual howls of youth rutting like dogs and none for me, the overworked, graying, sudsy creek, the grassy campground reduced to tread marks in mud, the clogged toilets and overflowing sewage taking us to the more, more, more of the times and a vaguely familiar excess. Oh, it was all too much all right, and there we were, hell bent for more, just up the road.

Well, it was a lovely fucking time that made a big impression and fairly captured the long and the short of it. A small society based on fundamental need and over-stimulation screwed things up. The pleasure centers got singed, and we needed fresh perspective, just like now, in a society convoluting through far more layers, electronically socializing, commenting, interacting, keeping its eyes down on tiny screens, jamming buttons to score more.

Over the Mountains and Into the Sea

JOHN'S RIDING SKILL was evident again, or maybe he wanted out of himself more urgently. Taking curves with abandon we raced across the foothills and over the plains for long, demanding miles through liberating hours. In the mid-summer of youth, exhilaration and rebirth are readily available. Life in abundance effused energy, stamina and lust into the mountains and up. Away from where we'd felt like Donovan's caterpillar, our departure the same as shedding our skins, yet doubts loomed in the miles ahead. Would we reveal the butterfly within?

I kept up as I could, into curves over my head, learning from the best teacher, experience, about engine braking and not locking up the rear wheel and dire consequence on a twisty mountain pass. Pushing the motorcycle down to lay it over as I'd seen the old French guy do in Biarritz, we finally dragged on asphalt. It felt too cold for sparks but I double clutched as well to better free the flywheel between shifts. John loosened up too, and so we flew.

Numbing summit passes hampered clutch and brake functions as our hands froze, so we pulled over to lean forward and grasp our exhaust pipes where they came out of the engine. John had seen this technique in a war movie where the Krauts were grabbing the hot pipes of their beemers, and he thought it was bullshit, but he always wanted to try it. It cooked our gloves but restored hand flexibility for the miles remaining at altitude.

Andorra was non-descript, a gingerbread tourist stop with many cultural items for sale. With some olives, coffee and a roll I sat on a curb to thaw and eat. John paced, watching traffic. Heading down the road we could easily monitor for them, but a town with side streets called for a keen eye to keep a red VW camper from slipping past. He couldn't believe after so many curvy miles so fast we hadn't caught them.

They had to spend the night somewhere too. She couldn't have been upset enough to drive all night. Could she? Equally rattling were prospects for Chas and Billy rounding out a new quartet. John was smitten, in pain. The only antidote: action. "Come on. They're up ahead," he announced, mounting up before I was half done.

Passing from Spain to Andorra and from there into France with no passports sounds crazy in today's world of security agents with accents patting down citizens of the United States of America, touching genitals and peeking into your skivvies for the good of the nation. But the world had not yet devolved. Passport checks and borders were relatively new, a holdover from WW II, growing in layers of complexity and control.

Marseilles would have been forgettable with flat topography and industry, but a Midwestern kid on a motorcycle rode alongside the Mediterranean through a major industrial port with the world at last in his heart. Pumped with urgency to embrace it all as if on a deadline, every mile felt new as gift. Marseilles back then had just met gridlock, its many arteries clogged by more traffic than the arteries could handle. Not to worry, with many new arteries under construction. The red van was not to be seen. Who knew if they'd come through Andorra or taken the coast road through Barcelona? Who knew if they were headed to Florence at all? Who knew if they'd be on the coast road past Marseilles?

In and out of town we rode with a few other motorcycles, first five, then fifteen, twelve, eighteen, brothers in the bond, some commuters but mostly adventuring youth, some American and some European. BMW, Moto Guzzi, all the British bikes, the odd Husquevarna and Royal Enfield and a few unknowns, we cruised in unison, in a common spirit of the day. The 60s had thrown off the yokes of difference and sameness, of prescribed life schedules, of convention and expectation. Palpable among us at fifty miles per hour was a common light of youth, wanderlust and spontaneous potential. Riding a motorcycle was always removed, but in those days we felt like advance couriers of the new word.

The southern coast of France was dramatically beautiful when first glimpsed from a distance. Gritty and dirty up close, it felt dirty, bare-breasted and abused. Humanity was comfortable by then with convenient packaging discarded out the window—packaging made of plastic that would linger for ages. And cigarette butts, because the taste of springtime, come up to Marlboro country, all the way up, Lucky Strike Means Fine Tobacco, Chesterfield, Pall Mall, Viceroy and the rest had become filtered. So many butts in the sand allowed no footfall to avoid them. It wasn't the Riviera imagined. The naked women seemed far away, surrendered to a starker bareness and sadder gravity.

Then came Monaco, hub of millionaires, castles and legendary casinos. Swimming pools. Movie stars. We didn't exactly feel like the Beverly Hillbillies, because they had a beat up old truck with Granny riding in her rocker on top. But the cultural disjunction was the same—with raccoon eyes from days on the road and grit, grease and bugs rounding the white circles behind our sunglasses, we looked unapproachable. Traveling with minimal gear is a blessed skill of young people, and we couldn't have been lighter, making do with no change of clothes. John finally relaxed beside the teeming traffic; no way they could have beat us to this border. No fucking way, not with the hell-bent riding we'd done since Pamplona.

The border crossing was a wide spot on the coast road with a tollbooth of sorts, where people stopped to show passports and entered Italy. Like most border crossings then, it was a formality. Anyone who could manage normal behavior for a few minutes could pass through. The sidewalk also widened on the Monaco side, though foot traffic seemed unlikely. The road on the Italian side went a few miles along a wooded shoreline with no sidewalks, no stores or stops.

We pulled onto the widened walkway near the customs booth and parked. The hillside to the left looked painted with castles and casinos. To the right, a seductive sea shimmered under blue skies. Boats cruised or swung idly from moorings here and there. Such luxury and opulence made that glittering patch of Mediterranean as different from the Midwest as a soybean silo from a motor yacht.

John had grown more macho in the few weeks I'd known him. He felt supported in this endeavor by his accomplishments, logging many miles and having sexual relations many times with an older woman. He'd proven his grit, and so he insisted that real riders sleep on their motorcycles—it was commonly known and practiced. What? You didn't know that?

I tried, propping my head on my backpack and crossing my ankles over the handlebars. A center stand would have been easier, but I wedged a sweatshirt under the left side, butt and back, to shim things up to level, kind of. At dusk a guy came around hawking sardine sandwiches for sixteen hundred fifty liras, about a buck, which seemed steep, but he had us. Chopped sardines, onions and olives in olive oil on a hard bun, its fulgent taste perfectly blended the elements of that long, forever day and life on the Med.

Nobody could sleep, but John felt it best that we stay awake anyway. They couldn't pass into Italy without seeing us, but they might see us and pass anyway. So we lay back and watched, wondering if they would see us and pass anyway.

By midnight we slept. In the morning we agreed that they wouldn't have driven in the night. If they had, they would have seen us and stopped because, after all, Jane couldn't hate John's guts enough to put him in a fix just for slipping her the salami and not telling her he was nineteen. Could she? Nah! We didn't think so. In fact, she might by then have reconsidered…

Well, that didn't matter. The sun climbed higher and the day got hot, and with youthful impatience, we wondered how they'd beaten us to the border. It didn't seem possible, but then they had a big head start, and a four-wheeler goes farther between rest stops and covers more miles in a day. Hell, you can practically nod off driving a four-wheeler and still cover a few hundred miles a day. Because a motorcycle wears you down. The wind and sun take your energy, and so do the rain and cold. A car has a windshield and a roof—and a heater and windshield wipers and three hundred miles on an average day, maybe four hundred. On a motorcycle you have thrills and chills, leaning and scraping and road fatigue in two hundred miles or two fifty. Or three on a push. We'd pushed.

We knew they'd beat us by mid-morning. We waited till noon to come up with a plan on impulse. Approaching the border on the Monaco side two German guys rode two up on a little one-lung scooter. Like Hans 'n Franz, the driver looked muscularly miniscule, while the guy on back bulged big. They too no speaka too gooda de English, but they pulled over as requested to hear our story and maybe comprehend our proposal. Our charades conveyed our need—they got it. John wanted them to pass through the border station as they had planned. But instead of riding on back of Hans' little scooter, Franz would drive the Thunderbird. Franz could do this, because the world was a simpler, better place at that time.

I would ride my moto through the border station with Hans 'n Franz. Once safely across into Italy, we would ride a mile or so down the road, out of sight of the border crossing, where John would meet us and take his motorcycle back from Franz. Eyebrows today would rise at this juncture, which shows how much we've lost. Back then the world of youth was one, unified with a common nemesis and a common goal. That language of simplicity may suggest oversimplification. And it's true that such a concept would never work today and may never work again. And therein resided the magic, in people wanting to be free, as they should be, in peace.

What is now a hokey, passé lyric by the Rascals from a half-century ago said it best. Back then we lived in that world. That sounds vacuous and sometimes was, but on that day, Hans 'n Franz shared a nod. Franz said something like, *Yah! I ride der grossa moto! Yah! Unt den we halten on der uder side.*

"Wait a minute," I said to John. "What are you gonna do? Hide in my backpack?" I didn't get it.

"I'm gonna swim it," John said, backing chronic macho with the man walk. I sensed a Hollywood rendition of the man walk, as seen in *Von Ryan's Express*, *The Great Escape* or any silver screen classic starring Frank Sinatra, Steve McQueen or John Levy.

I stared in disbelief that he would risk his life in the spirit of screen magic or the spirit of finding a little paper and cardboard document or getting laid again, maybe. I laughed short. I did not restate the premise because John was two layers in and peeling to his skivvies. With no further ado it was, "Here. Take my shit." He ambled down the stony path and rock-hopped the shoreline and jumped the fuck in. I looked left and right, fore and aft. Nobody noticed. Nobody cared. What if they did? A guy needs to go for a swim sometimes—alone in the Mediterranean. With no beach, murky water and a bunch of huge boats and people in white pants and blue blazers staring at him. He swam out a long way, what looked like a mile, and hung a left. I lashed his stuff onto the back of the Thunderbird.

And so it came to pass that Franz got fulfilled straddling a big British moto. Hans 'n I mounted up and followed through customs, showing passports and nodding yes and crossing in three minutes. We waited a half-mile down on the shoulder where the trees opened on a sea view. The border guards could have seen us but weren't looking. We posed no threat. It didn't matter. It was only a crazy, fucked up kid from LA swimming across a border because his ex-girlfriend had his passport, because she split in a hurry, pissed off that she was a grown woman of twenty-two and he was a teenager, nineteen maybe but hardly the man she'd thought him to be and bucked into midnight with.

I don't wonder where Jane is now, never have. But I doubt she ever humped a man more man than John Levy, who swam straight out with no hesitation till he shrank to a speck of flotsam beyond the boats. He churned on a strong, steady stroke showing no hint of heading in. Do they have sharks in the Med? Did they have sharks back then, before the Med died?

John wasn't going for it in the mode so popular a few years later but applying a spirit to a task, coming into manhood on practical necessity. John crossed the border with no passport.

Hans 'n Franz and I rode up another half-mile to the next clearing, because John was not turning toward the shore. I waved his shirt in the air, and without waving back, he turned in. He took another half hour to swim to shore and amble out, staggering and dripping. Hans 'n Franz hung around because they loved the action, pulling a goof on a major country in the spirit of the Revolution—and on motorcycles to boot. It was the action that defined us, that bonded us as brothers, which served as a magnet to any gathering of kindred spirits in that magical time. We'd won another skirmish, and John's celebration was brief but solid. Climbing back into his funky duds, it was black power handshakes all around and back on the road, double clutching for Florence.

Finding a red VW van in one of Italy's biggest cities would have felt nearly impossible, but *Europe on $5 a Day* listed three campgrounds in town, narrowing the search considerably. The first was small and easily scanned. "They're not here," John announced, dropping into gear before I could speak. The second campground was vast, a few acres on a hillside with scenic views and a creek. I scanned, wondering if it would clog on toilet paper. John tore through and in a few minutes came back. "They're not here."

"Whoa!"

"What?"

"They're here." I pointed down and to the left, just yonder. In another few minutes it was sheepish blushing all around. It looked like Jane had indeed horsefucked Billy, and there was John boy again—but wait a minute.

No, she hadn't. Maybe Billy wanted to—hell, yes, Billy wanted to—but she couldn't get old John out of her mind, and there he was.

John was worse, love sick and no two ways about it. He said she'd ripped off his passport.

She said she didn't fucking rip off any such fucking thing.

He dove into the red van and under one of the fold-down berths, and there it was. "Oh yeah?" What a relief, kind of.

"I didn't rip it off. You left it there."

"Yeah, well. You didn't have to leave so fast like that."

"I was mad."

John grinned. "You mean you're not mad anymore?"

She didn't grin back, but everyone saw a crack in the wall. "Not as much." It was like she'd never be completely satisfied, but a hardy round of groin pounding right then and there might help rectify the situation. John nodded like he'd seen John Wayne do a few times and headed back into the van. Jane wagged her head and followed, mumbling about boys and their fucked up needs.

Rianne sorted her laundry behind the van, which also seemed like a relief. "Billy and Chas out for lunch?"

"They split."

I squatted nearby to better watch a small masonry cupid pouring water from a blossom. You can't beat Florence for sculpture. "Doesn't seem like them."

"We got tired of them real fast," she said.

"You mean they got invited to split."

"Not really. Jane told them to get the fuck outa the van. I think she's in love."

"I guess you're not."

"No. That guy was a jerk. What are you gonna do?"

"I don't know." But I did know what I wasn't going to do, which was stick my peepee into Rianne's teetee, luscious as she looked. I hadn't yet sorted that aspect of the romance/love/sexuality continuum either; I anticipated the distinct scent of gumdrops and man goo. She seemed weak and soiled. Maybe she wasn't, but maybe my instincts were correct. Social disease in those days was the clap. The end. Oh, you could get syphilis and warts and some other nasty, exotic stuff, like the guys in Vietnam were bringing home, but you really had to go dredging the ditch to find that stuff. It was most often the clap and some penicillin, over and out. But still, she'd lowered her standards so hard and so fast. Chas was a dirtball, a clod and the worst kind of a loser, one with a big mouth. I wanted to nestle up to someone, but Rianne seemed somehow on the mend, airing out, freshening up. That's how young men think. Given a few decades, it's easier to process life's foibles, like Rianne giving it up to an asshole from Oregon. I've done the same with as much failure of character as Rianne could ever show. I'd played Chas's role as well, because given the time, most people play most parts.

John and I parked between the red van and a white car that belonged to Rayanne, who camped alongside. What an amusing confusion with Rianne on the one hand and Rayanne on the other. It seemed cosmic on a molecular level, like comet dust had settled on what was meant to be. Craving sexual relations with Rayanne would be obvious for any male. I craved the chance for Rianne to hear us.

Oh. Don't stop.

Those were the days. A sprightly nymphet pretty as a buxom pixie, Rayanne was a drop-dead cutie who could return a flirtation with the best of them. Oh, it was an invitation to a lovelock if ever a doubtful boy saw one. But things are rarely as simple as they should be. Rayanne held back. She didn't want to hold back. Holding back was against her instinct and better nature. Rayanne embraced the sexual revolution and wanted in—make that back in. She'd jumped in some months ago and got knocked up and ran into trouble on a tubular pregnancy with a cist on an ovary and a complicated tumor and surgery including hysterectomy and some other removals.

Rayanne was on the mend but still traumatized, her travels meant to rejuvenate her youth with renewed perspective on the rest of her life. Who wouldn't love a holiday after what she'd been through? Months of anxiety and pain had left her restless as a racehorse at a starting gate.

Oh, Rayanne wanted to run. But the world back then had no arthroscopic, lathroscopic or anyoscopic surgical procedure. All surgery required major incision, excision, stitches and scars. She would reveal her body to nobody, or, as she put it, "No pussy for you. Trust me. You don't want it in this condition." Which of course led to pathetic insistence that I did, and then to the inevitable dilemma of whether special relief should be merely anticipated or directly requested.

Rayanne didn't need that foolishness. I shrugged. It was only a simple question, and I couldn't really fault her for not wanting a schwantz lunging at her tonsils. Then again…

Never mind, she slowly unbuttoned her frilly blouse, then reached back to unhook the harness. The front loader was still a few years into the future. Anyway, with no further ado, rack revealed, she said a suckle would be lovely—not the one I'd requested but with my puckered lips on her two jugs. It was her version of a better idea. I complied and found it—to coin a phrase of the day—neat. But strange—Rayanne wanted lips on her nipples, any lips. I sensed difficulty a few minutes in, which is a long time to suck on tits. And I realized that she wanted lips sucking indefinitely.

I doubt she had come to terms on the rational plane. She craved nursing in post partum compensation, and though any lips applying suction would have done, she especially liked a hundred thirty-five pounds o' motoboy with a Lightning Rocket between his legs. It compensated her loss on a new mode of fitting in, kind of.

Fuck.

And alas. Things soon seemed askew.

Post partum blues leveled out on hummed lullabies. She cradled my head. Don't get me wrong; I still think of Rayanne, but five minutes was plenty, ten minutes more than enough, fifteen an imposition. She held me in place.

We soon reached an impasse, a repetition of non-variable friction points that could not possibly achieve resolution.

In coming weeks another young woman would sit next to me on the bus from Piraeus to Athens. Carolyn, like Rayanne, would fill the bill on intellect, articulation, womanly wares and an impressive balance between adventure lust and mental stability. But she would also fit into a pattern, call it a set piece on the evolution of romance. Also about my age, Carolyn would seem more mature, and she wore a dress. I loved that. We talked easily for hours and checked into the same hotel on arrival. She said to give her a few minutes, like twenty, so she could freshen up. Then I should come on down. To her room. She pecked me on the lips.

When I went down, she was gone, checked out. I still don't get it. I can't. The curse finally lifted in Tel Aviv with a girl who wouldn't shut up till she did, who kept rattling about the heritage of Zion and our continuing struggle. Wasn't it great? Being there in the Holy Land at that significant moment in history was…significant. And historical.

Our physical exchange was neither, ending in four to six seconds in a more prodigious mess than taking the top off the blender halfway through a smoothie. We thought that was normal.

Not to worry; only two months later the most beautiful campus female in Middle America plucked my heartstrings as deftly as Betty Boop had done when I was merely a lad. Engaged to be married in Boston, she asked if she could come over for a study date. I shrugged. Why not? Betty was smart and a better student than I. We studied all night, mostly physiology and sociology, including the great goodwill and public service that make the world a better place with special relief all around. But, I get ahead of myself.

John and Jane were on again, though she asked him to please keep his fucking mouth shut on the age thing. So we all hung out for a few days in Florence, visiting the original David and the huge flea market, where you could buy a Nazi SS uniform in mint condition for about twenty bucks, maybe from the original owner. I scanned the crowd for old Nazis. They weren't so hard to spot.

Rayanne was a triumph of the spirit but wasn't enough. Primed for all of her, I got only wet tit and a cold shoulder. So it soon came time again to hit the road alone.

The last time I set out solo was parting company with David out of Paris, with loneliness in waves. This next solitary departure felt like cleansing, and growth, like letting go for endless miles. On the far side of the mountain, my motorcycle and I could meet the wide world in anonymity and faith as everyone must, sooner or later.

A sign of the times was that the lyric of the times could adjust to any occasion of the times.

Maybe Jackson Browne was camping in Florence that summer, composing *Fountain of Sorrow*. My solitary departure had been forlorn and confused out of Paris, yet it would repeat itself in confidence. I would be all right. The Florence campground filled with arrivals from Pamplona and Marrakech. It felt like a repeat scene. John seemed keen on settling in one more time, smoking dope, relaxing and having sex with Jane as often as possible. Jane went shopping every day.

I rolled out of the Florence campground to the backdrop of John and Jane squabbling over limited space in the VW van and all this crap stacking up so you couldn't even lay down anymore, but whose crap is it anyway?

Whose fucking van do think it is anyway?

Fade to the soothing syncopation of pistons gaining rpm on the way out of the campground. Maybe they worked things out. Rianne glanced up from a chore to wave goodbye at my rearview mirror. And so on out of town.

I hit the Autostrada del Sol just south of Firenze early in the morning, bound for Roma. I had no plans other than seeing Rome. I wanted to round a roundabout and stop for an espresso any old where. Things were easing up, what would later be known as manning up. The world eased into friendly terms, and the adventure was hardly begun.

On a long straightaway in mid-afternoon, somewhere south of Baschi but north of Orte, deep in the groove of life in movement, I heard a knock, knock, knocking but not on heaven's door. I killed the engine because I knew what it was as it got louder and uglier, like hammers on anvils, tearing cylinders asunder. It sounded too late. Life had rolled down an Italian highway to beautiful horizons till it clanged, banged and clattered to a stop.

Bummer. A surly little guy from Manchester who described himself as a BSA mechanic had adjusted my tappets at the campground in Pamplona and then test-drove my motorcycle at a hundred forty. I thought he was bullshitting but wound it out myself and thought he'd done it right. Two weeks later it didn't matter. I found neutral to avoid seizing the tranny too, then coasted to the shoulder on a rattle and shudder. I didn't have a degree yet but was already thinking like a college graduate: I needed help.

It didn't take long. The Autostrada had help phones every mile or so, so it was a short hike to the next box, where I picked it up and asked, "No speaka too gooda Italiano. *Parlez vous*, humma humma?" On an earful of highspeed Italian I culled for a single syllable of English or maybe French. I found a few here and there and sought meaning. Then I took my only course of action: hang out and wait. An hour later a flatbed pulled up with a ramp and tie downs. I didn't get it. That wouldn't happen in the Land of the Free. I rode shotgun, and before too long, somewhere south of Orte, we pulled into a rest stop.

This too was different than your average interstate relief station. Instead of a parking lot, bathrooms and many children, this place was an olive grove with a terrace café overlooking a lake. The driver explained something in Italian and led the way to a table in the café, where he introduced an old man who sat there. The old man told me to sit and ordered a round of *Fernet-Branca*. The driver drifted off. Who knew? Into that beautiful setting the drinks arrived. *Fernet-Branca* is a liqueur, black and thick as roofing tar with a dash of mud and sugar, served in a fine, thin jigger with a lemon twist.

Well, it'd been a long goddamn day, so I put it down the hatch. The old man watched to see if I'd drop dead. When I didn't, he ordered another round. We talked, kind of. In sparse French he said he spent his days there in the café—*toujours dans le café*—but it wasn't always like that. He'd been in the *guerre*, WWII. "Ah," I nodded. "*Tu est un fascist.*"

"No!" he bellowed, winding up to swat me. But then he laughed and ordered us one more round. In an hour the driver came back out and we were on our way. I was not allowed to pay. What a day. What an old soldier. What a gut bomb, but never mind; what hospitality and peace of mind.

Back on the Autostrada, the driver asked many questions.

"The fuck, man. I don't know."

So he slowed down and got down to English, kind of. "You moto. Is *que?*"

"It's a BSA. 650cc. *Seis cent cinquante centimeteur cubique.*"

"Ah. *Seicento cinquanta centimetri cubici! Sei feefty!*"

"*Oui*. I mean, *si.*"

He plucked his CB radio from a sun visor cradle and barked a few words, waited and went into overdrive, so fast I couldn't catch a syllable. He stopped to ask, "You moto. *Issa Treeomph?*"

"No. It's a BSA."

"Ah." And back to the CB. "Bay assa ey…" Spaghetti, fettuccini, bon giorno, cinquante, no parlo, Alfredo, salami, pastrami, risotto, minestrone. Who knew what he said? Then he said, "*Molto bene. Gratzi. Si. Prego.*"

He grinned and nodded, with certainty, I thought. So we penetrated Rome. Traffic thickened and streets narrowed. Huge roundabouts with many lanes felt like a challenge and a threat. Who would ever go to the inside lane with maximum travel of three-quarters of a lap? Crazy. Yet a tiny car on the inside lane ahead seemed intent on ramming a scooter, as the scooter wanted farther in and the car wanted out. The scooter stopped abruptly and the driver got off, forcing the tiny car to also stop, and that driver got out too. They went toe-to-toe, yelling and flailing even as they turned and got back in and remounted and went their separate ways, to the inside and outside of the roundabout. The tiny car driver flicked the tip of his thumb off a top front tooth. The scooter driver let go of his handlebars to grasp the top of this left elbow with his right hand and thrust his left hand upward. "*Bah fangoo!*" He nearly hit another car, causing him to refocus his accusation and bitter claim on that driver, and so they went, round and round.

Most amazing was that the other lanes of roundabout traffic flowed around the squabblers while rounding the roundabout.

We turned onto a narrow street with an inch to spare on one side and barely a scrape on the other and stopped at a narrower alley we would never fit into. Not to worry, the moto mechanic was only a short way down, and he came out with the usual entourage of kids.

Once unloaded and parked inside, my motorcycle went through some brief tests, primarily of putting it into gear and rolling it. Metal fragments clattered inside, followed by wincing, cringing and head shaking all around. It looked like a set-up but sounded like the real deal, a blown engine. The mechanic conveyed the likely damage: maybe it would not be total on the bottom end and so it might not need pistons, cylinders and maybe a new main bearing. Maybe the damage would be only on top—heads, tappets, lifters and valves. He wouldn't know until tomorrow, because it was already late in the day. But he would tear it down first thing and then call London for parts and get them ordered. With luck, I could be out of there in a day, or maybe three days.

Afraid to ask what it would cost, I asked where to stay cheap. He nodded back up the alley at the city. My flatbed driver waited. The mechanic spoke to him in casual Italian, and we were off again in the flatbed, this time to a park a few minutes away, near the coliseum. I winced, seeing the park crowded with campers. It was Pamplona redux but bigger with more exhaust, body odor and garlic, a challenging blend of scents but infinitely better than shit. Maybe this place had a sewer main.

I got out and shook hands with the driver. He hadn't mentioned a fee, so I asked, *"Combien ça coute? Quanto costa?"*

He shook his head. I still didn't get it. What a country, to care so deeply for its youthful motorcyclists out making contact with the world. The idea at hand was that a country should care for its visitors who would carry home lasting impressions, visitors who were, after all, spending money. The service seemed casual yet today is recalled as far away in a strange place.

A few thousand kids camped on the ground. I didn't know anybody but neither did they. So I ambled in, looking for a few square feet to unroll my bag and lay down, comforted by the easy move to horizontal, surrounded by an atmosphere both benign and welcoming. Yet a random selection in a crowd of kids would foretell fate for the near term.

On one side were a striking couple, Erik from Scandinavia and Gretchen from Germany. Very few young people had body fat then, because it was a more healthful time in general. We'd grown up without computers or video games. We'd spent youthful years playing outdoors, low tech games like tag, freeze tag, hide 'n seek, piggy wants a wave, red rover, crack the whip. A hallmark of youth BC (before computers) was the parental call at dusk. *You get in here this minute, and I mean now!* That was in from outdoors, where pulses surged and life was vital. Thinness was also part of the youth culture because of the speed freaks, but recreational drugs seemed less tragic than the obesity epidemic a few decades down the road.

All the rockers were skin on bones, with a standard physique useless to any purpose under heaven except for twanging electric neon Jesus out of heavily amped guitars and banging on drums. Erik was better built than most, handsome and suave with blond hair, blue eyes and a perfect nose that looked superior. Erik turned to Gretchen, whose blue eyes, blonde hair, perfect nose and stunning posture could make men twitch in fear and longing. Together, they were like data meant to prove an Aryan theory.

I imagined her in form-fit leathers with a whip. *"Veh iss yoh peppahsss?"* She spoke with soft deliberation, commanding the eyes of males, a dominatrix to make men cower, to make men give and hope for some discipline too.

She took my hand and gazed into my eyes. Erik asked if I was traveling alone. I said ya, I mean yes. He looked at her. She watched me. She asked, "Do you have the Eurail pass?" Maybe a third of the kids traveled by train that summer. A Eurail pass was a few hundred bucks depending on class of service and countries covered. For one price a pass allowed open travel within certain boundaries and dates. "No. I have a motorcycle."

They traded another glance, seemingly asking each other, *Eina grossa moto? Vas is los?*

"A moto. Varoom! A BSA. Six-fifty. Lightning Rocket."

"Ah!"

"Ya!"

They looked around, puzzled. Where did I park? I told them it was getting an oil change and would be ready tomorrow or the day after. So Erik leaned in close to confide like men in the bond, that he and Gretchen were travel companions, but he would at that point be forced to leave, but she wanted more, so to speak, so if I wanted her—his words—she would be my travel companion.

Wait a minute. If I wanted her? Who wouldn't want Gretchen? Who wouldn't crave two out of three falls with Gretchen and a sure loss? Or three out of five? Or some mud wrestling and feather dusting? "Yes. Okay." And so it was set. Gretchen gathered her things and moved them the few feet from where they'd been alongside Erik over to the snuggle place next to me. I hadn't yet experimented with psychedelic drugs in the summer of '69, but Gretchen's willingness to let me "have her" felt as removed from reality as anything I'd known. Erik watched and smiled, perhaps recalling his own disbelief at this sudden jackpot. I imagined the works yet wondered why Erik looked so relieved.

Well, he was obviously not up to the challenge. So much woman requires a hefty hunk o' man to balance the needs of the first party with the supply of the second. I felt confident, pushing twenty maybe but feeling seventeen—twice a night or a baker's dozen would not challenge the catering department. I wanted to clarify that we would, you know, do everything, but it seemed obvious that we would, and clarifying seemed so…American. She held my arm with two hands and rubbed it. A guy came around hawking sandwiches, so we bought sandwiches. Erik excused himself to go down the street for some wine, and the evening was made. Gretchen showed me a pose, twisting her torso to advantage, though I could not imagine a disadvantage. She stared at me. She batted her lashes. She blushed at will. She caught my eye and glanced at my crotch. I lay back as Erik returned with the wine. We drank. We moaned and agreed that things were good and we were part of it.

I woke up with Gretchen clinging to me. I caressed her hair. She smiled. I touched her cheek. She murmured. I reached…under her blouse. She giggled. Then it was time to rise.

Back at the moto shop in the alley my motorcycle lay splayed, disemboweled. Then came the news: total annihilation. The oil pump had stopped. I was consoled by assurance that it could happen to anyone at any time—that an engine running dry would last a mile or two before seizing or throwing a push rod through a cylinder wall. The mechanic lifted my mangled engine from the workbench, grunting and huffing to say it would make a nice pendant, and he had a chain big enough to hang it around my neck. The assistant mechanics laughed. On the bright side, he could make it new for a hundred sixty-five dollars, about a third the cost of the motorcycle, two-thirds the cost of my charter flight. But fractional values meant nothing. I didn't have the bread. I nodded and asked when.

He asked where I would go next. I shrugged. Maybe south, maybe north. He told me to go ahead to Greece and have a good time, and when I returned, my moto would be ready. He would need only two days, but the new engine would not arrive for two weeks. I said okay and left.

Odd as it sounds, the youth brigade of the world that summer communicated via American Express. A few decades prior to computers and cell phones, we had Western Union and telephones with dials and cords. Most kids didn't carry credit cards then. Most cities in Europe had an AE office with a bulletin board and message services. So I went to AE in Rome and sent a telegram to Mom:

All OK. Great fun. Moto broke. Send $165. XXOO to AE Rome c/o me.

What else could I do?

I went back to the campground to tell Gretchen we could now relax on trains or hitchhiking. She looked concerned, so I explained. Her head wagged into a shake. No, she could not travel with a boy who had no moto, not when he said he did have a moto. No. It was not possible. She gathered her things into a bundle and moved them back to the space by Erik. Then she went to find Erik.

She was willing to trade snatch for a ride on back, and I was dumbfounded that I would get no snatch without a back to ride on. Ah, well. I lay back, too young to be so tired in late morning with burdens to process.

The world spun to the other side of my sleeping bag bivouac, to Bruce and Kevin, two Jews from Juhrzy—no disrespect intended—who had watched all three acts. Any Jew can attest that your Jersey Jew varies significantly from your Hoosier schmoozer. Bruce and Kevin were not surprised at the outcome between the *Hitlerjugend* and me, guaranteeing that the Aryan femme fatale would have turned sooner or later. They'd camped there for a day and a night before I arrived, and neither Erik nor Gretchen had spoken a word to them.

Not. One. Word.

Because Bruce and Kevin were Jewish. "How could they know you're Jewish?" I asked facetiously, as if blind to the noses, the eyebrows, the kvetch and shmageggy?

"Who can't tell?"

"I'm Jewish."

"Wha! You? A Jew?"

"Gazundteit."

"No way!"

I shrugged and turned to profile. Turning back I confided, "*Ma nish tah noh, hi lie loh hazeh.* Okay?"

"Listen, Bubby. She would have found out. Then she would have…she would have…"

Gretchen and Erik returned to see me commiserating with the Jews. Erik wagged his head.

Kevin whispered, "She'd have bitten your little schmekel off!" He and Bruce giggled.

Erik sighed in disgust, disappointed to be back on the hook or disgusted with the Jews. Or the Chews. I watched him quizzically, trying to see the difference between a Swede and a Chuhman, I mean German. He and Gretchen packed and left.

Bruce asked what gave Kevin the idea of how big or little my schmekel might be, but Kevin shooed him away and said to me, "Hey. We're going to Brindisi. You want to go?"

"And how do you know his schmekel would have been in her mouth?"

"What's Brindisi?"

"It's way south. You can catch the boat to Greece from there. You want to go?"

I shook my head. "Three guys can't hitchhike. It doesn't work."

"We have a car!"

I nodded. Why wouldn't I want to go? It was the frequently asked question of the day. And with that we were off, after lunch of course, because it was time. They'd found a little café up the street and would surely miss it. We stashed our stuff in their car and went for sit-down, nice, with a tablecloth and glasses for the wine and as much time as we cared for every delicious thing. Travel with Bruce and Kevin was like that: slow, celebratory, joyful and fun. And quaintly civilized, bringing me to the realization that I hadn't dined at a table with a cloth and niceties in weeks.

At the car they quibbled and nagged over who should drive first and who would sit in back and who had more lunch and by rights should be sleepier and who knew his way around town better, as if we three were equal. They looked at me for an opinion. I told them I could drive if they wanted, but in all honesty I couldn't find my ass with both hands. They giggled again. I wasn't sure why.

Historical context is again pertinent; gaiety had not yet come on line as a hip new wave of radical behavior, being or identity. It was neither spurned nor defended but remained simply odd. Call me naïve—and I was—but I didn't think of it. Until a few miles down the road when it was my turn to drive and Bruce's turn to sit in back, and

Kevin decided to sit back there too for the little smidge of extra room, so he could stretch out more. He was so sleepy. I felt great, driving a car, missing my motorcycle but loving the comfort of a seatback and a windshield. Goddamn! That felt good, on par with a tablecloth and glasses and chairs for lunch. I glanced at the rearview to see Bruce asleep, his head on Kevin's shoulder. Kevin snored softy, drooling onto his shirt.

We arrived in Brindisi late at night to empty streets and a deserted industrial port. The low scrub landscape behind the town seemed suitable, so we drove a short distance out, parked and unrolled our bags under the stars. Some wine, some cheese, a little piece of hash I'd managed to score in Rome, and the world glittered anew. You get nights of beauty your whole life, though that summer of '69 they came like clockwork as though the supply were endless.

In the morning we learned that deck passage to Piraeus was a few bucks and just that, passage on the top deck. The ship would leave at sunset and cruise all night. Since it was early, prime deck spots near the smoke stack—for the warmth—were still open. Kevin and Bruce found a garage to store the car, and we were on board by five. The youth brigade of Americans, English, Italians and Greeks made up the manifest in equal measure, happily awaiting departure, snacking on sandwiches, souflake, giros, olives, pita and hummus.

I ate underway, picking freely from the smorgasbord of untouched delectables left on the dining salon tables. Then it was time for sleep in the mildly pitching sea and salt mist, so we curled up in the smoke stack's three-foot radius of warmth all night. Could it get any better?

It seemed so in Piraeus, moving from the dock to the bus with a warm farewell to Bruce and David—they aped discretely when Carolyn, the formidably beautiful and articulate woman who would vanish directly, rushed in to ask if I would mind terribly if she sat beside me. "Not terribly," I said. "Can I ask why?"

"Yes. You can. A man is following me. He may not get on. But I think he will. Just in case."

"Not to worry. We'll pretend to be on our honeymoon."

So the road happily unraveled into Athens, the bus bouncing nicely along the Greek countryside on a beautiful sunny day, as my future wife and I got to know each other—till we checked in, and she checked out.

The first of two salient events of that phase occurred while strolling an Athens sidewalk that afternoon, wondering where to find a pension or hostel. I'd checked out of the hotel once what's-her-name split, because it was twenty bucks—four days budget! Ain't love strange? I stopped to scan a park that looked inviting, but I saw no campers. Being first could set you up for arrest, and we knew even then about what happened in jail and what they invented in Greece. I squinted at what might be some backpacks and people near some bushes and stepped nearer for a closer look when a familiar voice called out, "Hey! Beezer boy!"

There under a parasol at a sidewalk café table sipping a Nescafe was David Rayall. Yes, we'd had some friction, but a reunion never felt better. He arrived three days ago from Rome, where he'd been since Madrid. He loved Greece.

"You visited Bruno and his mother?"

"Yeah. It was… It was…how can I say it? It was…real Italian."

"What the fuck did you expect? Lower Slobovian?"

"No, I mean the language, the cooking, the wine… Taken together it was a…a unified context…you know…you could really…" David became Professor Rayall, his first symptoms of lecturing condescension occurring there on the streets of Athens.

"So. Was he sad to see you go?"

"Not at all."

"You guys fall out?"

"Why would we? Bruno is most reasonable." He nodded up behind me, and there was Bruno. They'd flown to Greece, which didn't so much piss me off as, well, yes, it did piss me off. David could cry poormouth with the best of them, and here he was popping for double airfares when he was too cheap to spring for gas money on the motorcycle. He'd complained that I was driving anyway, and having him on back couldn't account for more than a few pennies, so he'd buy me a pack of gum or something.

Ah, well, I was glad to see Bruno and glad for him. They had tickets for the next morning on the boat to Mykonos, where everyone was camping on the beach and eating at these amazing beachside huts where they cooked the fish and brought in the wine. Bruno was excited and happy as a poor, resourceful man would be. And he spoke Greek. "You didn't say you spoke Greek in Spain."

"No person of Greek speak in Spain."

"You speak English now?"

"Yes. I hav-ed to learning."

Bruno had found a place to camp—across the street no good. Too much polizei. No good. So it was old home week once again. I got my ticket for the Mykonos boat around the corner and a block down, and it was set. I had longed for a long night with my future wife, but she was gone, and I have to admit, getting loaded with the boys under the stars felt as good as one more time ever could.

We ate free on the boat to Mykonos next morning, and once ashore hiked the few miles to a far side where rocks and scrub lined a sandy beach area. I had foresight even then to bring a mask, fins and snorkel of adequate quality that I bought in Athens, and though I saw only a single fish, she seemed to expect my arrival with a welcome from Poseidon, god of the sea. She was blue with black bars and big eyes that asked for help, with the Aegean already mostly dead.

We drank, smoked, ate fried fish, swam in the ocean, told tales and lolled the days away. We ate free on the boat back to Athens, where we camped again.

The next day we would catch a bus to the airport and fly to Tel Aviv, David's idea, or rather David's compulsion. I told him that Jews aren't like Muslims; they are not required to make a pilgrimage. He insisted that real Jews do, given the chance, and being this close to God and then not stopping in for a visit would be nothing short of an insult.

"What? You think God lives in Israel? You think he's got a nice flat uptown? Fuck."

Ah, well, it was another eight inches east on the map, and we'd heard about free love on the kibbutzim, and Bruno was eager as well to try a society that served up breakfast and lunch too, and provided a bed and clothing, even a hat, and medical services and, well, everything in exchange for a few chores. He thought the answer to his economic situation might be waiting in Israel. I asked what was wrong with hitting the tarmac in New York and opening an Italian deli. Or wait! He could be a wood carver named Geppeto.

"Fangoo. I no like'a New York. Too many Jew."

We laughed and drifted off anticipating another adventure.

Tel Aviv was too much like New York, with a preoccupation on bombs and instant death so pervasive that it colored every minute. People threw trash on the ground, because trash everywhere would make no difference if you were dead. They weren't yet dead but could be dead at any moment and would surely hate to waste the effort of cleaning up.

We took a daytrip to the Red Sea and sat up in the water with no flotation. We talked with a lonely Arab whose hotel had been shot to smithereens by both sides. In Jericho we saw fourteen-year-old boys in open shirts and flip-flops with machine guns slung over their shoulders—boys with no youthful innocence or adolescent machismo; these boys seemed war weary. Anxiety depression prevailed. Joy seemed isolated and out of context. Even the prospect of sexual fulfillment at last seemed best postponed, except that such things are not rationally processed.

Well, it was a great burden to be rid of, not so much the physical build up as the peer-pressure burden. Unfucked during that summer indicated abnormality. A grand tour was meant to alleviate inexperience on all levels, and the doors were open to opportunity. Still, those of us who took awhile longer to cross that rudimentary threshold were relieved of a significant burden.

Crossing that threshold for my associate in sexuality and me was a coarse, quick exchange between a madly lusting boy and a young woman of uncertain depth or substance. She insisted on what she knew with oscillating chatter. We arrived directly at premature ejaculation and nothing more to say. I was glad to be rid of the pent up pecker juice and she who'd played her part. I'm certain she'd hoped for more romance, more attention, more cavalier wit, more of anything to value in her memory trousseau.

David and Bruno had discreetly left the room to grant some privacy to my partner in desperation and me for the few minutes we would need to lighten our mutual load. They came back and wanted to know how it was. I lied, telling them it was great. It wasn't great, but it made room for another try with less urgency, more deliberation and maybe better company. Things could develop more slowly next time with more exchange, maybe, I thought. Then again, that's what happened in Spain and failed on deliberation where a pounce and fucking were in need.

Well…

We turned in at ten. By midnight I woke with a gasp, hardly able to breathe.

It was my first night indoors in eight weeks. Staggering to the window I leaned out to gulp the fresher air. I'd seen movies with wild boys who couldn't sleep in beds. It was true; anything less than the great outdoors and all that air was stifling.

The next day we took a bus to Jerusalem and found a cheaper place and met Abraham, an Arab our age who envied the youth brigade and wanted in. Abraham asked if we liked to smoke hashish. We nodded like pups, and he smiled in camaraderie. If we harbored distrust, it was what we had learned, not what our instincts told us. Abraham said he would take us to a tea parlor behind a café, both operated by his uncle. And we were off, down the yellow brick road.

Abraham turned to face us near the café with a warning: we would be offered hashish to buy, but we should decline, no matter how great the quality or the bargain, because the Arabs offering were in cahoots with the Israeli police, who would arrest us. They would demand a huge bail from our suburban parents and then deport us— and then return the hashish to the sellers. What we smoked, on the other hand, could not be used against us.

Abraham at nineteen or twenty was one of us, an instant ally on the road to adventure, a brother in the youth brigade, because that's how it was. Not so much as us against them—though there was plenty of that—those times recollect as us united, based on the simple virtues that will not go away: youth and idealism. Youth goes away on a personal level, but it remains immortal as a font of idealism, and I think of Abraham steering us around a certain disaster, because we were brothers in the bond in that holy bonding time. Oh, we would have shopped that bargain! We may have changed since then, though I believe the fundamentals to be intact, and a peace pipe would be a lovely thing to share again.

Uncle Tenouse was a perfect host who led us through the café to the space in back, enclosed by three short walls with a partial trellis and hanging vines for a ceiling over a sawdust floor. On stools around the perimeter sat Israelis and Arabs in common society awaiting the pipe. Abraham's cousin Farouk entered with a flourish, grasping the pipe in both hands. The impressive hookah captured our fancy and fantasy. Would they ever believe this one back on the farm? Ali Baba tassels and Arabesques dangled in festoons among the leads. Little brass charms, figurines and cymbals clinked, as a briquette of hashish wisped in the oversized bowl. Inhaling like a billows, Farouk stoked the briquette till it glowed red, till his eyeballs slumped toward his warm smile, and the glow gained radiance with a life of its own. Farouk delivered, rounding the patrons on their stools. To my left a geriatric Arab smoked and mumbled, "Hubbly bubbly. Hubbly bubbly."

The other customers pulled like seasoned veterans, exhaling in billows. What was not to waste? The briquette, about two by two by two of red ember—and I don't mean centimeters; that was inches—wouldn't fit into the bowl for a while. To our left two middle-agers introduced themselves as former pilots. That they were Israeli was foregone; nobody else had pilots except the Egyptians, who wouldn't likely come to Jerusalem to smoke hash. I leaned over and asked a pilot, "What is hubbly bubbly?"

He shrugged, "Good shit." Was it true that we would be arrested if we bought any hash? He said it couldn't be truer, because the Israeli government considered hashish a severe threat and a great ally. That is, many Arabs were stoned—all the time stoned, and even though the Soviets supplied advisors, explosives and guns, the Arabs could not figure out why setting a bomb on the ground three feet from a building only blew a hole in the ground and left the building unscathed. Now how would it be if the Israelis started smoking hash too and messing up the fundamentals of endless warfare?

"You're smoking it."

He shrugged. "I'm retired. And I won't buy any either."

The cost of the session was one Israeli pound, about 28¢. As if that weren't enough, an exotic beauty of the Middle East, Abraham's other cousin, served mint tea and fresh melon slices. Stoned to the gills, we ogled, we dreamed, we sipped and ate. And smoked some more, for the sheer, abundant richness of the thing.

Abraham asked, "Is good. Yes?" He grinned hopefully, seeking affirmation that we were one, among the youthful wave meeting the world on fresh terms of peace and love all around us.

"Yes. Is good."

Strolling through the underground market I bought a burnoose and keffiyeh with a tasseled band I wore for years on Halloween. It was a real hit four years later during the first oil crisis, when the costume got a rope belt and some empty oilcans dangling from it. I had to stop wearing that outfit many years later when terrorism displaced the love all around us. Halloween could be so fickle.

We walked up a steep hill to where a guy waited with some camels. The guy was another friend of Abraham's, maybe another cousin or uncle, and so we too were in the fold. We dropped another pound on a camel ride, which was a goof and another stoned gas. Our friend Abraham was kin to Abraham, Isaac and Jacob, and don't forget Sarah, Leah and Rachel. Ishmael fairly completed the arc of the Revolution in replacing historic conflict with newfound friendship. Ah, youth. Our dromedary cloud made time immaterial down to incidental eons drifting by as we drifted past olive trees said to be seven thousand years old, which seemed very old but then not so old in the geological view. In fact, human time seemed momentary, a still life like us. Fingertips brushed olive branches that were already two thousand years old even back then, when

> God said, Abraham, kill me a son.
> Abe said, Man, you must be puttin' me on.
> God said, Abe?
> Abe said, What?
> God said, You can do what you want, Abe, but...
> next time you see me comin', you better run.

Abe said, Where you want this…killin' done?
God said, Out on Highway…61.

A young Jew in Hoosierville had faced tough questions from tough, inquisition-hearted people: *What is a Jew? Why are you Jewish? Why does anybody need Jews? Why did you kill Jesus?* Oh, yes, the little playmates at Hoosier Elementary had wanted to know, had wanted to fight, had wanted blood revenge. Everybody knows now where this line of questioning is headed, or they should know, if they're Chewish. The answers often began with *er…uh, well, it's like this…* Maybe it was only imaginary that things changed when Bob Dylan captured the essence of Jewish history in a few lines of lyric. But concise, eloquent language down at street level can change perspective and understanding. The Jews were the first culture/tradition/belief system to codify behavior on human sacrifice; it was not cool or good. It was bad— thirty-seven hundred sixty-one years before Jesus H. Christ it was bad. God delivered the message by example to Abraham, who proved himself devout but would have been wrong. Such is the beauty of Judaism, with its unique flexibility allowing the rules to be bent in times of extreme circumstance. Rules? What? Rules. Sacrificial offering from that time onward was deemed best made with a goat, a scapegoat who would carry the burden of our sins. The irony of the beauty of Judaism is the practice of scapegoating Jews; they're so convenient.

These and other orbital perspectives drifted on out to Highway 61 where thoughts got splayed like offspring on the sacrificial block to the deity of altered consciousness. Those days and clouds and camels and new friends and family and Bob Dylan took us farther from suburban influence than we'd been or imagined. We'd smoked too much dope, and many days of it made for a paltry deposit in the memory banks. Yet we became vested on a heady accumulation of feelings of well-being, of fulfillment in fun—and in the most important component of those years, no matter how lost it now seems: the love all around us.

We lived with abandon in a spirit of accepting the whole wide world, celebrating its many-faceted freedoms, its layered realities, its amazing quirks and beautiful blemishes, and yes, its endless opportunities for goofing. As in all cultural phenomena, the clothing, nuance, body language and behaviors of the time were a demonstration of who we were and what might be—faith in these things felt natural. Many souls remember that faith, those wild times and amazing scenes. We did not ponder the poor guys in the jungles trading fire that very moment. We did not resent them or dislike them in any way. We heard, like everybody else, that we'd spit on them, as if spitting on the Viet veterans was aligned with our views and feelings. It didn't sit right; so hostile and warlike in a crowd committed to peace.

Decades later we learned how freedom of speech is easily abused—nobody spit on homecoming vets. The spitting story was a pioneer effort of warring interests to influence perception and mold collective consciousness into mob rule. Modern attempts of the technique include Kenya, socialism in the White House, death panels as part of health care and a range of vitriol to remind us of our roots in the 60s, when we got grounded in truth.

We didn't know reality as perceived by the Viet vets, because they went, so they weren't like us. We sympathized, especially with those who realized too late the difference between martial law and civil law, and that they should have declined when they had their civil rights.

Those who made it back were viewed curiously at first—keep in mind that the My Lai massacre occurred in March of '68, and the military covered it up for over a year. Up to five hundred unarmed villagers of all ages were raped, otherwise tortured, murdered and mutilated. The direct cause presented by the military: war stress on valiant troops who broke with so much evil coming at them. In the end, events at the village of My Lai were deemed a massacre, all the murderous carnage pinned on one soldier sentenced to twenty-two years for so much mayhem. He served three years of house arrest.

How could anybody participate in a massacre? Oh, wait; they weren't feeling quite themselves. They'd become killing machines by necessity, and you're bound to have a massacre or two in those unfortunate conditions. Or some such.

Concurrently emerging in those pivotal years, two other events eliminated the tiderip between the two major war resistance camps. The first of those events was general. Fragging occurred frequently as a quirk and soon becoming a pattern, then a phenomenon, then an explosive act of opposition. Wikipedia today defines fragging as:

> In the U.S. military, fragging refers to the act of attacking a superior officer in one's chain of command with the intent to kill that officer. The term originated during the Vietnam War and was most commonly used to mean the assassination of an unpopular officer of one's own fighting unit. Killing was effected by means of a fragmentation grenade, hence the term.

The jungle war spawned movies of profound impact—*Full Metal Jacket, The Deer Hunter, Good Morning Vietnam, Platoon, Born on the Fourth of July* and many more, including the benchmark of reasoned insanity, *Apocalypse Now*—

> *...suddenly he'll grab you, and he'll throw you in a corner, and he'll say, 'Do you know that if is the middle word in life? If you can keep your head when all about you are losing theirs and blaming it on you, if you can trust yourself when all men doubt you'... I mean I'm... no, I can't... I'm a little man, I'm a little man, he's... he's a great man! I should have been a pair of ragged claws scuttling across floors of silent seas...*

Dennis Hopper found himself in a character truest to type, and *Apocalypse Now* was rendered in masterstrokes, adhering to a tried and true literary gem, *Heart of Darkness*. Touching on Joseph Conrad's key characters and lines—like *The horror, the horror, the horror*—*Apocalypse* captured the drift of reason from secure moorings in war. Marlon Brando as Colonel Kurtz pegged Conrad's Mr. Kurtz but then stepped out—and up to sainthood with the most reasoned defense of men engaged in violence. Such a lengthy statement seemed like a monologue or worse, a diatribe. But drastic conditions in war called for drastic measures in drama, and Marlon Brando delivered the message of the ages adapted to the age:

I've seen horrors...horrors that you've seen. But you have no right to call me a murderer. You have a right to kill me. You have a right to do that...but you have no right to judge me. It's impossible for words to describe what is necessary to those who do not know what horror means. Horror... Horror has a face...and you must make a friend of horror. Horror and moral terror are your friends. If they are not, then they are enemies to be feared. They are truly enemies! I remember when I was with Special Forces...seems a thousand centuries ago. We went into a camp to inoculate some children. We left the camp after we had inoculated the children for polio, and this old man came running after us and he was crying. He couldn't see. We went back there, and they had come and hacked off every inoculated arm. There they were in a pile. A pile of little arms. And I remember... I... I... I cried, I wept like some grandmother. I wanted to tear my teeth out; I didn't know what I wanted to do! And I want to remember it. I never want to forget it... I never want to forget. And then I realized...like I was shot...like I was shot with a diamond...a diamond bullet right through my forehead. And I thought, my God...the genius of that! The genius! The will to do that! Perfect, genuine, complete, crystalline, pure. And then I realized they were stronger than we, because they could stand that these were not monsters, these were men...trained cadres. These men who fought with their hearts, who had families, who had children, who were filled with love...but they had the strength...the strength...to do that. If I had ten divisions of those men, our troubles here would be over very quickly. You have to have men who are moral...and at the same time who are able to utilize their primordial instincts to kill without feeling...without passion...without judgment... without judgment! Because it's judgment that defeats us.

The jungle war classic movies were still a few years away—gestating as we watched events unfold, as the madness of the moment became known, widely viewed in thirty-minute segments each evening on three networks. But specifics beyond geographic coordinates and body counts remained sparse, until fragging. Fragging was an act of refusal, the ultimate rendition of: *Hell no, we won't go.* Well, the poor fucks were already there, a tad late to say no, but they did what soldiers do, distracted by evil in critical mass, killing commanding officers who insisted on another night patrol. The most frequent victims of fragging were first lieutenants. James Calley, the single conviction from My Lai was a first lieutenant.

On college campuses across the nation young men were offered military advantage in the Reserve Officer Training Corps. Only a few hours of military education each week could teach many useful things about weapons, marching, chain of command and war. It could earn a few bucks monthly *and* give a guy that certain leg up as a first lieutenant. After all, college grads were smarter, and the smart guys should call the shots, so to speak.

Fragging was war resistance and military breakdown with a uniquely American spirit, far removed from the Nuremburg defense, that *ve vass* only following orders. Our guys were better than that. Lyndon Johnson felt the pinch and bailed out on another term as your President, live on TV. His heir would be Vice-President Hubert Humphrey, a skilled politico who may have stopped the carnage but was hamstrung on Johnson's graces, such as they were. The end result: riots at the Democratic Convention in 1968. Chicago looked more like Dresden than a windy city, more like a repressive regime than an urban center—but tear gas, rubber bullets and billy clubs were a walk in the basil next to the jungle war. And who showed up on the Chicago front to defend the country they loved? The Viet Vets.

Spit on them? The fuck you talking? They were part of us, bearing witness as only they could do. The Doors put a heartfelt tragedy into a lyrical love ballad, *The End*, lamenting the love lost between a generation and its country. Whether love gone awry is better or best or even comparable to Rosie the Riveter and a kinder, gentler patriotism is infinitesimally incidental to the hard cold fact that we felt this sentiment. Viet vets against the war lived this loss. So when anybody calls "the 60s" a lost opportunity, he does not reflect the true loss that defined the greatness of those years for what they revealed.

Another Vietnam classic decades later weaved a compelling thread of Viet veteran opposition. *Sir, No, Sir* shines a light on American military might and what it still wants to keep in the dark. Viet vets pushing seventy share the truth of the country they loved and fought for without question.

Many draft dodgers saw the truth first or were afraid. In any event, even if young, naïve and drug-addled, draft resistors knew that Vietnam had no link to the USA or its defense, that "winning" the war would warrant occupation, billions more in defense contracts and a corporate/cultural beachhead to make Southeast Asia free for consumer products. Hail, Coca Cola and Big Mac.

Losing the war would make the world no different than it had been, except for making it more peaceful.

And so it came to pass.

It's not fair to criticize anybody for missing the point and the action, even a career-minded journalist with impeccable credentials and potential. By the same token, a network up-and-comer cannot criticize his government or the leaders he must interview objectively on any tender subject, especially a jungle war with no clear objective. But the inference is clear on a book entitled *The Best Generation*, and that gets tricky for Tom Brokaw. The WWII guys were the best, and so were our guys, with a challenge uniquely layered and complex, with a cultural rift demonstrating the weakness and strength of America in a topsy-turvy reversal of power in regard to guns and flowers. We were not meek and did not turn the other cheek or inherit the earth. The war protest was both violent and disobedient, running the gamut from Students for a Democratic Society and the Weather Underground. They blew up buildings to let us know which way the wind was blowing

So many fragmented groups had it up to fucking here that incendiary exchange could happen as soon as not. Sticking a flower up your gun barrel or flashing a peace sign to a hardhat were taunts, so a few hippies got clobbered, proving the hippie point. Fringe extremes were most often embarrassingly violent or soft and felt as stupid then as they still do today, maybe more so, because that was an original time.

Yet through the din came Donovan's soft, sweet dirge in a lyric so poetically removed yet specifically compelling that it soothed the aching spirit of a generation in a lullaby with a heady downbeat. Yes, the elders of our time had chosen to remain blind, and way down below the ocean was where we wanted to be—*she may be.*

Undulating rhythm over the pulse of the revolution affirmed the value and victory available to those who would tune in, turn on, drop out. Psychedelic drugs likely influenced more people outside the military than in, but that's conjecture, and the demand for psychedelics in Vietnam was formidable. Who of the right mind or whatever mind remained wouldn't want a change of mind, away from the jungle war? Vietnam soldiers were swamped, fighting for life in a hostile environment. They needed time away, to see a reality above and beyond a chronic reality of extreme violence—the world they'd been drafted into. Who wouldn't rather gaze on *Lucy in the Sky with Diamonds* than kill or be killed?

A milestone was the baby boom transit from adolescence to adulthood. It came fast and slow, with the best and worst the world had to offer. Lasting impressions formed from the crucibles of limitless fun and horror.

What was manhood? It was a toughness that few boys were up to but all were required to attain. Manhood got knocked down on all fronts. In some quarters it got back up. We were warned to trust nobody over thirty. Thirty was out of it or worse: thirty took its marching orders from the most extreme military/industrial mentality America could conjure, beginning with Lyndon Johnson, ending with Dick Nixon, suffering William Westmoreland on the way. Johnson got duped; Nixon and Westmoreland were dupers.

That was the world unfolding in the summer of '69.

David, Bruno and I hitched a ride to a kibbutz that made knives—stamped steel butter knives you might see in any diner. The place was nice enough and hospitable, even welcoming with open arms, embracing, nearly grasping. The managers reminded David and me that we were landed citizens in Israel, because we'd been born Jewish by definition, meaning that our mothers of record were Jewish. A Jewish mother could be verified and, *mazel tov*, qualify us for Israeli passports. We could stay for life and do God's work, if we chose to do so. David pondered the offer. I thought, ho boy.

Our host seemed giddy with prospects and further assured that Bruno's lack of a Jewish mother was not a problem. Bruno seemed like a good boy and a hard worker and would be welcome, and immigration would not be difficult, if we chose to stay together. It felt like another draft.

We stayed a day and a night and hit the road with no real objective but to find a kibbutz with less fervor and more females. We found another kibbutz a bit higher off the desert floor, a cooler place with fewer dorms and buildings but much more land. More green-ery at elevation felt more inviting than the desert floor. We spent three days pruning, aerating, tending and picking the acres of pear orchards on this second kibbutz. Hard work was rewarded with three squares daily and a bunk bed with clean sheets. A bonus was a warm welcome to social events, including group discussions on God, the State of Israel, the meaning of Jews who live in the land of Zion or elsewhere, the ways of the world and working together. Then came the naked swim.

The kibbutzers loved us, mostly as a polite means of loving Bruno, the exotic Roman Catolica; he was so strong, warm and hard-working that his other talents boosted his stock to new heights. In mere days he already exchanged words and phrases in Hebrew and actually attempted jokes by twisting the language incongruously in a way that made people laugh. Was that accidental? He did it at will, in a language he hadn't heard till last week. Some people stared; he was so hung and uncut.

In three days came a memorable event, unanticipated as a sudden turning point and no big deal really, except that it was, when Bruno realized he was home. A seeker for years who couldn't resolve needs with skills had finally arrived. He stayed. He may be there still. David cried in farewell. Then Bruno cried too. I told them to get a grip and didn't look back.

David and I caught a bus back to Tel Aviv after being warned about hitching. Wha? Two Jews from America? Are you nuts? We stayed one night at the King David Hotel, and it didn't blow up.

We flew back to Rome the next day and got a huge room with an incredibly high ceiling in a massive pension with Doric columns surrounding an interior courtyard where a writer in exile surrounded by Italian antiquity could knock back espresso and Fernet Branca and table-grade Chianti that went down like lemonade.

The next day I picked up the money old Mom had wired to the American Express office. At the moto shop in the alley, my BSA 650 Lightning Rocket sat out front looking brand new and ready to go. I kicked it over to hear it rumble sweetly.

David said he needed to go north into Germany. I didn't want to press him and knew his motivation, his morbid—to my mind—drive to visit some concentration camps. Okay, maybe morbid is the wrong word, but I didn't need to go and didn't want to go. I was born a few years after the camps were shut down, and for all I knew, what with Buddhist inclinations, I'd been there already. The dormitories, work places, showers, ovens and mass graves made me shudder and resist.

He said nobody was required to go, meaning he wouldn't insist, and he wouldn't mind riding on back if I wouldn't mind. We'd both grown, successfully avoiding condescension.

We crossed Northern Italy into the Alps, staying at a youth hostel on the top of a mountain and riding the next day into Munich, where David retained his tact, rising above rancor or regret. "I think you may be one of the best motorcyclists in Europe, but I can't ride with you anymore. It hurts my back, and it's scary."

I matched his simple honesty with understanding. "I think I've had enough too." I had no plan for shipping the thing back—hadn't even thought that far, typically of the day and age. Shipping it would cost hundreds more and present another thousand miles from New York to the Midwest, which would have been incredibly cool a few months ago but at that point the idea sagged with fatigue. So who knows? Maybe I was well into transit too.

We rode to the Neumann Center that operated as a youth hostel around Europe then, and you didn't have to be Catholic; but it didn't hurt. Where was Bruno when we needed him? The woman said to come back after three, so we cruised down to Schwabbing, the hip action boulevard of those happening times. Even then the Germans were a goosestep ahead, among the first to embrace post-existential nihilism in a holdover beatnik, chain-smoking, heroin-addled, tattooed radical world on the burnt edge of the hippie world. Schwabbing was lined with action places to drink, dance, eat, smoke, drink more and simply be. The angled parking places along the boulevard were a popular place to sell vehicles adequately hip to appeal to that market. So I angled in and put a sign on my handlebars. **For Sale**. It felt like treachery.

Did I really want to do this? But a gregarious voice coming up the promenade interrupted my doubts. "You can't sell that thing here! I mean of course you can. We are free to do what we want to do. But that motorcycle—it is beautiful, by the way—is British. I would buy it myself, but fucking Britain, excuse me, refuses to join the Common Market. If anybody in Europe buys it, he'll have to pay a 33% tax. That's right. I said 33%. How much do you want?"

"Five hundred dollars."

"Hmm. A bit high. Way too high with the tax. You know." His name was Dolph Dieter Helmann, but we could call him Dolph Dieter. "Oh, fuck, you know. Just call me Dolph. Why do you want to sell such a beautiful moto?"

"I don't, really. I need the money."

"Ah, yes. The money. Everybody needs it. And I suppose you are very tired of riding it. All the Americans end up here with their flashy motorcycles tired of riding them and willing to sell them very cheap." Dolph sounded like a set up. David stared at an obvious former Nazi. The Thousand Year Reich had marched up Schwabbing only thirty years ago. Dolph was about mid-thirties, too young, except for the Hitler Youth Corps. David couldn't help it, as his morbid motivation went to mordantly awkward compulsion. Maybe some things are necessary.

"Are you a Nazi?" The question sounded aggressive, even hostile and marginally stupid, out of place and time, but the subject lingered beyond place and time. It drifted in the ether like a mist, a sticky one that would not dissipate, a tangible essence in its consequence. And odd as David's sensibilities were, this *was* the very same boulevard where thousands upon thousands of Germans had stretched an arm in allegiance and abeyance to *der füehrer* for world domination forever…

"Nein! No, I was not a Nazi. I was too young. I was only Hitlerjugend. We was kids—*ve vas kids*—younger than you. It was like camp. We didn't know what it was. Oh, today they all tell you they didn't know how terrible—they all say they hid their Jews in the basement. They knew. But we was kids. We didn't know. You ask these kids around here today about Nazi. They will tell you, *Vas? Vas iss los? Nazi?* They know nothing about that. What? You think they learn it in school? No. What is to teach, that we made a mistake of character and judgment? No. We are taught that we went to war and we lost, and now it is over. My father was a tank commander, but he wasn't a Nazi. He was a soldier. In the desert. You know."

David stared.

I pondered Nazis and 33% tax and another eight hundred miles to Amsterdam and another thousand miles to Middle America. That's when Gary Cooper walked up with his trademark swagger and slow confidence to ask, "How much?"

"Where are you from?"

"Venice."

Gary had shaggy blond hair and was clearly one of us. Dolph said, "You don't look Italian."

"Venice Beach, man."

"Five hundred."

He nodded. "I'll give you five hundred if you can wait."

"Wait for what?"

"Till I get home, man. I got two hundred I can give you now, but I'll have to save the other three. Shouldn't take more'n a few months."

"This you can do," Dolph said. "Selling to another American has no tax. Who is to know?"

"But what about the title and registration?"

"Doesn't matter. You sign over the registration in his name so he can cross the border. Then you work out the money with him."

"You want to drive it?"

"Fuck yeah, man."

So Gary Cooper, whose name sounded suspiciously like a Venice Beach bid for Phase II stardom in Hollywood and an easy motorcycle hustle, roared up Schwabbing. That he turned around and came back was the big surprise, as I realized when he pulled out that the whole show could have been staged.

But it was a time of confidences. It was not staged. It was coincidence, or synchronous convergence, similar as two paths crossing in a snowy wood without the snow but with the same faith and trust. Yet again the age embraced the lyric.

The bigger surprise was the overwhelming relief when Gary Cooper pressed two hundred dollars into my hand with a handshake and a promise to pay the other three hundred in the next few months. We traded addresses and phone numbers, and he was off on my Lightning Rocket. I like to think that that's how it was in those days, though it may have been only sheer, dumb luck. I was dumb—tired and dumb. And lucky. And maybe it was.

A bigger surprise came in Gary's first letter some weeks later, saying that the motorcycle was about the most fun he'd ever had, all four hours of it the next morning, till a car turned in front of him from the wrong lane and he crashed into it broadside and went flying over the top but didn't get hurt, but the motorcycle looked like a steel pretzel. In the letter was a check for fifty bucks and a continuing pledge to pay the rest as soon as he could.

That's the thing about riding every day; if you don't get creamed in the first week or two, you probably won't, because you gain the second nature, a certain knowing that they will try to kill you given the chance. Gary was unseasoned, without road wits.

Meanwhile, back at Schwabbing, Dolph offered to show us a great place to eat and celebrate. We said we'd meet him once we ditched our stuff, but he tagged along. We wondered why but figured it out. Dolph was born too soon. He was one of us, technically too old to trust but he compensated with gregarious charm. He explained that he liked hanging out with American tourists, because they taught him about the world. Back at the Neumann Center at three forty-five, the desk *frau* said she had no rooms. "You said to come back after three and…"

She pounded the table with her fist. "I said come back exACTly at three! No room for you."

Dolph laughed, "Fucking Germans." Not to worry—he knew a place, though he cautioned: do not ask the man who would rent us the room anything about Nazis. The man greeted Dolph with an emotionless hug. He appeared to be early to mid-sixties and a very apparent colonel. In a bathrobe with no visible clothing under it, smoking a turquoise cigarette with a gold filter in a pearl holder that he held between thumb and forefinger, palm up, he seemed the essence of gentlemanly bestiality. "Are you…" He puffed his cigarette, exhaling as he scanned David and me. "…a couple?"

"Yeah. A couple o' knuckleheads," I said, quickly giving David a knuckle rub on the head. This behavior indicated removal from manhood—and removal from genteel bestiality; it dashed hopes for nostalgic reminiscence of the Third Reich while ass fucking. Which, when you think about it, was a seasoned move on my part.

We got the key to the room at the top of the stairs with a warning to be quiet and leave the key on the table in the hall.

Dolph took us to a place for bratwurst and sauerkraut and much beer, again deferring to David's check list. Dinner was superb. David said, "Gee, it's a good thing Germans don't fart." Dolph laughed, leaned over for an oompa pa and ordered another round, saying we'd have to leave if they started with the polkas, because he couldn't take anymore polkas.

The next day David took a bus to Bremen, where he would either book a tour or go alone to Bergen-Belsen, where his grandparents died. I headed to Amsterdam without asking what he would gain by staring at some Godforsaken ruins and ovens. Apparently it would do something for him, something he needed done. We would meet at the American Express office on Dam Square at noon in two days, or at five as a backup to noon.

We kept the peace by focusing on practical concerns, by discussing logistics for meeting in Amsterdam. Practicality seemed best, given his compulsive search for a physical connection to the horror or the lingering spirit or the lost souls, or all of the above. It remained amorphous and conceptual to me. The camps were a devilish stain on humanity—yes, already a few anti-Semitics were swearing that it never happened, which underscored the importance of proof and remembrance. Oh, it happened, and we're not so concerned that it might happen again, because it surely will if allowed to happen. The greatest concern now is that those hateful few must bear the shame for eternity.

Still, David seemed driven by a mordant curiosity somehow meant to flesh out a specific identity. I had mine. It was easy: a skinny young Jew hell-bent for adventure on two wheels. Nazi death camps? Where (the fuck) was that at?

Nowhere was the obvious answer, and I felt like I'd arrived at last, with or without the two wheels under me. Well, let it be. David was missing the motorcycle gene. I got along fine without wallowing in death camp horror.

I felt woefully average without the speed, the feeling, the look, the view, the centrifugal and centripetal forces gently opposed with me conducting from the podium. This was the World Youth Symphony Philharmonic—or had been till the music slammed into silence, which was better than a wreck, but left something to be desired. I practically wobbled through those first days of no motorcycle like a sailor freshly landed on terra firma, and so will ice skaters after only an hour at the rink. Coming down off the blades to the shoe-leather express is a grounding experience, a good one in some ways, allaying certain dangers but then removing the great rewards derived from risk.

On the bright side, optimism prevailed on plenty more hazard where that came from. David and I met again on the fountain steps in Dam Square among many youth gathered to share tales from all corners of Europe and North Africa. Many pipes wisped into a single cloud. We loaded a gram of hash into our pipe and joined the flow, giggling when a cop stepped carefully over our outstretched legs. It wasn't funny. It was the way things should be, with public servants serving the public.

We lost ten days in Amsterdam smoking hash subtle enough to assure that it would not impair. That time was not totally lost but lingers in the mists of amazing good fun. Two clubs then specialized in loud music in an auditorium with speakers at varying levels, floor to ceiling all the way around for total penetration of the stoned groove. Mattresses all over the floor let you lie down before you fell down, or you could fall to a softer landing. You could smoke your own hash or buy it there and lie down and roll over, Beethoven.

Oh, yeah, Chuck Berry sang it a dozen years earlier but emerged from the cloudbank with a downbeat perfectly tuned to what we felt, what we were. The groove honed more perfectly on Creedence, the Stones, Dylan, Big Brother, Moody Blues, Jimi, Janis—you name it. Nobody danced then, except alone when the muse inspired movement. The step of the day was the modified funky chicken, in which the dancer flopped around with no apparent concern—make that deliberate disregard—for conventional rhythm or grace in another compelling demonstration of nonconformity. David and I lay back on our mattress and giggled like hyenas one more time when a buxom chick stood up, stepped over and straddled our legs and danced for us. She wore no panties. We felt trapped, till she turned around for the scenic view and we slid out from under.

For me it was a time of perspective, looking up at a dimpled ass for a laugh and a goof I can still recall. Looking back was more than a recall of miles, people and places. That summer influenced what we might become. Applying the lessons would take time, but the non-stop nights and days of sheer, raw adventure begged a question: what just happened? I found myself more often alone by choice, rethinking events taken only on the surface in the first go-round.

Lifetimes are spent seeking unique stimulation, like at depth on the Great Barrier Reef so many decades later, where life in color, effusion and social complexity came on in waves too rich for assimilation in the moment.

The 60s was like that. Whatever the effect of those times, it rendered a changed fellow, a college kid who'd been around and had something to think about, a work in progress.

Off the Road Again

COLLEGE STUDENTS WERE redefined in those days of cultural convolution, division, distraction and practical maneuvering. For decades the stereotype student of higher learning had been a college Joe, either Ivy League landed or State U drunk. Other cultures took a bemused view; Americans seemed odd on many levels, but they did have money, and here they were, wasting four prime years in a classroom poring over books instead of getting a jump on life itself.

Well, many Ivy Leaguers took the baton of cultural leadership from their parents, often alumni parents. The baton assured greatness in what we hold most dear, which is influence and affluence. State U students were more practical, studying hard sciences or humanities to teach.

The war of the 60s kept greater numbers of male students in college as a survival option. Campus life became a postponement of war life. It wasn't real, but the alternative was all too real; it was like Romper Room for pre-adults, a new phase in the developmental process that strove for something other than success. Chronic anxiety characterized the challenge of draft-age males who avoided the jungle war by staying in school. The jungle war waited like a predator in a burrow. The jungle war was required. It waged dutifully, with numbing measurements of success and cold comfort in the enemy's exponentially greater sacrifice. Body counts came nightly, with every one of our boys worth twenty or forty of the strange men who scurried through tunnels and would not back down, unlike their countrymen on our side. It was a rough time emotionally, given to rough, hateful profiles, like *slant-eyed, zipper-headed gooks*—that phrase was a send-up on rightwing fervor from the movie *Candy*, based on Terry Southern's novel. The cast included Marlon Brando (again; talk about range), Richard Burton, Charles Aznavour, James Coburn, John Huston, Sugar Ray Robinson, Ringo Starr—and Walter Matthau as the military advisor who also summarized the U.S. military view of enemies: "Mexicans. Albanians. They're all the same."

The alternative to the jungle war? Get high, get laid, get a C average, become a college grad. Studies, final exams, essays, pop quizzes and stuff could get tough but added up to a proverbial walk in the park next to the jungle belly crawl, with those pesky swamps, snakes, malaria, booby traps, night patrol, heroine addiction, social diseases unknown to the western world and friendly fire.

Back in school, a lively social calendar helped suppress the rising tide of anxiety. So the great wide world shrank back to mundane rigors and distraction. One subject resonated, because of a graduate student instructor clinging to ideals in art. Ted Schaeffer at twenty-nine taught beginning narrative and seemed older, verging on old, yet he captured the writer's life with flair. Ted was married and had a kid and taught to buy time to finish his current book. And he could drink and carouse with us young'uns.

Creative Writing 404 with Professor Peden, on the other hand, was dry as toast, a humorless exercise in witless rhapsody on the famous people he had known as prelude to promoting the pHd and its vast benefits. Or was that the PhD?

The difference between those who can and those who teach wasn't new. But the 60s rendered many who thought they could as campus captives. At least an art form helped remove the onus of both worlds, one at war, the other at school. Ted Schaeffer warned us against the PhD. But Professor Peden advised in favor of it: 90% of all National Book Award authors held the PhD. Ted Schaeffer said, "Yeah, and look at the books they write. They're shit! It's political. Do you really want to spend your life writing like that?" Ted had a point, and he risked his job assuring that prime years were best spent on adventures to feed our fiction. Fuck a bunch of bookworms.

Would we get high and laid as frequently in the outside world? We hoped we would and couldn't really see why we wouldn't. We felt late in making our way. We felt slighted, not as short-changed as the poor stiffs dying in the mud, but trapped in the egghead bunker. The place was stifling, except for the demonstrations.

Ah, well. Campus schedules, rigors and requirements were easily ignored. Wearing funny clothes, taking drugs and hanging out with a lovely, lively crowd was a blessed distraction. The jungle war would not go away but loomed nearer, with June graduation hardly nine months away.

We repress in the short term in order to move ahead, so we can process later with greater method what was repressed earlier by necessity. That was college think for never mind, I got other things to do. The sentiment hadn't changed from the junior, sophomore or freshmen years, but things changed over many motorcycle miles, adding nuance and a certain mystique. Unique boots helped, and so did two uncommonly cool leather jackets from the Florence flea market. The first was dark leather in a sport cut with lapels, probably a Gestapo model. The second was a flyboy number with a fleece collar, likely salvaged from a downed flyboy, likely one of ours. Oh, the coeds saw, the coeds cooed, the coeds circled.

Youthful days passed in oblivion. Death was among us, and we rolled the bones with abandon in a world of delusion. The romp seemed urgent, free and necessary, given the rip of the times. The sexual revolution merely responded to the greater struggle. Freedom of the flesh demonstrated other freedoms too, and the kids were eager. Bio-function was common, repeat as necessary—or available.

About that time a batch of Stanford clinical acid arrived from Charles Silverberg just a few months before he killed himself with a shotgun at age twenty-two when his girlfriend called off the romance. She was forty-two, so the romance was mostly his. She showed him a few things he'd never imagined much less seen with a coed. He was in love. She was more practical, albeit amused with such a witty, feisty little guy. For all we knew, she had his best interests at heart. But probably not. Charles was way too crazy. He looked crazy, his yellow orange hair sticking out like he had his finger in a socket, his woolly eyebrows and bulging eyes and shit-eating grin made him look crazy and hungry for more. Well, she showed him a crazy thing or two.

Charles wore his love on his sleeve as he freely told of the crazy times they shared and the shit she pulled in the craziest places. Rod Stewart sang a song about Maggie May, which was unreal, because it was late September, and Charles really should have been back at school. Charles was a medical student at Stanford and knew the guy in the lab who mixed up the lysergic acid diethylamide. Talk about a fur piece from Ray Haney's baggy full of purple powder; this stuff had lift-off smooth as comet dust on a clear night and leveled at sixty thousand feet above the earth like an orbit in an overstuffed chair. Oh, we saved the Stanford clinical for special occasions or Saturday.

We fairly envied Charles, what with a full grown, full blown, no holds barred woman to have his way with and better yet to yield in every way to her way. What a marvel is the human mind, and a more insistent marvel is what a young man takes to be his mind. We assumed everything, including the wrecked bed and difficult mornings, when she did kick him in the head.

That Stanford clinical acid introduced us to acid potential—and, as they said in mid-Missouri, it "plumb ruint us" on the regular stuff for ever more. High quality was a standard that would not be met again, but doors appeared to open.

Three weeks after returning from Europe I got a call from Betty Boop. We were friends. She was engaged, untouchable and way too beautiful to blemish with sexual abandon but she needed a study date. I felt lucky; we had big tests coming up in American Realist Literature, requiring insight and analysis of Mark Twain and Henry James. We also had Shakespeare, the comedies. Betty sighed: *at least* we didn't have the tragedies. Boy, they were *really* tough. I knew she could walk me through to the C that would avoid the jungle war.

A few study dates later, Betty sighed again, recalling the process of choosing the right study partner. Youthful lovers like to remember the formative phase. She said it was my style, the boots and jacket and honesty, however brusque. She wanted to tap into it. I did not reprimand her inverted imagery. I was too grateful tapping in.

So the weeks passed, studying into the nights. Who doesn't remember that first blessed visit to the candy shop? Betty stood apart in afterglow, introducing a dynamic aspect to the sexual component of the greater revolution. Good friends could get it on if they wanted to, and it was okay and then some. It was an extension of everything being everything. And they wanted to.

Was that a simplification of sex without love? No, because I did love her—valued and cherished her. Twenty and beautiful she was easy for a guy to cherish, on fragile footing in the real world, perhaps, but generous in romance. Then came her unique, obscure yet often dazzling wit.

I did not want to marry her, which she needed someone to do. I would commit to be her one and only forever or until boredom or a dynamic new horizon do us part. Why not enjoy what we had into the foreseeable future? For my part, we should have done so. Why would we mess things up? Marriage? Marriage was for parents. The world was a few years past the archaic social dictum that required married couples to stay together till the principals found somebody else, usually also married. Then came a round of divorces to make way for new marriages. Fuck. We were smarter than that.

Betty accepted my terms in the short run, so we could build foundations for a more lasting regret. She made me realize what I declined—what I would soon do without. Confidence with her footing as any woman, affirmed by gasps and whimpering, she brought us along in a small step for man, a giant leap for manhood. Beyond the squish and her singular beauty we achieved a rounded exchange. Maybe such frequent frolic indicated long-term commitment, so formalities would be foregone, if only I'd say as much.

Maybe we'd still be together, despite the odds, but she got married in March on spring break, ahead of schedule. She laughed too loud for comfort on her return, asking, "Why the fuck not?"

Her boyfriend posed the question first. They were so ready and willing, he said. So, why wait? Why not just…get it over with? Repeated to me, the question seemed personal and moot; Betty had moved beyond an answer. I was willing to resume practical relations for mutual relief and the betterment of the world in general but got another laugh, this one short, sardonic and also rhetorical.

We didn't learn much that year beyond the stark alternatives that life presented. Campus days could be loved or suffered. My girlfriend could trump all logic in her perverse compulsion to be what her parents wanted her to be—what we, as a cultural force, wanted so dearly away from. My college mentors could trump all instinct by discouraging a natural bent for adventure and settings way out of town. My government could trump all logic in its will to wage war and require my participation.

One side used duty and patriotism to frame the Vietnam War. The other asserted that the government was largely bought and paid for by corporate interests, primarily defense contractors with billions to lose or gain. The government would make the world safe for democracy—and for mixed free enterprise in lucrative new markets. McDonald's and Coca Cola were mere icons, like the oil companies for that matter. It was billions in weaponry that had the world by the balls and still does. I chose not to go, not for Dick Nixon or anyone.

Who would choose to be in a jungle trading fire with someone never met over an ideology applied far from home at best, over mercenary interests at worst? I would not. I would be elsewhere. It was time to decide, because a letter would soon arrive, opening with *Greetings...* That's how the draft letter began.

Back in '69 at Marcia and Betty's a month or so prior to New Year's Eve was another night of nights. We gathered round the tube without the crazy snuggle Kenny Visser would feel up next to the fishbowl. On that night in late autumn we watched the first draft lottery broadcast on TV. The Selective Service System attempted to make the process formal and transparent, to infuse the process with random chance, so the draftees could feel lucky or unlucky rather than simply oppressed. Three old men in suits and a woman with pearls and a hat hosted the ceremony. They're still viewable on-line, and the grim aspect of the little exercise is still laughable and tragic.

A nation preoccupied with war got nightly broadcasts with battle scenes, death tolls, exotic names, explosions and continuing bloodlust grist for the media mill. The nation divided further, as it had for the Civil War. Families and friends suffered rifts over Vietnam. People fought over the rightness and wrongness of fighting that war. So the first lottery was neither joyful nor celebratory. Yet it provided relief as intended. Those with numbers within the projected quota cutoff number would be drafted. Those with higher numbers would be spared. The lottery freed half of the military-age males in the country to proceed with their lives, barring unforeseen developments. Freeing up half the vulnerable population served to ease pressure on the Federal government, not nearly as much as the all-volunteer army would do. But the all-volunteer army would take a while longer to figure out.

A host plucked ping-pong balls from another fishbowl. Each ball showed a number that corresponded to a day of the year. Each day was then recorded in the order its ping-pong ball was drawn, to determine the order of conscription to the United States military draft—the first stop on the journey to the jungle war.

The third date called was Kenny Visser's. He smiled, stood and left, as if to pack his bags for the trip.

I remember Kenny V as a stoned and happy guy, a smart guy in silver- and purple-striped bell-bottoms and ruffled shirts. He wore his long blond locks in a pageboy and never said no to a reefer, and confided once as we drove from mid-Missouri to Denver in a Volkswagen Bus that sundown was a tough time for him. He didn't know why, but it made him anxious and depressed, even though he knew he'd feel much better by nightfall. Even that strange confession came with a smile. Kenny was the complete hippy and one of the first guys I knew to cross over quick and clean—over the border to a new life in another country, that is, and cross over from reefer, psychedelics and coed leg to real life with consequences.

Kenny had another two years of student deferment before his lottery number would take effect, but he left the country soon after his birthday was drawn from the fishbowl, gave up the U.S.A. for Montreal forever or until Jerry Ford issued amnesty. I knew he was headed out and asked him why the rush, when he had another two years of deferment. He said the student deferment was a piece of shit, a waste of time and life, just like school at the State U. Yeah, sure, he was having a great time, but he was hanging out, just this side of hiding out, and he needed to be somewhere he could call home. He wasn't certain where that would be, but it would be somewhere he wasn't afraid of being drafted.

He told me to look around—look at him and myself and all the misfits we hung out with, all of us refugees from a world at war, hiding out on a campus. "College? For us? Fuck, man. We should be out there getting started."

He loved hanging out but hated the classes and the hours wasted on empty talk with nothing to teach or learn. He hated school.

I assured him he'd hate the jungle worse. He nodded—no argument there, but it only boiled down to two choices if you let it. He had a bad feeling about the whole situation—the United States of America situation, that is. Kenny was a conspiracy theorist, often melodramatic and sometimes correct. He proved true to his convictions and spirit.

He vanished a few months later to Canada.

It felt like a death in the family. Premature departure made it more poignant, cold and anonymous. One of the guidelines for crossing into Canada was no talk beforehand, no communication or indication after. Close friends disappeared, as if by choice. The Federales went north on clues to bring potential soldiers home.

The seasoned among us knew that drugs could expand the mind, yet we had to keep that expansion within boundaries, with sustained connection to the non-tripping world we lived in most of the time.

Obviously, some failures occurred, though acid burnout was mostly attributed to excessive frequency and/or dosage. Both culprits were triggered by the rock 'n roll mentality of more, more, more. If one hit was cosmic then two hits should have been galactic, or something silly—make that stupid, with nine hits revealing the face of God. So it was. Those burnouts looked crispy—and insane.

The point was that the drug of the day would magnify many things, so the drug should be avoided if those things were dark, or in any way doubtful, apprehensive or anxious. A situation rife with challenges and complexity should not be compounded with LSD, mescaline, psilocybin or peyote. The alternate realist should wait with faith that happiness runs in a circular motion; in time the circle would come round again to a better place.

Donovan was soft, nearly quaint, getting it every time. So we waited a while. But how long could we postpone a major distraction, with life already on hold? And what about the boys in the jungle war? They couldn't very well wait for some blue sky and daffodils.

It was a time, a time it was and all that with the love all around us and flower power and demonstrations two, three, five times a week, where a college guy could get laid by being draft age and keeping his mouth shut. Joan Baez advised the girls—before the girls became women—to just say yes to the boys who said no, and so they did. It was a political statement, well received.

But imbalance was the sign of the times in a nation virulently divided. The love-it-or-leave-it crowd could win the scuffle on any given day, and the hippies and war protesters could dominate the airwaves on the next day. This was no yin/yang harmony, because both sides buckled under the yoke of war. A great nation with co-opted leadership was overriding its headlights, barreling down a dead end road. Barry McGuire assured over and over and over again, my friend, that the end was nigh on most AM stations. FM was more lyrical, nuanced and softly threatening with imagery like a hard rain that was bound to fall.

Most people felt the painful truth, that the eve of destruction had begun, and the hard rain was falling. Bob Dylan foretold the reckoning as well. The hard rain pummeled with rhetorical questions on the whereabouts of a blue-eyed son, a darling young one who was all too easily imagined far away in dire straits.

Lyrics moved minds. Lyrics infused hearts with pain and suffering in the sweet bye and bye. Creedence also asked who would stop the rain, as the body counts, fire fights, napalm and bombings went on and on and on. Another Dylan lyric effectively captured the mood, the sentiment, the feeling and direction. Jimi Hendrix had the same view from the watchtower, backed by guitar and a haunting voice pleading for a way out of here, immersed in chaos and inverted values, meaning and truth.

A tough situation bearing down generates anxiety. Richie Havens picked up the pace and touched a nerve in a song called *Freedom*, repeating the word freedom over rhythm guitar as a concept. Richie Havens pulled no punches, and let it all hang out with handsome Johnny marching to the Concord war with a flintlock in his hand.

Handsome Johnny marched to the Gettysburg war with a musket in his hand, to the Dunkirk war with a carbine in his hand and, oh, fuck me, to the Vietnam War with an M-15 in his hand.

These pages can't sing *Magic Carpet Ride* or pound the hard driving downbeat that got us down that dark and lonely road. But we remember. Slinging pizza and beer pitchers at the Hoffbrau House paid a buck and a quarter and hour—that's a dollar and twenty-five cents, not the buck and a quarter of decades later that could range from a hundred twenty-five dollars to a hundred twenty-five grand, depending on how things played out for any given hippy. Those who sloshed beer or gobbled pizza or sat and stared at the universe unfolding or danced the funky chicken alone in the cosmos—they too were one with those who served, all part of everything as everything. Steppenwolf stepped aside for a crossfire hurricane that gave birth to *Jumpin' Jack Flash*, and it was a gas. The toothless, bearded hag was on us. We were drowned, washed up and left for dead—nobody illustrated the agony and the ecstasy better than the Rolling Stones, who put a spike right through my hea-ead.

Mick got it to a T on what had befallen us and who we'd become. It was a pulse to match, a consensus boiled down to jungle rhythm in defense against a jungle war. It was exhausting, a pressure release in our rebellion that had come to a boil. Arlo Guthrie took the lead from his old man Woody, going against the grain and the law for small victories in ballad form, coming into Los Angeles with a couple of keys—which weren't keys to the city but kilos, two point two pounds of smokable salvation.

Hard-driving anarchy was the antidote, and those of the 60s heart and soul know where they were, what they were up to when certain hard-driving rhythms play back.

Pearl diving was a common job in those days—taking a shift in the kitchen, clearing the plates into the garbage and setting them in the big sink to soak a few minutes before loading the big rack and sliding the load into the commercial dishwasher for the scalding, then pulling the hot rack out to stack and prep for the next wave.

Sometimes you had to hit the kitchen for some pearl diving if the mescaline was coming on strong. It was enough to make you wonder who in their right mind would pop a psychedelic at the front end of a shift—oh, wait! Did you say right mind? There was the fucking problem! The mind wasn't right! What a goof!

The paranoia/hallucination interface could get extreme in a hurry, with nobody watching but you and the ether people. Well, they could gang up too, and sometimes you'd hike on out into the cold, friendly night to get a breather from the chaos, not by choice but by necessity. Not to worry, job security was not an issue, because the huge fucking mess would wait right there till you got back, and so would the piece o' shit job. I hated it but oh, for one more night of it—to feel the juice surge and wane and surge again, to achieve forgetfulness on a hard-driving downbeat in a crowd clamoring for more, as all hands on deck joined the chorus to shout down what stalked us. This was the process of becoming some-one else in another time and place facing something other than the future bearing down, dead ahead. Despite our experience with alternate realities, the reality upon us defied our grasp.

So we reached a might further.

Soon after the lottery the Selective Service projected a draft quota with a disclaimer that it could not be certain one way or another, but number 195 would possibly fulfill annual needs. The monster would be fed at that point, maybe, but it might need another course or two.

I drew 198. Dicey. What could you do? Get a job? Draft counselors were listed on a bulletin board at the Commons—I picked one and called. We made a time to meet at his house. How strange, seeking help in the suburbs, penetrating the cul-de-sac, split-level sameness we'd been goofing on those many semesters, parking on the set of *Leave it to Beaver*, walking through the picket gate and up the trimmed, flowered sidewalk and knocking on the stately front door.

He opened formally, pointing to his overstuffed living room where real life seemed sparse. His family remained unseen, appar-ently instructed to stay back while Dad pursued his patriotic calling. I sat, fearful of soiling such a bogus chair. He showed me a paper-back book. *1001 Ways to Beat the Draft* listed a thousand more or less practical pointers. The cover price of five or six bucks was the same as twenty-five today bucks. He paid, chump change to save a life. He'd plucked my copy from a case of books and folded it back to the 1001st way to beat the draft:

Learn to chew tobacco with your asshole and keep a chaw tucked in your cheek. When the proctologist tells you to turn around, bend and spread, do as instructed. When he comes in close, spit tobacco juice right in his eye.

I laughed, on cue. What a visual. He was a family physician, practiced in delivering difficult prognoses—so went our review of grim options in a series of sessions at his house. He assigned the book, calling it the most important homework of anybody's education. We would review and develop those ideas that seemed appealing, except for the last idea of chewing tobacco. "You're on your own there." He chuckled. What a relief.

We reviewed choices and consequences, including sentencing patterns. That would be prison sentencing. He called it a serious game; with luck we would avoid the dead serious.

In a short time packing up and heading north seemed like the best option, but an interim option emerged. By refusing induction, civil rights and civil law would not be forfeit. Draft counselors across America had focused on induction refusal in one place, clogging the court dockets there, allowing more time for the God-forsaken war to end. The strategy was based on faith that the madness must end, though it seemed eternal, without conscience.

It would be another fifteen years before Journey would capture the love that lingered for San Francisco, an icon of the most lovable components of American culture, including tolerance and the informed intelligence to consider differences among people. San Franciso could pluck heartstrings coast to coast on a reference of lights going down *in my city...*

The tune recalls the love all around us in a lyric of refuge, rendering the essence of home, as in home free. San Francisco made sense, so I—*we*—would make the pilgrimage, because we belonged there…

Bolting to Canada was a last resort, to be implemented only after refusing induction in San Francisco, the interim strategy. First off, we would attempt to avoid the Vietnam War by failing the pre-induction physical. Here too draft counselors across the country ran the odds on failing the physical. Strategy was based on statistics—all in the days of the telephone as the single form of communication, when all phones were wired to walls. With no cell phones, no internet, no email or social networking, no 24-hour news, no nothing but the fervor of a few good women and men, we wended through the maze, feeling the love all around us where we least expected it. This was justice in America in a compelling mobilization of conscientious individuals. This was a golden, glowing opportunity of historical magnitude, realized.

In short, hippies were a phenomenon becoming a subculture around the Summer of Love in '67. But in spite of non-conformity as a golden standard, nearly every inductee tried to fail the physical by being a hippie—stoned, dressed funny and talking cliché. The army couldn't draft a bunch of hippies, except that it did.

My draft counselor, a short, squat, unimposing fellow of impressive skill, pushed his black glasses back up flush and poo-pooed the hippie idea. No standard precluded military service on the basis of looking or acting strange—to a point. Of course that point was the difference between normal and genuine strangeness. With thousands of would-be failures showing up daily as hippies, he could not recommend the hippie approach.

He advised psychiatric treatment. We had time for a series of sessions that would be billed and paid for—don't worry about the expense; it was covered. Following those sessions, the psychiatrist would document severe instability and/or psychosis in a letter that I would take to my physical. The rest would fill in. Read the book.

I read, developing my strategy and awaiting notice as June graduation and death approached, inexorably. Its arrival at last was a relief.

Greetings... From *1001 Ways*, draft counselor guidance and personal improv, the strategy was ready for unveiling. Every inductee was allowed to postpone the physical. We could count on one postponement. We could request a second postponement and might get it, but we could not count on the second postponement. We got one. Every inductee was allowed a change of venue on the physical, especially with a hardship factor. The closest Selective Service exam center was St. Louis, convenient but deathly in its low percentage of failures. This pattern may not be related to Missouri's political inclination, or maybe it's an accurate reflection. Denver, on the other hand, only seven or eight hundred miles away, had a favorable failure rate on the military induction physical. I applied for a change of venue to Denver based on hardship, to help ailing Uncle Fester or some silly shit. Any reason could be suspect. How could anybody need to be anywhere when they were *going* to be in Vietnam in two shakes? And they knew it! Come on.

I got Denver with a six-week lead on my physical. My draft counselor called this timing perfect, and it would also allow for more planning on a move to San Francisco to refuse induction, if I passed the physical. Meanwhile, I wore long sleeves, long pants, shoes and sox and a hat to avoid the sun, to become white as a shut-in. A month out, early August, I ordered a bag of Dexedrine from Brother, a stand-out stoner of the western world. He felt that five milligrams daily would do the trick over a month. I weighed about 140 in those days. My counselor said the actual number of pounds would be incidental to the hollow cheeks and eyes, the gaunt physique and skeletal demeanor. Oh, boy. I ate nothing. It was easy, because Brother fucked up, oops, and got a bag of thirties instead of fives—that was thirty milligrams of Dexedrine, with the teeth gnashing and electric energy that did not sit well indoors. He blamed it on those fucking tiny numbers. I could not survive thirty-milligram dexies daily, but that was okay, because success and failure merged. I threw in the towel on the whole fucking Dexedrine deal because I was ready to die at home and didn't give a shit about anything but seeing another day, even if it was in a jungle war. By then the dexies had done their deed. Oh, you can spot a speed freak.

Goodwill was good for a lime green shirt with a texture, faint puke stains and long sleeves, along with some baggy, straight-leg pants with cuffs—nobody had straight-leg pants but deviates and derelicts not welcome near a playground. Goodwill was also good for some ragged wingtips. I ground holes into the soles and took the heels down to half on an odd, pigeon-toed angle. I stopped clipping finger-nails and toenails a month out and chipped half the buttons on the shirt with pliers, because *1001 Ways* said chipped buttons were a sure symptom of fucked up crazy insane. I put these clothes on ten days out. So that was the end of bathing too.

Strung out, wired up, ribs sticking out like a xylophone, I stopped brushing my teeth eight days out. Six days out I dulled some scissors so they could chew the edges of the nails. *1001 Ways* said chipped nails were as fucked up crazy as chipped buttons.

I got a crew cut and stopped shaving four days out. I hadn't eaten much, but a bowl of beets three days out made a terrific juicy dump just in time to cease anal hygiene on a high note. It felt good, with a sense of completion, like a forty-yard pass to the end zone, kind of, but without the marching band or the pompom girls. Two days out I scraped a few chewed fingernails up in there for some beet shit resi-due—gently, to avoid injuring the tender sphincter membrane—and I sat in the glow of yet another great play in a great drive down the field. Yet that golden interlude darkened as I wondered how (the fuck) I could get through the next two days. I'd jumped the gun.

Then again, that level of commitment would have made Betty Boop proud—dropping to 122 from a skinny 140 in so few days, jacked up on amphetamines, dirty, hungry, raw and eye-popping bona fide creepy, I realized all over that I hadn't jumped a god-damn thing but finally grasped the reality upon us. Kenny Visser confided that he was scheduled to split a few months earlier and then rescheduled to split in July. He rescheduled again when my strategy developed, just to drive me to Denver. I couldn't very well drive myself. As it was, I lay in back on the floor next to the spare tire. Kenny called it an honor and an ultimate goof. He stayed in a groove, listening to tunes, turning the radio down near sundown to confide his daily depression.

I passed the physical. Bummer. Unbelievable. Kenny Visser had the good manners to squelch the told-you-so, but he couldn't resist a wry eye on passing the joint on the way home.

My draft counselor wanted a complete debriefing. I told him the war machine needed too much fresh meat, that my delivery, appearance and demeanor at the induction physical had been impeccable—that the guy administering the written test begged me not to wig out. The guy had come in close to the little desk where I slumped and stared to whisper that he was A-OK with acid and anybody who wanted to take acid. His whisper went loud enough for everyone to hear, because he was getting emotional in his effort to avoid a scene, because a scene would look very bad on his report. He swore to God that he was pulling for me to fail, please God let me fail, but please don't freak out in his part of it. Please. *Put down any answers you want or no answers at all but don't freak out.*

The written test was also a challenge.

We live in the United States of

        a. Mexico
        b. United States
        c. America
        d. all of the above

And so on. Many guys in the testing room took all the time allowed to give it their best and get it right.

The army shrink asked the questions we'd rehearsed. What would I do if an intruder broke in and threatened the lives of my family? I shuddered in response and told the shrink I'd kill them.

Kill who?

What?

The army shrink scanned the crumpled and shit-stained letter I'd brought from the psychiatrist. "Who paid for your sessions?" I stared, trembling to the negative.

My draft counselor did not commiserate but went directly to Plan B, refusing induction in San Francisco, reminding me that the San

Francisco district court docket was backed up four years. Four years loomed like another round at the State U. But this four years had to be better. San Francisco was the birthplace of the love all around us after all, and it was a vibrant setting of a dynamic culture where a young man could find himself in productive pursuits. My draft counselor ended that phase of counseling by assuring me that San Francisco was our target city by choice, not chance.

In those days of *Love it or Leave it*, Dick Nixon's "silent majority" demanded that "America" be defended. The majority was never asked to fight the jungle war. Some military personnel came from silent majority families, but the vast majority of silent individuals did not volunteer for combat action.

Weighing choices became tedious and depressing. Continuing debauchery helped to distract thoughts from the jungle war. The year after college saw college grads swelling the work force—not the professional work force. Positions weren't available to a guy as good as dead, I mean drafted. Pearl diving, slinging pizza and pitchers, picking up pop bottles for the 4¢ redemption, working the orchards, parking cars, bussing dishes, trash pickup, anything for a buck and a half an hour to pay the rent and buy some groceries was what we'd come to.

Some did not feel deprived. A regular job—something to develop—was not a logical next step for many persons veering from the common career path. Are you kidding? We wanted away from that. As free spirits we could live forever. Work was unsavory by definition, something you could not feel but spent your time doing for money and stability. And security.

We worked hard but didn't call it work because an art form offers no security. Experience could be an art form in itself. It rarely paid. Months passed on assessment, rationale and waiting.

Into the Wilderness

COMPARE AND CONTRAST 17th Century metaphysical poet Andrew Marvel to the appearance and/or reality of the prosaic meter and/or iambic pentameter rhyme of Shoo-fly *or* Frogdick. Filling a composition book stone-cold ignernt on a topic—any topic—felt natural. Loaded for bear, a successful student of the times could view final exams as an exercise in superiority with the mental dexterity most available to the young at heart. The view from the cloudbank led to passing grades and a college degree with a major in huff and puff. Or would that be puff and huff? The 17th Century metaphysical poetry professor wore a bow tie and a cheap suit for his monotone lectures, extolling one stanza or another for exquisite meaning. Metaphysical poetry in mid-Missouri? What an amusing juxtaposition!

We felt so clever, goofing our way to a college degree—but it was faculty mercy that got us through. Professor Bowtie freely gave the C- to keep errant, goofy boys out of the jungle. Alas, I passed my physical to become another college grad qualifying for house arrest. I scoffed at the State University's invitation to graduation. What would they do? Praise my unique achievement? Predict leadership into the future? Assure brimful potential? Fock.

Running into an old flame from high school after four years of world-changing events felt like a milestone. Our mutual worldly development gave rise to intimate discourse on topics we'd hardly considered in high school, and the old familiarity of youth was a certain comfort in challenging times. In a spirit of continuing discovery and repetition, we became friends all over again. That's why many people marry. I had no choice but to keep real life on hold, to wait things out, to hang around campus in limbo, working menial jobs, keeping up with the good times and goofs.

We rented an attic apartment and lived over the Wendell family. Geoffrey Wendell seemed old, forty-one already, and staid, with elbow patches, pipe smoking and chronic pondering. He ran the Audio Visual Aids Department for the University and observed without judgment the silly pursuits of wayward youth passing time. A prevailing theory of those days was that recreational drugs were illegal, because they allowed people to pass time in non-productive pursuits. Productivity seemed necessary for the war machine; such was the simplicity of our perceptions. A successful goof would utilize recreational drugs in the pursuit of nothing but fun. One huge success called for a card table setup near the street to display a dozen tinfoil cups filled with dirt. We tended shop on folding chairs, and the sign out front said:

Hot Mud 10¢
Just add water.

We watched the market pass by, applying our degrees. Sometimes we answered questions. Geoffrey was impressed that zero return could provide so much, and he caught on: the goof shall set you free. He took a chair at the hot mud table one day to light his pipe. We lit up too, as a test, kind of. He said nothing, passing with flying colors, because Geoffrey was cool. We suspected as much but felt gratified to be proven correct. When the joint came his way, he said, "I'm not just blowing smoke here." Geoffrey was a funny guy. I laughed. He smiled, "I've been watching. I hear what you say and how you say it. You're good. You could be the one."

"Which one?"

"You got a line ready."

"It's not a line."

"Take it easy. I'm not saying a line is a bad thing. Look. I'm sitting on more electronic broadcast equipment than any fifty-thousand-watt radio station ever dreamed of capitalizing. Do you know who makes money in radio now?"

That was easy. "The holy rollers?" The airwaves didn't hum with come to Jesus and *give*; they wailed.

"Bingo. We'll call them the evangelicals."

"You want me to ask for money for Jesus on the radio?"

"No. That would be fraud. Or, it should be. Do you know what cassette tapes are?"

Everyone had record albums then, but we knew about cassette tapes—space-age gizmos with little plastic spools that let you play the tape over and over without a conventional tape recorder. They were meant to replace records but we didn't believe it and didn't like it anyway. Replace records? Why? Besides, they were just another version of the clunky 8-track tape. Audiophiles stuck to records. "Yes."

"Cassette tape is the ticket. We broadcast a radio show once a week for starters. All I have to do is apply to the FCC to occupy a vacant number."

"It's that easy?"

"It is for me." Those were the days. "At the end of the show we sell cassette tapes. Each tape has a show on it for five bucks. You can get the whole set of six shows for twenty-five bucks and save yourself five bucks right off the bat. I can get cassette tapes for about eleven cents, and the players for about three bucks. We'd have to order a bunch, but I can hide it. Once we settle in, I'll sell the tapes and players to us at cost. That'll account for the money."

"That's not fraud?"

"Only if we don't pay it back. Then I'll tell you what we're gonna do, because you love God and you love The Word *and* you love the folks out there listening. These cassette tape players would run you thirty dollars each in a store. But we're gonna send you the whole set of six shows—and throw in the player to boot—for forty-five bucks. Now you're saving yourself fifteen bucks. Get it?"

"Get what?"

"We sell entertainment and hope for a brighter day."

"You mean we preach?"

"You preach. You say whatever you want to say. I've heard you. Tell a story. Tell another story. Tell them God loves them. That can't hurt, can it?"

"Just go on the air and sell tapes and tape players?"

He nodded, gaining momentum. "Just about. I've been thinking about this, and the puzzle parts keep falling into place, not just kinda but perfectly. You're Brother Bob. It gets no better. It has a roll out the gullet with a pleasing feel and sound. And we don't broadcast from the university. We head twenty miles up the road."

"You mean to keep it legal."

"No. We'd be legal anywhere. Twenty miles up we'll be in Kingdom City. You don't think Brother Bob from Kingdom City might play like hell across the Bible Belt?"

Few people then grasped numbers relating to market share leading to dollars. Characteristic of the times, revenue was gross, but it made the difference between a hippie and a rock star. Rock stardom lurked in the collective consciousness; it could happen to anyone. Geoffrey's idea could have generated millions. I said no. I couldn't do that.

"Why not?"

"I'm Jewish for starters."

"So was Jesus."

"Not like that."

"Not like what? Jewish is Jewish. He was. You are. I don't get it? What's the difference?"

"Jews don't proselytize. Jews have no missionaries. Converting to Judaism isn't easy. It's very difficult."

"You wouldn't be proselytizing. Or converting. Or preaching anything Jewish. Or Christian. You'd be talking happy hope and glory. You'd be *selling*! I've seen you sell hot mud for chrissake!"

"We never actually sold any."

"But you weren't afraid to ask for the money! You weren't afraid to have some fun and share it! You think you might sell some light and hope? You think a Jew ever sold anything?"

"Yeah, they have. That could be another problem."

"I didn't mean it that way. It just came out wrong."

"It usually does. I just fairly well know how it would end up."

"Well, if you don't want to do it, that's okay. I'd always feel remiss if I didn't run it by you. It's a winner. You could be a winner, if you'd let it happen. I haven't picked too many, but this is one of them."

"You do it."

Geoffrey lit his pipe again, blew out the match and shook his head. "I'm too old. My voice sounds old. I can manage and I can coach. This calls for youth and a natural instinct. This calls for skills you might take for granted, but I see what they are. You could say the same things I could say, and people would smile for you but raise an eyebrow for me. Like I say, you're young, and you got it. Maybe I'll find somebody else. You never know."

It didn't grab me but I promised to think it over, and so I did, seeing myself in the chips, which didn't seem like a goof but could have been a cop out—going on the radio to say things I didn't believe to a people I didn't care about or like in exchange for money. It seemed calculated and cash based. I wanted no part of it, except for the money. The money would change everything.

Legions of draft age guys with no deferments passed the military physical in 1970 and waited the death knell, *Greetings...* War anxiety infused the first round lottery crowd with a pandemic of dark spirit. Into that cloud Geoffrey Wendell had planted a little seed that germinated to a vision. Imagine a right bona fide longhair with a penchant for improv. Just add money and you get way out front of the hot mud crowd. You get the farm, all new, with mobility and freedom, which was a delusion to be sure, but a welcome change from so much cultural oppression.

The problems of rock stardom had not changed over the ages, beginning with bloated self-esteem and skewed values. Geoffrey's idea changed perception of potential, enhancing our basis for happiness; such is the nature of greed, which is most often self-inflicted. Lust got confused with love. Emotions felt sincere, but new horizons viewed from our cozy attic tended to devalue our idyllic bliss. Pondering money, I believed I had the goods to cash in at any time, no rush. With money available, I could be superior to material needs. All needs would resolve with celebrity, though some needs felt well met at home. I'd never felt this way about one coed, so I presented a plan to shore up the base and keep us calm. It called for optimal sexual frequency. I thought true love warranted maximum potential, by paying attention to the cock—I mean clock. Any healthy young man will affirm that a rest between rounds is essential and can take two to forty-five minutes with about a twelve-minute average recovery. Like time and tide, recovery was a requirement of nature, an interval that must be accepted.

Ninety-minutes would be conservative, a cuddly interlude deemed mature in some quarters, and a recovery period of an hour and a half would render a brand new boy, ready to mount up one mo' time for another ride like no tomorrow. I approached fucking—I mean lovemaking—with method, often called methodology in your houses of academia. Make that academiology.

Never mind. We would do it, wait forty-five to ninety minutes, and then do it again. Round the clock.

By paying attention we could get in sixteen to thirty-two fucks per day, which wasn't realistic if we factored eating and sleeping, which could occur in the intervals, but the regimen seemed more reasonable to block off, say, eight hours for personal stuff. Make it ten hours for unanticipated stuff, like a rigorous broadcast schedule. That would still leave fourteen hours, yielding nine to eighteen goes a day. Think of it! God, how satisfying would that be?

Topping it all off: the money. I didn't mention the money to my sweetie just yet. I was saving the news of my decision to become a radio rock star for a special celebration.

The girlfriend looked troubled, annoyed and upset. She walked away, leaving me to wonder what. What?

Even eight times a day would be better than what we had, which was what? Two? Three? Ah, youth; taut as a drumhead and subtle as a pounding—and soon to be rich, rich, rich!

She announced soon after that she would head to Miami to be with her mother, and she left. Such was the fickle nature of showbiz. I liked her, supported her and tolerated her quirks. I could not imagine anything long term, but her departure felt like a loss of magnitude possibly greater than showbiz. She humbled me. I had nothing but picking apples and stealing pop bottles, slinging pizza when I could stand it, and roofing until springtime melted into summer. I could meet my pesky needs but felt foolish dragging dates up the staircase and pounding the jam into the floor/ceiling for Geoffrey's family to ignore like the two hundred fifty pound fuck in the attic.

It was the best of times and the worst of times.

Something had to give. Months stacked up, and those of us stuck in the campus/jungle interface felt like sitting ducks. Movement could change things, but the questions of where to go and what to do became circular and migrations became conceptual. The best option to confinement was upping the dosage.

We could sit and spin, with lyrics to facilitate our lyrical notions. In *Mr. Tambourine Man* our jingle jangle mornings got validated—as evening's empire crumbled into sand, and though we were not sleepy our weariness amazed us... *And the ancient empty street's too dead for dreaming.* I saw Bob Dylan not too long ago. The interviewer asked if he would consider composing more lyrics like those written in the 60s. Dylan said, "No. That won't happen again." Is *the ancient empty street too dead for dreaming*? Probably not, but the singular lyric of the 60s will be a long time coming back.

Meanwhile, becoming one with the smoke and pale light, we drifted, mostly on short trips around the bend.

A Flea-Bit Painted Monkey

ANARCHY IN CONFINEMENT was the Revolution in a nutshell. Young men hung out in university towns waiting to leave for Canada or Southeast Asia or maybe San Francisco. Meanwhile, we raised hell, goofed and made a scene. Or we gazed inward and beyond, wondering what and when. The dream began to end that year. Jimmy Levin failed college because he never went to class. We got by going to the first day of class, maybe a day or two during the semester and showing up for the final exam to fill a bluebook with nonsense. Jimmy was radical, ahead of the curve. Jimmy didn't fuck with any of that first day, last day, bluebook bullshit. Jimmy laughed, and then everybody laughed.

The cosmic goof in play was that neither the University nor Selective Service had connected Jimmy's non-dots. He fell through the cracks. Hardly a year or so later people would describe his life that way, but many thought Jimmy turned into a sunbeam and shined his way out.

Mick Jagger's plaintive song of *Mr. Jimmy* seemed obvious to those of us who knew Jimmy Levin. That was many, many people around campus and uptown. Oh, Jimmy was known. Why wouldn't Mick Jagger know him too? Mick's moves seemed to imitate Jimmy Levin in every way. Mick Jagger even admitted to *standing in line with Mr. Jimmy.* We did not take that as coincidence but we also refrained from discussing Mick's further revelation that *he said one word to me, and that was dead.*

A pioneer of the one-way ride, Jimmy was dead when they found him, cold but smiling serenely, like he knew, or had known. Jimmy seemed supremely indifferent at the end, when his surly, casual arrogance acquired depth and subtlety into the next phase, his body language softly saying, *Yeah? So?*

Jimmy overdosed on downers, Tuinals, which were yellow but weren't called yellows, not like Seconals were called reds. Both were trademark names, for what that was worth, which was millions to the drug companies and maybe had value for us too as a cultural component of what we'd fled. Or in Jimmy's case, pharmaceutical drugs were something to goof like no tomorrow. Mick Jagger narrated to a T one more time with *Mother's Little Helper*, a rock ode to barbiturates and the blessed acceptance they provided to suburbanites everywhere.

Chief among the images of the day was Jimmy Levin's Mick Jagger, with the slink and swagger, hollow cheeks and puffy lips. Jimmy aped Mick down to the hip hugger bell-bottoms with green and pink stripes and paisley usher ribbons down the legs. After mastering every cut on *Let It Bleed* that spring, Jimmy deferred to stardom with a new pair of pants he wouldn't take off, because they were leather, and at sixty dollars were known to be "the last pants you'll ever need!" And so they were.

Jimmy had zero body fat, just like Mick, though Jimmy stayed skinny by shooting speed, likely far more than Mick ever did, if Mick ever did. Just like Mick, Jimmy let his Elizabethan blouse hang open to show his ribs and concave stomach. He'd hunker down, sink his head into his shoulders, raise a knee and bring it across the other knee as if to counterbalance the emotion within. Pointing a rubbery finger at the future and with the other hand grasping a broomstick by the neck, his microphone, he matched the stereo in perfect synch, proclaiming himself to be a flea-bit painted monkey, proclaiming that all his friends were junkies. It was a lyric. It also rang true.

And so on through the groove, syllable for syllable, twitch for twitch, short-circuited but young enough to override the system on the polite disclaimer, confusing messianic with satanic, or maybe pointing out the similarity between the two. Oh, it was food for thought, but only for a beat before the next serving, the finale, where Jimmy squealed in a plaintiff pitch between falsetto and a rodent's death throes that he was, indeed, a *mon-keeeeeeeey...*

The accompanying percussion and guitar here fairly worked Jimmy like puppet strings in spastic hands, with agony and ecstasy appropriate to the pitch and sentiment of the moment.

Then he slumped with exhaustion in quick repose between tracks. Next came a ballad, a personal favorite, the one where Mick Jagger obviously had Jimmy Levin in mind for the sad ballad of getting what you need.

It wasn't all Stones, though *Let It Bleed* seemed to connect Jimmy Levin best to how it was. The Stones didn't exactly replace the Velvet Underground—they couldn't. The Stones simply went to a new phase, as yet unanticipated. Besides that, Jimmy needed a change from his Velvet Underground accompaniment, in which he and Heavy Greg Buckstein would heat their junk spoons, tie off, find a vein, get the register by drawing a little of the red stuff back up into the syringe, and then hold it right there while somebody— or maybe one of them—would reach over to set the other needle right in the very first groove on the record. Jimmy and Heavy Greg would have about three seconds of hiss, and into that unholy interval they would breathe deep, gather their wits, such as they were, and leap from their perch at the edge of the cliff, into the abyss. Pressing plungers they sent the drug coursing brain-ward. Ideally, Lou Reed came in on cue just as the drug reached the top floor, the Men's Department: hats, capes, boots and numbness… Lou Reed also seemed ambivalent in his reach for the summit.

Metaphors of the abyss and the summit were not mixed, and anyone who thought they were would only reflect the constraint of a conventional world in which gravity works downward, when in fact gravity and everything that is everything can work whatever way a true player wants it to work.

And so on to the money lines, leading up to Jimmy's bliss. Jimmy heard the cue and had the timing down—never mind—he'd come in and fade out, keeping the beat and waiting, anticipating, rejuvenating to the heady downbeat where he would light up with giddy fulfillment. Lou Reed's lyric deconstructed a single word down to three syllables *heh roh win* and the meaning of life and death, because death only triggers new life, check it out, let it go, get it on, if you can. A lyric of life beginning with the smack flowing would not be popular these days, possibly not even allowed. But who said the 60s was all sweetness and light?

Rhythm and rhyme flowed forth so unbelievably, profoundly true, and it was an album anyone could go out and buy and do the same thing with, whether they wanted to hit smack or speed or anything. Who cared which rocket fuel got you into orbit? What difference did it make with no rules anyway? It didn't, and it couldn't get any neater than that.

It did seem strangely practical in Jimmy and Heavy Greg's hard-drug, rock 'n' roll anarchy to save the Velvet Underground's ultimate cut for special occasions so they wouldn't get tired of the music—or too strung out on junk. Speed seemed easier to manage, and though the boys would have wilted in their boots at the first suggestion that their approach to partying down like no tomorrow was in the least *moderate*, they could still survive with honor. So they agreed that hitting speed instead of heroin most of the time for the synchronous beginning of *Heroin* would keep the Reaper amused but for the time being keep him at bay too. He could be such a rascal, insisting on the constant tease, though everyone knew that's where he would leap out of his apparent lethargy and take you quicker than snacks on the run.

Heavy Greg could not handle the idea of shooting LSD anymore than he could see the fun in stepping off the curb in front of a bus. But wait a minute. Greg was no pussy, no way—you think it was for nothing everyone called him Heavy Greg? But that didn't mean he was crazy. Shooting LSD? Well, of course you could. Nobody said you couldn't, and everybody knew you could shoot anything. We heard of one guy who shot peanut butter. Peanut butter, man! What a goof. But LSD? That was like, you know, using a Mack truck for a golf cart or a nuclear warhead instead of a cherry bomb or some shit. You know? Man, golf. What a goof.

Mainlining LSD was Jimmy's idea, Jimmy's modest proposal: "Hey. Would it be a fuckin' goof, man, or what, if we, like, spiked some Owsley or some microdots? Or some fuckin', some fuckin' sunshine, man? Uh huh! It'd be like the fuckin' astronauts, except faster!"

Jimmy saw LSD injection as the next frontier—as the ultimate defense against a world gone crazy. *Everyone* was eating LSD, and that was cool, but that was all it was, all these…college kids getting off to get their shit together. Jimmy needed more, something way out front, something to let him hang ten over the cutting edge, something daring, something to wake the Reaper from a sound sleep and slap snot out of that silly fucker.

Besides all that good fun—on a serious note—Jimmy had responsibilities, like, you know, to think up this shit and then check it out, you know, for the kids. He conjured it one day, looking around for something new to shoot up, till it hit him like a bolt of lightning—the idea of cooking up some LSD, drawing it into a syringe and spiking it. Realization spread across his face in a grin, perhaps in emulation of the grim one himself.

He called the idea original, or, as he put it afterwards, he invented it. *N*obody he heard of had yet hit acid with a spike. Now there was the space shot he'd been looking for. Besides, what could it do to you, take you out six dimensions on a bumpy ride? So? What's wrong with that?

So Jimmy hit some acid by himself, like a test pilot, kind of. Heavy Greg worked the record player, because once you hit acid, you can't really control the volume and wouldn't be able to tell if it was way up or whisper quiet or if you got it right, really, and if you missed the groove, you'd already be in the heavy Gs, where you could spend a day and night staring at the grooves in search of the lost one. So it was best that he had heavy Greg there to work the controls. Jimmy loved all his music as a parent might love all his children, each for its unique character and lovable quirk. He picked Led Zeppelin to shoot acid to, *You Need Love*; it seemed so perfect, and heavy Greg did not blow the mechanicals but got the needle into the groove at exactly the right spot with no scratches and optimal hiss. Jimmy pressed the plunger and slumped into the floor, leaning against the wall, staring and twitching.

Greg tweaked the treble and bass so the tone was perfect, then he untied Jimmy and laughed, "What's it like, man?"

Jimmy's mouth went all floppy, and he laughed too, kind of, and made some noises but couldn't talk too well, which everyone thought was similar to Houston Control losing contact with Major Tom. Then Jimmy nodded. He stared at the record player and said, "It's off."

Greg said, "It sounds off. That's all. You're accelerating, man. You're breaking out of suborbital. It's not off. Get all the way, man. It's on. It's right on…man."

We hung out for a while watching Jimmy get all the way, but then we started getting off too, maybe forty-five minutes later, because we'd only swallowed our acid. Then we drifted apart to roam the Universe. Some of us may still be out there. I think Jimmy might be. A few days later he had Heavy Greg convinced that it was a stoned gas and then some, and maybe, just maybe, anybody who didn't try it would never know, never *experience*, which would not do, which is what happened to our parents, and look how they ended up. So they bantered further, working together to get Heavy Greg pumped up to try it. Greg was game, already feeling a little bit second fiddle, with Jimmy telling everyone how it was, and he, Heavy Greg, grinning and nodding like a bump on a log while Jimmy debriefed on his journey to where no human had ever been and returned from: the outer galaxy. "It's like, man, you're just sitting there one second, and the next second, you're like…like…tripping your fucking brains in two, man."

What a nut. But what a dazzling character. Many called him a waste of everything. But he wasn't. He wasted his human potential in the material productivity arena, but that was exactly as intended, what he wanted most of all. Jimmy set out to blaze the ether. Till the day he died and maybe beyond that, he was a warm, fun loving guy who set himself apart from most humans by making a commitment—not to drugs; they were merely his vehicle. He wanted to be the tungsten in the light bulb. He stood out in the Heart of the Revolution by refusing to resent the seemingly silly, material lives his parents lived, with their suburban needs and fears, their addictions to creature comforts and so-called security, their tastes and fads that looked ridiculous a few years later and were in fact ridiculous in the moment. Jimmy Levin referred to his mother and father as pure parents, as lovable as parents could be, and he openly loved them back, more so for their foibles, which he found endearing and grist for his mill.

Jimmy's parents had gone out with all the 50's parents and bought split-level, ranch style homes and put plastic covers on the sofas and chairs. Mother wore her hair high. Father drank highballs. The country club proved their success, and all of life in America had big fins and plentiful chrome, because those things were evidence of the future upon us, which was superior and real by consensus and apparent reality, along with the prescription drugs Mom and Dad popped like M & fucking M's, man.

Jimmy's filial love was as radical in those days as a few ear staples, some eyebrow spikes, a nose ring, a tongue bearing and some lip brackets came to be decades later.

Oddly enough, I met Jimmy under far less friendly circumstances—not met, really, but saw him. Like so many state university detainees of the times, old acquaintances from high school reappeared as different people in a different world.

Jimmy wrestled in high school for Ladue, our archrival. He was small even then, wiry and punked out decades ahead of the punk fad. Two severe cowlicks clipped short rendered a spike-headed kid with an aggressive smirk who remained undefeated at ninety-five pounds near the end of the season. Surly and arrogant, he was easy to dislike, stepping out of his team circle, walking halfway to ours and staring, till he picked out Nick Geiss, his ninety-five pound opponent. Then he laughed, pointed and sneered with ridicule, in fact aping Mick Jagger even then, a few years before Mick did it.

Nick Geiss was my good friend, also undefeated, so this match would preview the district finals, with the winner going on to state tournament. Jimmy was a villain. He pinned my good friend and made it look as laughably easy as he'd predicted. Then he did a little strut with the smirk and pinched face that would stay with him on to the state university, where he wouldn't wrestle but would become an icon in other circles. The same misunderstood sneer would be there when they found him.

Yeah? So?

But I get ahead; characters and events and interplay, often influencing what came next.

Reconnection with friends from childhood well into the revolution often disregarded former identity. It had to by necessity. What came before was a goof of no goof, a joke in which we had been the butt, till we cast that burden aside.

I don't think Jimmy went through a formal thought process of dismissing our pasts on opposing wrestling teams. I think he came on like an old friend recognizing a current teammate. He carried on over several drugs coming onto the scene, some new, some untried, some thrillingly anticipatory, while others presented refinements over what had been known. Drugs were the adventure of the times in general and of his times in particular. He didn't remember me from Adam or the peanut gallery when he pinned my friend, as the cheerleaders for his school chanted: *Jimmy Levin! Get the pin!*

I never asked why he was such an asshole back then but merely mentioned that I'd wrestled for my high school and saw him wrestle Nick Geiss. He didn't reference his win or the pin or his progress to the state finals but lit up with a smile. "Oh, man! Nick Geiss! How's he doing, man?" Jimmy's humility was impressive—and that was a cornerstone of the higher times: ditching the ideas our society thrived on, competition being the biggest culprit. If you didn't know how good Nick Geiss was and how easily Jimmy pinned him, you could just as easily miss Jimmy's discounting-of-self in passing. His cumulative presence, however, was formidable. Jimmy didn't just take drugs; Jimmy learned what the drugs could teach him. For a long time the good things were learned, with a few bad things in time that came with the territory, if you stayed with it. Jimmy would eventually learn about overdose, maybe.

Sure, it was part of the times to set aside conventional concepts like winner and loser. But few people mastered it like Jimmy. He was a spirit to reckon and a natural born leader in our new world at war— scratch that—our new world of goofing like no tomorrow. What could possibly be a better antidote to war and the military mindset than a big fat goof? With a big heart and a few fatal addictions, he also delivered humility and friendship. In all the drug-addled haze, Jimmy Levin knew what to value. Like a rock star in our bumpkin neck of the woods, he would greet anyone shuffling in from nowhere with a laugh and a welcome to join the fun.

The high school matrix wove tighter that strange season of our disconnection when Stevie Getman missed his own college graduation by a few key credits, and college was not for him a goof. Stevie had family money to take care of, so his degree in accounting would factor significantly in family and country club perceptions. Stevie had gone to my high school and did not wrestle, but Jimmy Levin was an old familiar, because Harold and Jeanette Levin were ta ta friends with Sylvia and the Wolfman—that would be Mr. and Mrs. Wolf, Stevie's mother and her new husband. All four parents had occasion to observe and discuss *the children* at the club, including Heavy Greg Buckstein, whose parents not only waved ta ta from their golf cart; they actually worked very hard at *reducing* their handicap—even as the club tournament approached!

What a goof: golf, Republicans, country clubs and parents, with their cocktails, Cadillacs and pills.

This is not to suggest a Jewish revolution as subset to the greater revolution but that Jews factored prominently on the front lines of both sides.

As if by coincidence Stevie Getman got a new apartment for three months of summer school to get his last three accounting credits at the University of Colorado. With summer upon us, blood stirred. I advised Geoffrey Wendell that I would forego his attic for a pilgrimage of sorts, next stop San Francisco, to pay homage and check it out. The Selective Service office had not changed its quota projection through April, which seemed propitious, since springtime generally increases all activity, including war and killing, but the jungle war held steady.

Greg and Jimmy were on the road together, possibly to review potential in Boulder, where drugs of extreme recreational value were said to be available. Soon in Boulder we began our summer of disorientation by celebrating no future to speak of and a past that didn't count or matter. Everything relative to time and space was on its head. Or rather in its head, man. I hitchhiked, because you could make better time without a car and hardly ever waited more than two or three minutes for a ride, because the sisters and brothers were on the roads that summer. Make that five minutes or ten, because I had my bicycle, because a guy needs transportation. The Peugeot UO8 retailed for about eighty bucks and re-introduced a generation to the joy of bicycling. Mine got stolen in Boulder three days in—which is still a laugh; not the theft—that was a bummer—but the sheer freedom of hitchhiking with a bicycle. "Yeah. That's cool, man. We'll strap it to the roof." One ride after another tied it to the roof or stuck it in back of the microbus. Then we got stoned, heading west. We all got stoned on meeting and stoned on parting ways. We got stoned like first Americans, sealing a deal, affirming our subscription, buffing the view to better roll down the road.

That was the year Heavy Greg got nicknamed after Magnavox came out with a new TV, the Quasar, aggressively merchandized for easy access to its vital components. The Quasar was the TV with its *Works in a Drawer*. Heavy Greg became known as Captain Quasar, because he had his works in his drawers. He and Jimmy were hitting junk with greater frequency that summer in Boulder's first infusion of heroin and the associated crime wave. Junk was not cool, mainly because it segregated the brothers and sisters from the junkies, in most cases. Greg and Jimmy were exceptions, remaining cool, because they had the good sense not to mention junk in any company but that of other junkies, though they didn't consider themselves junkies. Junkies needed the cure at very demanding intervals, and both Greg and Jimmy had gone three days without to prove their point and could do so again. Any time, man. Besides that, both had money and credit cards from their parents, so they didn't need to be out on the street stealing stuff.

Their parents wanted them to stay out of trouble after all. Heavy Greg and Jimmy were as well discreet enough to hit up in the bathroom, because heroin was still very, very heavy, man, a certain taboo even among your major hell-raisers, and good breeding and upbringing didn't count for nothing—not yet anyway.

Still, everything was a goof, and Stevie Getman and I giggled like hyenas when I reminded him of the shit-fit Sylvia and the Wolf man would have if they knew who was running smack in Stevie's bathroom. Sylvia and the Wolf man were dead fucking ringers for the portrait of Ike and Mamie Eisenhower and held the pose far longer than Ike and Mamie ever did.

Some clinical grade mescaline and a Leon Russell concert seemed like synchronous events right on the heels of so many synchronous events. We'd all arrived within two days. My bicycle got stolen. I got way bummed—I had a few thousand miles and many happy memories on that bicycle, and eighty bucks wasn't chump change. But then Leon Russell rolled away the stone on his way into town, and some high octane mescaline came down the pike as if by chance to make me feel better, to help things let go of their material claim on each other, to loosen up the firmament and let the universe proceed with expansion, beginning with our minds.

So we took some and went. Leon Russell looked like the old man on the mountain in a top hat even then and was a rhythm 'n' blues god, and Mary McCreary, his eventual wife, had a body that formed up right there on stage, direct from everyboy's dream. She sang and danced in the front line, her Amazon-African physique a certain jaw dropper for the boys gaping up from the front row at her perfect melons bouncing to the pulse of life while Leon fired off a shoot out on the plantation. All the joy and light, the insight of Truth and Being filled us with a warmth and camaraderie like never before till the show was over, and we were spent but still tripping, or rather all tripped out with nowhere to go. Most people experience at some time a silence of audible dimension, yet sitting in that room after the show was a level up, so to speak, buzzing along to nowhere as the room went empty.

Into that lull Heavy Greg asked the thin air among us, with his distinct downward inclination, "God, man. I wonder what it's like to be dead. Man. It must be the trippiest fuckin' trip in the world, man. It must be like...like...."

Dead? What the fuck was he talking dead for? Well, maybe dead was cool. Nobody said anything, because we were tripping and not nearly as seasoned as Greg or Jimmy, so we couldn't talk—or at least not with any confidence, and besides, we had to scan the files for dead and trippy, since anything could be cool. We liked the Grateful Dead, with the skulls and everything. They were cool, and tripping was definitely not your usual life form, and tripping was cool, but dead was not like tripping. No way. So we sat and stared, fairly stymied, until Jimmy summarized the situation:

"It's not like anything, man. You're fuckin' dead." The guy was full of surprises.

You're the Reason I'll be Traveling On

—Don't think twice. It's all right.

BOB DYLAN PRESENTED a few new angles on a tough situation. By letting things go we could have faith in the road as a place to be, a place where life unfolded in continuing adventure, where brotherhood came our way along with a few sisters. Ah, youth; if not for the presumption of the thing, more kids might embrace it.

Well, times seemed tough. After riding my bicycle three days in the Boulder Mountains I had no bicycle. Leon Russell through the mescaline lens was an impossible act to follow. Stevie broke the news to Jimmy and Heavy Greg that he had to study to graduate, because. Hey, that's cool, man. They left.

Bummer.

Jimmy passed me a card on the way out, not a business card but a credit card with the name Leo Denton. Cards were such a goof. Business, credit—the fuck? Jimmy got this card from a guy in Boulder as collateral on a balance. Jimmy knew that balances were bullshit and always tilt, unbalanced, and he was done with the guy. Maybe he sensed something without letting on, just as he knew of his wrestling skills without letting on. Shrewd yet humble, he smirked, pressing the card into my palm. "I got a card, man. I'm giving it to you. Be cool."

That was cool. What do you do with a credit card? They were a goof and then some, like another trick to get you into debt you'd never be able to pay. Then again, they were magical. Credit card companies sent live cards unsolicited to random consumers in the 60s. Many recipients welcomed a new way of life, strapping on the harness in the new American plan, providing instant mobility at only a point and a half—rotating. Many people thought they'd arrived at last, at the financial mobility they'd always expected to have. The credit card promised fantasy fulfillment on the more, more, more. What could be so bad? 18% annual didn't really count, because you'd pay your bill monthly. Why wouldn't you?

Credit card transactions at that time occurred on plastic boxes with rollers requiring some muscle and no electronic capture. A few people with hot cards cost the card companies millions, but the companies soaked up that loss as a nominal cost of doing business.

I had Gary Cooper's number from when he bought my motorcycle in Munich the summer before. He still owed me a few bucks, which was cool, and I called him on Stevie's phone to see if I might crash on his couch there in Venice a few days. That call was a major event in those days known as long distance. Back then dinner and long distance both ran a couple bucks, but Stevie wanted to study. That was cool, especially since the Wolf Man likely picked up Stevie's phone tab.

"Sure, come on," Gary said.

It was on again, hitting the road to Mecca with an LA detour on the way. San Francisco glowed in the distance. If Gary Cooper paid his debt, I'd be flush and on my way to Freedom Central.

Stevie drove me through town to avoid what he called the urban hassle, out to the main artery heading south. Pulling over at the on-ramp he said don't worry, he could head down to the next exit and get off, because I'd fare best at the on-ramp, where cars slowed down. I felt generous, letting Stevie explain the ways of the road. He didn't get out so much, and there he was studying accounting in a prime fillet summer. Fuck.

We shook hands. Flipside, motherfucker. And the freedom freeway opened again on anything possible. A grown man on an interstate on-ramp with a rucksack and a cardboard sign that said LA might doubt his meaning in life today—he might question his place in society, his contribution and his value to anything and his long odds on getting a ride. Back then, waiting on a ramp was like a line in the water—perfectly baited over a deep hole with surface ripples indicating lunkers down there; who knew what might come along? I could feel things working out and getting higher, not just on reefer but on the evolving beauty of road society. That wasn't the same as a natural high, because a natural high required no reefer. I couldn't quite get that one. Besides, if we could get high with no reefer, then a little reefer on top of that would be really nice.

But chronic reefer wasn't a problem then, what today would be called an issue. 60s dope had less THC, so you could smoke more and adapt more easily. Life felt higher in general, away from campus delusion and intellectual confinement. Smoking dope had been a means of dulling the edge during the student deferment. After graduation, before the physical and adrift in the DMZ, dope smoking felt like a natural supplement to life on the road. Just as a water colorist uses a tinted wash as a pleasing backdrop, so the dope put tinted pleasantry on the world in movement.

Every brother was a trip in those days, when brothers came in all colors, and every trip unfolded with ups, downs and revelation as the puzzle parts of peace and unity tried to fit together. Every sister enjoyed equal status in what we shared, which was everything. If the chemistry was on, a brother and a sister had sexual relations, which wasn't incestuous or any kind of nasty. It was natural and set us apart from a nation of suburban inmates. We felt free. They seemed envious.

Take Susan Bromberg, a lanky girl from Boston nearly a head taller than me. Experimenting with the road as a place of being, serving her internship to the age upon us, Susan crawled into the back seat of the soulful Volvo that had picked me up from the on-ramp. We'd driven a few exits down to an off-campus apartment complex where we pulled in for Susan, who hugged her friends and put her pro-model backpack with lumbar support into the trunk.

The two guys with the Volvo had posted a ride on a bulletin board at the University. Susan had called and arranged for the ride. It was organized and civil with expectations clearly stated. When the Volvo boys pulled over for me, one asked if I could help pay for gas. I pulled Jimmy's credit card halfway out of my vest pocket. He opened the back door.

So the four of us were on our way to LA till one of the guys turned around to ask Susan and me how we felt about veering off to check out Taos. Taos had become a gathering point, a haven for the happening and what might be happening next. Susan actually put a knuckle on her chin before nodding ponderously. Sure, she could be cool with Taos. She'd heard it was a groove, possibly a gas. She'd heard of the hot springs at Taos. They were supposed to be *really something*. That pegged her as suburban with parental influence, out for an adventure with the other kids, sampling the Revolution before settling down to a real life of stability, security and convenience. She'd just graduated Boston College, and boy, did she ever feel relieved, finally done with studying and stuff. She would begin pursuit of a master's degree in psychology only two months down the line, so Taos seemed like a spontaneously perfect spice for her adventure soufflé. Her brief bio ended on a groan that she didn't even want to think about more school, not until she had to anyway.

"It's not like you have to go," I said.

She laughed short with resignation. "But I do," she said, pegging suburban coordinates one more time.

The two guys in front also hailed from the east coast and said they too had recently graduated in the *Bahstin* area. Small world, but Harvard was not what it used to be and, frankly, they were ready for some action before hunkering down on legal careers. The Harvard degree could not guarantee the presidency of the United States of America or the Supreme Court for that matter, but, really, you had to respect the stats and be ready.

Stick thin and tall with impressive posture, Susan Bromberg did not slump to better meet her peers. Apparently sheltered, she had keener instincts than the average princess. Surely Daddy would have fixed the frizzy brown hair and arched nose, as surely she resisted. With such good manners, she was easy to like. She eyed me back and blushed, pretty in her way, but no, I did not want to be an item with her. I admired her womanly attributes, as hormonally crazed young males have done since forever. But prospects for intimacy with Susan Bromberg seemed distant, objective and impersonal.

"So we're cool, sharing the gas three ways?" The dude riding shotgun turned and squared his torso to better pose the question. Susan deferred to my apparent seasoning on such a rude opener. Ivy League University graduates may have required elaboration on an attempted ass fucking, but those of us from the State U did not. Susan had already agreed on the phone to share gas expense three ways. And surely I'd counted to three the moment I got in, after agreeing to share. "Besides, gasoline expense wouldn't begin to cover wear and tear. Tires. Oil change. Grease. Lube. Battery. U-joints. Points. Plugs. Condenser...windshield wipers..." The guy already sounded like a candidate.

"Sharing is cool," I said.

"Great. Okay, we were planning on LA, but we have to get back. But we do want to see Taos. So we can take you that far if you share the gas. Okay?"

Susan shrugged, wondering instantly if this would play out as us against them. They seemed unusual to say the least, removed from the spirit of the day. I said, "Sure. We can use my credit card. In fact, I'd just as soon use it for all the gas and you can pay me back." Six eyebrows rose. So I pulled the credit card all the way out of my shirt pocket. The shotgun dude said, "You want to put the gas on your credit card, and we pay you in cash?"

"Yeah. Why not? My fucked up, downed out father pays the tab. So why not?" A personality defect had come to the surface; I'd matched their division by three with a sleight of hand and pre-empted follow-up with another great offer. "Tell you what: you guys just pay me a fourth. What the fuck. Dad's a rich fucker. Know what I mean?" Oh, they knew, so they went along, shifting in their seats, seeking comfort on the advantage just gained. Was it the fair advantage they chronically anticipated? Susan looked me in the eyes, making me feel immoral, until she cracked a fractional smile.

The crux for some was revolutionary behavior short of crime that could result in conviction. I felt beyond, pondering flight from the country.

We camped that night in the full flavor of the times—in a clearing off the secondary road to Taos, around a campfire with sandwiches, chips and sodas. It was peace now, right on, fuck the pigs and down with the establishment at the expense of a combo gas station/grocery store. Everything went on the card, gas, groceries, some stretchy seat covers, a couple quarts of oil, some windshield juice and fuck it, throw in some that fruit juice too, and a deluxe snow scraper, because you never know—oh, and some new wipers while we were at it. Why not? I assured the Volvo boys that the crusty old fucker wouldn't feel it anymore than a princess might feel a dildo under her mattress. They didn't get it but chuckled on cue and agreed that a seventy-five percent discount didn't come along every day.

Giddy with victory, the *Hahvahd* boys scanned for what else might be granted as the attendant walked around back to write the license number on the voucher. I thought the jig was up. But the boys chortled, like the car was hot or they'd actually graduated from Beantown JC with a major in drama. Or maybe Dad was so connected that credit card fraud would be a trifle. They talked of tires, an oil change and a battery.

I could not imagine anyone so inured to common sense—what we at the State U called stupid. With a tinge of guilt I wanted to suggest a good story for when the credit card company came calling for payment. But the campfire blazed with future prospects. The gifted young men fairly crooned over career potential and political contacts. Names dropped with the dew as I yawned my way to horizontal. Susan stretched out beside me. At some point she nestled in for warmth. We woke at dawn, startled in our snuggle. I assured her it was cool. She sat up, perhaps prodded to do so. She ignored me admirably and softly suggested that, in her opinion, we would be better off hitchhiking rather than traveling with the Volvo boys. I asked what she thought was wrong with them. She looked me in the eyes again. She shrugged.

Two hours later we rolled into Taos and another service station. I told the boys that Susan and I would say goodbye, because we'd decided to stay in Taos for a while. They nodded and turned away, then turned back to ask if the credit card might be for sale. Karmic consequence seemed balanced, and one of them flashed two twenties—they wanted to rack up a road trip on my father's credit card in exchange for forty dollars. Their worldly way made the answer easy. "Why the fuck not?" I felt like a courier getting paid. Old Dad died ten years earlier, which somehow seemed right.

We watched them head out, flush with greater potential, highballing into a dazzling future. Susan and I hoofed a mile or two the other way toward a village. Hiking down that solitary road, I asked if she felt better. She said, "Yes." The bond between us was silent and tangible. In a minute she said, "I'm around those guys all year. I didn't come this far for more of the same. Besides…"

In another while I asked, "Besides what?"

Togetherness sometimes happened. Sometimes it flowed. Susan was easy, deferential on some things, taking charge on others. She knew where to make camp, what to buy and who to trust, applying her smarts to the road like a veteran.

We hiked to the truck stop in the village where the word was that "we" were camping by the springs another two miles out, and so we went and sure enough. Another blessing of the road was discovering "us" in another homecoming of brothers and sisters. One of us at the springs was extra dirty and tough, with his hair pulled back and woven into pigtails bound by a headband with two feathers out the top in back. His hair wasn't simply naturally dirty; it looked like he'd poured dirt on it. Some beads and dangles off his leather vest in front did not make him look like Willie Nelson.

Mental and dark; assessment took a fraction of the usual moment required. Snake Who Runs drove a new Buick Electra 225 convertible with the top down. Some of us were familiar with the Electra deuce 'n a quarter because of establishment-based parents, or we had friends with affluent parents. This guy seemed way outside that realm, but he seemed sincere in saying, "Hey, come on. Throw your stuff in back. I need help with the groceries." He spoke directly to me. Susan took the groceries we'd bought at the truck stop. She would find us a spot and get us settled. The simple act of keeping my rucksack with me reflected the vagaries of the day.

I wanted to stay by the springs, where many young females soaked naked. Why would I want to go help with the groceries with such groceries at hand? Besides, Susan was looking better, and I knew she wanted to peel and soak. But the code of the times called for pitching in for the greater good, and when Snake Who Runs jumped over the passenger door and walked across the front seat in his muddy Dingos, I felt his urgency. I felt foolish opening the door and getting in, but a few home habits hung on.

We hightailed it across the plains lickety split, thumpety thump, fuck a bunch o' roads 'n shit. I wanted to say something, like this seemed an odd place for a grocery store, or this must be the shortcut, or I love Mom 'n Pops that are way out of the way, but I wasn't that dumb by nature and hadn't graduated Ivy League. I knew Snake Who Runs had something in mind, like groceries without the grocer or the store, and I was afraid I knew what it was. Bouncing like a jumping bean and holding on with both hands, I would've had to yell anyway. Besides that, Snake Who Runs yelled first, "I love this car! Picked her up in Denver! I'd never buy one, though. Fucking piece o' shit! It's gonna fall apart before you know it! Just you watch!"

We'd been pounding sagebrush and tumbleweed at forty to fifty mph along the base of a steep hillside and deep arroyo when Snake Who Runs hung a right hard enough to peel the tires off the rims. The tires stayed on, and when I glanced over, I thought I saw him nod in admiration, till he winced when we pulled a hit and run on an old saguaro, her arms raised in futile surrender against the onslaught, who was us. I braced both hands against the cushy dashboard briefly for the crash and splatter. The impact nailed me to the cushy seatback, and I glanced to see the Snake man grimacing in sheer gratification. We sure as fuck wouldn't take no shit from no fucking cactus. And uphill we roared, spewing contrails of dust and debris, our hood hardly dented and not too schmutzed and lumpy with blood and gore from the old saguaro's innards.

We slowed to cruising speed about halfway up, but I soon realized it was more stalking speed, till we turned left to run parallel with the tree line below some grazing cattle who stopped grazing and looked up with grave concern that was well founded.

Cattle here and there vocalized, "Mmmuuhh!"

Snake Who Runs eased us in as close as he dared before jamming the shifter into park and leaning over my way to reach under the seat for a handgun, a big sumbitch. I didn't think he was queer and going for my crotch, and when he bolted back out and pointed his gun at my head I didn't think he actually aimed to shoot me. But he would have shot me had I not ducked under.

Two shots slammed overhead, and I sat up to see a big steer felled just uphill as the others loped away. Snake Who Runs was up and out, jumping over me and drawing his fifteen-inch, calf-strapped Bowie knife on the way. Like a seasoned field butcher he sliced out about a forty-pound section, say three feet by five feet, maybe two inches thick, with practiced long strokes of the razor-sharp blade. Hoisting the meat slab clear of the carcass he lugged it on short steps huffing and puffing to the car, where he flung it into the back seat.

It clashed. Blood red on chiffon lime? Come on.

"Top sirloin, man. We eat good."

"What about the rest of it?"

"Fuckin' wolves 'n coyotes. They gotta eat too, don't they? Fuck, boy. I gotta tell you everything? Hell, they oughta eat good ever once 'n a while just like us. Don't you think?" He pulled a t-shirt out of my pack to wipe the blood off his arms, adding with a short laugh, "Snakes too." He wadded my shirt and pitched it in back on top of the meat. "Don't you worry. That shit'll wash out."

I didn't complain.

Then it was back to the springs and just in time, because the local contingent of itinerant workers had arrived for the show of naked hippie chicks up at the springs. The workers had gathered round a few tailgates to drink beer and wait for the emergence of fresh-soaked naked women right there free for the ogling and who knew what else. These were hippie chicks after all, and everyone knew they liked some hot tamale in their taco. The naked females had remained submerged till help arrived, which was us—or was Snake Who Runs at any rate.

We pulled up and were almost stopped when he sprang from the car much like Jack comes out of the box, except that Snake Who Runs jammed the brakes and crunched the deuce 'n a quarter into park before leaping out, flashing his giant, gleaming blade. Was it a warning? Not really, except for the capacity presented by a rough and tumble, dirty, shirtless man ornamented like an Indian and splattered with blood as he waved a knife bigger than most forearms. Leaning over the back seat he stabbed the meat with sincerity, like it wasn't yet dead, then hoisted it on the knife up and out and onto the trunk.

The itinerants murmured and rustled about, but Snake Who Runs sliced off a few square feet of top sirloin and offered it up as a most amazing and unexpected steak dinner—"Yeah, motherfuckers. I'm talking top sirloin! On me, motherfuckers!" So the peace offering was made. A few stray threads and foam core of Buick Electra 225 upholstery and some chiffon lime paint flecks looked like meaningful garnish. Make no mistake; the meat offering did not reflect the love all around us but rather proved the power to the people. That meat was not meant to signal the green light on our women. The clear and simple message was that every man among us understood the sweetness and danger of fresh pussy, and we could all eat steak and enjoy a lovely fucking evening, or you're gonna die, motherfucker. *Comprendez?* The itinerants accepted the dripping, congealing, fly-swarming slab on short nods and murmurs of *Gracias, Señor.*

Snake Who Runs could have been in politics too, running against the Volvo boys. His verbal skills weren't articulate, much less loquacious, but neither are most congresspersons and senators. And the Snake man could have spiced up CSPAN with his diplomatic skills. He seemed insane and well intentioned, so maybe it could have worked out.

I don't know how many of our women wanted to give themselves to Snake Who Runs that night, but it was a few, till he grunted one last time and then snored. Susan had wisely bivouacked on the periphery, away from the main fire. I found her there drying her hair, having changed into clean shorts and a blue shirt with no bra, an enticement framed in personal comfort. Looking back it frames as opportunity lost. She saw me staring and said she didn't eat meat. She unpacked an impressive little camp stove along with a mess kit and a bag of brown rice. She cooked a cup of brown rice, and I had a square foot of sirloin to keep the peace. We talked of where we'd been and what we'd seen. She said she didn't feel any too sure about that snake guy. I told her everything was cool, but yeah, we'd best keep an eye out. She made no bones about curling up next to me, though I slept sitting up till first light, when Boy Who Leaves Early woke his travel companion who gathered her kit quick and quiet. We strolled up to the main road to sling a thumb east, back toward the interstate.

Susan and I parted ways in LA after three days on the road camping one more night behind another service station. Dirt and fatigue cancelled curiosities, and she said thanks, getting into a cab to a friend's place just off the interstate. I suspected her friend was female and felt slighted when she didn't invite me to stop in, clean up and relax, so I didn't ask for her phone number or invite her down to my friend's place in Venice Beach. She wanted to check out the University psychology department, which sounded chronic, but I didn't press. What was to check out in a psychology department? I hitched on out to Venice thinking I could find her later if I wanted to, and I went over to UCLA a few days later to look around, just for a goof. I couldn't find her, no loss, except for the bang that likely wouldn't have happened anyway. And then came the worry that maybe she expected me to invite her down to Venice, because Venice was hip elite, and she didn't want to seem pushy. That loss could have occurred in any decade, yet a reunion with Susan would be more than friends remembering; the context was so great.

Gary Cooper and I were pen pals by then. He'd sent three checks for fifty bucks each and said he ought to have the rest by the time I got there. He didn't, but he had a Kawasaki 350 he was trying to sell for two bills, a fair deal that could pay me off and make me road flush. Meanwhile, I could crash at his place and hang at the beach and check out the crazy scene there or cruise on his Cow. I toured town one day, amazed that anyone would ever buy a two-stroke scooter and a 350 at that, with the smoke screen and all that *wing a ding ding ding ding... ding ding ding*. But it was great to have two wheels below and great to cruise some new tundra, even urban tundra—it was Venice Beach in 1970 after all. I pulled in to gas up and a guy working at the station said he'd been looking for a 350 to restore. Had I given any thought to selling it?

Restore a Kawasaki 350? Why? Was I missing something?

I didn't ask, but in another synchronous cohesion I said yes and cheap, only two fifty. He took his lunch break to ride back to Gary's, and the deal was done. Gary and I split the extra fifty bucks to seal our friendship. I never saw him again, but he still stands tall.

Hanging out at the beach a few days more was easy, ogling the sex kittens with the huge racks, watching the muscle guys pump up and stare at their arms, roller skating, playing in the waves. It got old, and a major topic was rampant theft to feed the heroin habit creeping into the neighborhood. It did not feel fresh or free but more of a mutation. It felt like time to move on, a recurring theme of those days. Time to restore the soul at the Mecca of our freedom.

On the road to San Francisco with my thumb curled north and my pocket thumping with cash, I figured life might well stay sweet till old age. I'd be rich and famous by then and could deal with challenges more easily. Why not?

I thought about friendships and counted those solid enough to count on for a day or two of shelter, so if I wanted to stay on the road, hitchhiking cross country and back and around I'd have a place every few hundred miles or every night, whichever came first. I still think about Susan and would have called her a few times over the decades.

Traveling indefinitely only seemed like a viable concept the first few days out. It could get old directly, but most things do, and the biggest challenge seemed to be in keeping things fresh and lively—and happy, in spite of the topsy-turvy world crying out for equilibrium. Call me old fashioned; I could stand on an on-ramp and watch a hundred cars whiz by with no chance of getting a ride to San Francisco, because unity got so diluted in your urban centers, especially LA, where everybody was in such a hurry to begin with. And I didn't care.

Never mind. I could hit the groove in inner space on the Moody Blues, Quicksilver Messenger Service, Country Joe, Joe Cocker, Joni Mitchell, Arlo Guthrie or any of them. Or shake a tail feather to Motown or Memphis. I'd visited both and understood the soul groove and the funky groove too. A well-rounded repertoire was invaluable to a roadman going coast to coast, border to border. Insight came easy on an on-ramp in summertime, which felt like another Summer of Love, after all. Watching the world speed by, casting fate to the wind, you could hear reassurance on the breeze, see clouds gambol overhead and know that a ride would come along, likely in a van driven by a sister or brother.

It would be another two years before America would capture the age we were born to. The boomer wave was the first generation to say that war is bad, that we won't fight without a direct threat to family or country. We learned this from raising hell and waiting for a ride to the next happening on *Ventura Highway, in the sun...shine.*

I could sing along with America or the Marvelettes, confident that life would shape up with more and greater insights. In a few rides I got into San Francisco and delivered to a house of many friends, where new friends could crash on a couch. That was cool. Everything was everything, and San Francisco was about as stoned as a groove could get. The house was friendly and tolerant and more or less stoned with an open kitchen and brown rice on the stove and coffee on, and if you could make a contribution, all the better.

I got warned to look both ways before crossing the street—any street. I sensed an early and rare opportunity to apply my degree and got further warned against stop signs and traffic lights appearing to manage traffic. Do not trust stop signs or traffic lights. The neighborhood had discovered reds, not commies but downers—Seconal—rendering many people numb or half asleep or dead, and some of those people were still driving cars. This development undermined my faith that marijuana and LSD would be our platform of redemption. Downers seemed wrong by sheer logic. How could you get high if you were down? That was tough to figure, considering how many people smoked dope with their downers.

Still, anybody could see that it took a place like San Francisco for everything to actually be everything, with brotherhood and sisterhood and an entire generation standing against a war so blatantly corrupt. Widespread consensus sustained the values and commitment of the times across the land—the Bay Area land. The spirit was naïve and simple and deadly accurate. Walk out to the road and stick your thumb out. Walk into the kitchen and pour another cup of coffee to perk up for another joint. Walk outside with a paper cup and ask a brother or sister for some spare change.

It worked, kind of, but broke down substantially with the Tate-La Bianca murders in Los Angeles. The murderers looked, spoke and acted like hippies; hardly the first whack job hippies with delusional psychosis, but their grisly behavior threatened to end the love all around us on a single night. It was official: we were not all brothers and sisters, and the times had begun to change back around.

The only positive aspect of that cultural milestone was the absence of 24/7 news channels, cell phones and the Internet. It was big news on all three networks for a half hour a day, without horrific images dividing rampantly as aberrant cells and metastasizing through the system.

Most streets in Berkeley were under construction that summer, torn up with deep ditches for one amazing convenience or another. Dirt and rubble got piled alongside every ditch and diverted pedestrian traffic to spaces available against building walls or weaving around parked cars or into traffic. Traffic sounds and jackhammers allowed murmurs here and there, "Spare change."

"Help a brother out."

"Got twenty-seven cents?"

"Speed. Acid. Weed."

"Spare change?"

It was crowded, and the love all around us was hot and tired and pissed off to the verge of violence but not like the jungle war.

Hardly a month later it was mid-Missouri again with a few more milestones stacked up. Most profoundly, Selective Service said it had not changed its quota projection. It would not, could not guarantee that the quota would not change, but coming on to September felt like the clubhouse turn. A new year would bring a new lottery. Then began the grueling prep for the pre-induction physical.

Another sign of the times was a few miles outside the town where I'd done my time on the student deferment. Mid-Missouri was rich with beautiful countryside then—what would become the subdivisions and strip malls of the immediate future. But at that time the foothills rolled freely from pinnacles to pasturelands. One place of refuge where some friends had lived for a year or so was a communal setup they called the Farm. The group at the Farm changed occasionally with departures and arrivals but remained constant in bliss and the love all around. Pro rata rent shares varied according to the desirability of a room or outbuilding. Thomas Strong was a strapping, likeable hippy with loving values. He seemed born to bib overalls, a billy goat goatee and a happy approach to life and any tasks—especially a man-sized task. He glowed along with the love of his life, Sarah, a blonde beauty whose energy and good looks focused on Thomas. She could not be near him without hugging him, clinging to him, caressing him. She got some overalls too and added soft patches inside to spare her nipples. Sarah wore only overalls, and the guys could see her breasts as often as not. She laughed, as if at the free flowing love between her and Thomas. He laughed back, so wonderful was the joke they shared. Nobody had to sneak a peak once Johann was born, a good baby by all counts, even with his yen for the tit, which Sarah flopped freely at the first whimper.

It had been a set piece till mid-summer, soon after Johann's first birthday, when Dugan showed up. A surly, swarthy hippie with a wild black mane, a shaggy black beard and hairy shoulders, Dugan asked Sarah if she wanted to join him yonder in a field. He had something he wanted to show her.

Sarah admitted soon after that she really, honestly, could not believe the length, girth and stamina of Dugan's dick. She said, "I've never seen a dick that big. It was scary and so amazing when it fit." She said she "balled him" as a goof, because he really wanted it, but she would in no way hurt Thomas, who she still loved madly and always would. Thomas hung his head and blushed, maybe in deference to the love all around us that sometimes must be shared.

Everyone saw where things were going, back to the field and then back to the outbuilding where Sarah, Thomas and Johann lived—on the way to the ditch. Sarah and Dugan laughed at their frequency, saying that sometimes a man and a woman "just have to get the balling out of their system so they can get on with their lives." Sarah frequently proclaimed her eternal love for Thomas, and soon Dugan did too; Thomas was so loving and so understanding of the harmless nature of the thing.

Thomas had "split" from the Farm a few days before I visited. I saw him in town, clean-shaved in pants and a shirt and shoes, a circumspect guy whose wife had run off with a freak. He had Johann—Sarah had agreed that Johann would be better off for a time; she was so busy with Dugan.

Endings seemed more frequent.

I split for St. Louis, a gray sprawl of suburbs surrounding a hollow core. They built an arch in the center to balance the void. It was something to look at. A classified ad described a job at Laclede Gas Company paying eighty-five hundred dollars a year. I'd never imagined eighty-five hundred dollars much less seen eighty-five hundred. I knew it wouldn't come in a lump but would be doled out and largely spent in the process on basics like taxes, rent, groceries, insurance and new clothes. I applied. I didn't get the job.

Fock! I felt like the guy in *The Deer Hunter* playing Russian roulette.

I phoned the girlfriend who got discouraged with my frequent fucker plan and got the nod to come on down to Miami. She seemed lukewarm, like she'd hoped for a better catch but needed rescue at any rate from life with her mother—a dire and aging Republican who would not shut (the fuck) up on the glories of Dick Nixon and the horrors of the hateful hippies.

I went, hardly expecting a family embrace but surprised at the anti-Semitic reception. The girlfriend's mother had divorced the father many years prior and shared sparse dialogue since. Yet they agreed that Jewish and broke would not do for their daughter. The summary indictment: daughter had fallen victim to the worst combination, and for what? She'd been a pompom girl, which is nearly a cheerleader. She could do better. The mother required that the daughter address her as her Aunt, so men suitors wouldn't know she had a daughter so old, so men wouldn't think her so old. The father was born Jewish and fairly defined a certain class of Jew, post WWII, embarrassed by hatred coming his way when, really, he wasn't like that at all. He'd changed his name to a generic, suburban version unidentifiable as Yidloch, which surely the Fourth Reich would have nailed him on, had it arisen under the light of a single, dangling bulb as the electrodes shot sparks from his sweaty nipples... Don't get me started.

Meanwhile, the daughter had a job in Miami. I rented a studio in North Miami and two days later she moved in.

Evenings were best, when the heat slacked off and the geriatrics turned in soon after the early bird specials. We toured the "alleys" on clunky bicycles, stealing citrus and avocados hanging in reach. We rode bicycles to Biscayne Bay to snorkel, my second time since '55 to revisit another reality only faintly recollected. On the way back we passed a crazy man on the bike path. He looked berserk with urgently wild eyes. A minute later a young woman staggered out of the bushes. She'd been beaten and raped.

Witnessing a capital crime gave purpose for a while—another beginning on another ending. Detectives called and stopped by to insist on the critical nature of eyewitness testimony on behalf of a rape victim. We had to be sure of the I.D. and sure to follow through, knowing the prosecutor would seek the death penalty. It got so tedious that I turned to a detective slogging through the process and said, "Hey. Are you worried that I won't want to see this guy burn? It's not a problem. Okay?"

"But you said you were a conscientious objector. I mean, that's why I..."

"Vietnam is not WWII. I'm not a conscientious objector, and even if I was, this ain't that."

They had the guy fingered, picked up and in a line-up in no time. The victim and I scanned all the guys in the line-up a few times and separately identified the same guy. But I got to the courtroom to learn that the rapee had changed her mind; she couldn't be sure; she'd been so surely flummoxed by the defense. The case was dismissed and the guy walked away.

She knew he was the guy but got stuck on the death penalty. She got stuck on many people insisting on absolute certainty, because a guy was going to die, and it would be on her. They broke her down. I saw it coming and wasn't surprised.

I had a job in North Miami pumping gas and waxed a few cars on the side at fifteen bucks a pop. Shit, six cars a month would cover rent, and the cars lined up for gas and the asking. How perfect could it get? With free fruit and avos and squids at forty-five cents a pound, life wasn't so bad for the short term.

The cops came back around to ask if I might have a chat with the victim. Why not? It was brief. I told her I had no doubt on the defendant—he was the guy. I pointed out a few details: the dark, greasy complexion, a single spit curl up front, one dimple, except that it wasn't a dimple but a scar with a small star tattooed in the crater, evil eyes under bushy, sloping brows. But if she didn't want to see him die, then she could let him off.

Between a shit and a sweat herself, she hung her head to ask softly if it would be terrible if he walked and then raped again?

I said yes, it would be terrible, and we were done.

It seemed like a waste of time and pathetic. She got raped twice. I sensed something in the making and fed a blank page around the platen to begin. That was tough, waiting and watching, like the words would appear as they had on New Year's Eve, 1969. They did not appear. Instead America came on the radio to preempt my narrative on social irony with a lyric of greater sadness on a more personal irony. We had loved the road, yet it led us to a dead end, to a place where spirits went away. The key line in Easy Rider was, "We blew it." And there we were, outsiders in a world growing more practical, idealistic with no prospects at twenty-two, gazing at nothing but arid desert and heat ripples *on a horse with no name.* America captured every facet of the revolutionary years, even the end song.

Which just goes to show how quickly an era can end, can fold over into what comes next—how quickly a brain can throw a rod. With comforts met and a reasonably tolerant girlfriend who did not begrudge me every few days, I despaired. Cheap rent, warm weather, free citrus and avocados and semi-regular leg would not last, and I knew it as surely as a fresh page would yellow. Maybe a rapist walking free triggered my personal depression. What seemed more likely was a mutual failure with a wrongful society.

He Had All the Breaks

OLD MOM SENT clippings over the years on school peers, each time noting in the margin: *He had all the breaks.* The breaks included a stable home with adequate money to meet suburban standards. The clippings were invariably about success for one dipshit dullard or another who had feared to step out and risk anything. In routine confinement, furnished, all expenses paid, they lived the norm as expected, waiting to take the family baton.

Mom could not see the gain in a life of freedom, a life of no regimen. She sent a clipping when Charlie Dunham became president of his father's company. Charlie was a pimple-faced nitwit whose father died long ago, but the trustees could not give Charlie the helm till he was "ready." At twenty-two, Charlie got the money and helm. Mom inked in the margin: *He had all the breaks.*

Another guy made partner in his law firm where he'd worked since marrying the senior partner's daughter two decades prior. Yet another guy had a part in a community theater play and expounded on community and theater. Every guy was noted for all the breaks. I went to Sunday school with Tommy Rosen from '57 to '62. Mom sent word that he'd made "a fortune" as a CPA and had a heart attack and fell over but would likely recover after having, of course, all the breaks.

I asked if she admired those forgettable boys. Of course she did; look what they'd done. I asked if she could sense anything, uh, er, boring in what they did. She said, "You're crazy. You smoke that LSD and take so many risks." She hung her head on that critical note to allow, "But what you had to go through, with those miserable jobs."

I took a lead from Jimmy Levin in cutting Mom some slack. No way could she see the light of the 60s. I could not rub two nickels together and come up with 15¢, but I got by on marginal return. Things can get tough for anyone, and risk remains ambient, because nobody has nothing to lose. A man pays sooner or later, and I paid sooner. The clippings showed no risks. Now it's later. They're paying. She shakes her head, still concerned. Old Mom got over no lawyer or doctor in the family but could not value a free spirit who stepped up to adventure.

Parents of the 60s suffered a split-level, cul-de-sac frame of mind. Many of their children got haircuts and jobs on first reasonable offers. Some offers were wildly lucrative but of questionable ideals. Copping out was idealism surrendering to stability, security and appliances. Many 60s youth co-opted. Some claimed to have fought free of war, not comfort, or that the 60s introduced peace and love as building blocks for a better future. But back then, the future remained on hold.

I saw Jimmy Levin the day before he died. He was staying at his parent's house for a while to get his head together and figure out some shit and maybe get his shit together and then maybe get his trip together, you know. I was just back from San Francisco via Taos, and LA and hadn't seen Jimmy since Boulder, when Stevie Getman got ruffled over balancing his books or some shit.

Jimmy remembered. We laughed. He didn't know if Stevie had graduated summer school yet. I was in town a few days and didn't know what I'd be up to but heard Jimmy was living at his parents' house. I wondered what that deal was about, so I stopped by for a goof, to smoke a joint and see what was up. I mostly wanted to see where Jimmy's wizardry had taken him and how he'd maintained his leadership position on the cutting edge of radical drug experimentation while holing up in suburbia, like the Beaver but with no rules.

Jimmy's mother did her best not to look, sound and behave like June Cleaver but failed—couldn't help it. She chirped cheerfully that Jimmy was "in his place," the garage, converted with a bed, a small fridge, a table and chair, so Jimmy would be comfy at home, not confined.

I went on around. Slouching over a bowl of cereal, he slurped from a spoon an inch equidistant from the cereal and his mouth, his head askew to make room for the cat, who sipped the milk more daintily from the opposite side of the bowl with no spoon.

"Hey, Jimmy."

"Hey, man. Want some cereal?"

"Nah."

"I'm into cereal. Do you realize? Cereal, man. It's too much."

"I used to eat cereal."

"Yeah?"

"What are you doing?"

"Nothing. What are you doing?"

"Nothing. I don't know. I might go back to Columbia tonight. Nothing going on here. You got anything going on?"

"No, man. I heard you were going down to Florida to find your girlfriend."

I laughed. "That's funny. I haven't heard that yet. I been thinking about it, but I don't know. Maybe I was thinking out loud."

"Yeah. Hey. I got an idea, man." He sat up to check my reaction to breaking news, that Mr. Jimmy had a new idea, which he considered dynamic, radically forward-thinking and possibly a few inches out front of the cutting edge. "I'm gonna hit some Tuinals." He didn't ask me if I wanted to try it with him, because I wasn't on his level; he knew that and most likely didn't want to embarrass me with my predictable answer. It was cool; we understood that I'd be welcome to hit some Tuinals with him, but it wasn't likely in the cards, because I never hit anything, because needles wigged me, whether they were stuck in me or anyone. But it was cool. Everyone knew what level everyone else was on, and what kept things cool was the ultimate freedom from judgment. Everything was everything, and that included the potential to be cool. Jimmy was on the ultimate level with drugs, not only comfortable with any drug in any mode but hungry for something to test, something that might break out, break in, *break on through to the other side*…

Jim Morrison was still rocking out and would continue for another year. But I didn't do needles, didn't want to and in fact couldn't watch without the dizzies. Besides that, I couldn't handle downers. I once tried a red Mike Dunn gave me. He stole them from his mother, who had full bottles and didn't miss a few. He popped two and advised the same dosage, because one Seconal wouldn't get it. I told him I'd try one and then take another in a while, as necessary. The one turned my legs to jelly, then my hips, torso, arms, eyes, brain and so on. I eased back in the grass, paralyzed, and got up six hours later with severe sunburn and a hammering headache. Mike asked, "Cool, huh? You want another?"

"No, thanks. I think I'll cut back for now."

"You sure?"

"Yeah. I'm sure."

"Suit yourself."

"Okay."

Meanwhile, Jimmy waited for my reaction—my amazement and admiration—but all I could muster was my one go with reds, or rather with a red. So I nodded slowly and said, "Hitting Tuinals. That'll be like...jumping off a cliff."

"Yeah, man. That's good, because it's downers. I mean it's all like a big cliff with anything you hit, but like with downers, you jump off and keep on, you know, going down."

"Yeah," I said, though I didn't know. This was years before bungee jumping, so I didn't imagine springing back. I only saw a nosedive at terminal velocity.

"You like downers?"

I shrugged. "I couldn't ever get into downers."

"Yeah," he said, turning back to the last of the cereal.

"Well, I gotta go. See you, Jimmy."

He nodded, slurping, but he called out when I was at the door. "Hey, man. I'll let you know how it went."

"Yeah."

Dead by the weekend, Jimmy let everyone know how it went. Nobody could be too surprised, but death is always a surprise, even as it seems foregone. Sadness filled the airwaves as old friends called with the news. Jimmy dominated thoughts till the first notes of his mother's lament, stock audio from the bereaved parents file: "Such a waste!" Jeanette and Harold had been oblivious for years that Jimmy got wasted long ago. Denial compounded in her claim that Jimmy was about to join ranks with the *Doctahs* of the world; or maybe the *Lawyahs*—an *Accountant* wouldn't be so bad. Blind to Jimmy's hunger for pharmacopoeia and blind to his emaciation after six years as a speed-freak junkie dabbling in downers, Jeanette had spent those years effervescing. She'd believed that Jimmy would snap out of it and go to his room for a nice club tie and a Brooks Brothers shirt. Then he'd marry a nice Jewish girl and begin a family. And why not, Mr. Smarty Pants?

WWJD? What Would Jimmy Do? Or say? Harold and Jeanette Levin died within a month of each other some years later from old age and broken hearts—what Jimmy would have called their usual routine. Harold was quiet, not so much unthinking but tuned out—like Jimmy but with nothing else to tune into. Jeanette babbled to the end, her blue bouffant and oversized costume jewelry sticking her in time like an old joke.

Jimmy would have summarized their life and demise in a unique blend of cold compassion and liberal understanding: *Yeah. That's cool. They never were really, you know, into much.*

Jimmy's obituary came as another clipping in an envelope from Mom. It called him a college student and loving son, survived by his parents Harold and Jeanette Levin of dry goods fame and longstanding philanthropic support of Jewish causes in Israel and the Jewish Country Club—not the upper-middle class reachers and schnorrers but the real hoi polloi club with the old money and solid sterling silver and Lincolns, not Cadillacs, just like the goyem. In the margin I wrote: *Your son is making out like a bandit, considering how Jimmy Levin had all the breaks.*

I sent it back to Old Mom, and she agreed that it just goes to show you. She moaned and remembered: *What you had to go through.* Parental kvetching gained depth in the 60s with far more pitfalls for tender youth, what with the drugs, the war and loose shiksas.

What if the 60s Never Happened?

The South Fork

TIM LITTLETON WAS forty-one already and a real businessman, homey as Burl Ives with the folksy goatee, and he was fat, warm and humorous as a Burl Ives song. He tipped me off one day that the Savannah paper wanted coverage on our little island corner of South Carolina—not a stringer but a staffer. "Every New York news hound'll be on it, once they find out. Cold, miserable bastards." I got the job.

Savannah journalism was who, what, when, where and the facts with no style, no flourish and no irony. *Who the fuck you think you are, bubba? We don't need that shit.* Making slightly less money than rent and groceries, two years felt like a long time. Seeing prime time fade away, it was time to take a stand, time for a novel—time for a labor of love with no check on Friday. Time for the saving grace—and poverty, just add water.

Nobody quits art. Art is set aside for practical reasons. Then art fades away, sometimes. I stayed friends with Tim Littleton because he understood artistic aspirations, and because he gave me work, writing a monthly article for the Chamber of Commerce magazine he'd edited. My special coed had put up with an attic apartment in mid-Missouri, with subsistence living in Miami on stolen fruit and menial jobs—with artistic delusions and a low budget oyster roast billed as a wedding in our South Carolina back yard. We'd moved up the coast a hundred miles to Charleston, where a fellow stood far better prospects for revenue than on a resort island.

Hot mud was still laughable, even as a fossil remnant of a long gone age. Still, how tough could real business be? Businessmen didn't do shit—anybody could see that. They hired out the work.

This conclusion followed the data; on learning that the city magazine in Charleston would not be a source of income, because there weren't no city magazine. But a city with no magazine would want one. So it was settled by virtue of logic, free will and flight of fancy in a package deal that felt like a legacy.

City magazines were new and Charleston, South Carolina was picture perfect, a still-life of lovely bones marinated in scotch whiskey, bound to history, inured to innovation and obsessed on non-identity and chronic regret over the Great Misfortune, meaning the Civil War. Who gave a shit? Charleston was the town that time forgot, especially the 60s—that would be the nineteen 60s.

Always friendly and eager to meet new, white people, the place welcomed with strange, warm greetings. *Yenna? How you do-een. Whatcho fittin' a do?* The upper crust defined itself in khaki pants, Weejuns and blue oxford cloth shirts with button-down collars. The uniform uniformity indicated social status and defended against devilish influence from yonder, meaning the world outside the city limits. Egalitarian charm transcended social strata, as in the most frequently asked question around noon. *Jeatchet?* (Have you as yet engaged in luncheon?)

Ah, the beauty of it all—a young man with gusto could ease in and make money on a one-horse burg in a pickle jar that loved seeing itself in a mirror and didn't mind a few mixed metaphors if they shone with pride and commitment to fight on and have another drink. A hippie in Caucasian clothing could take solace in the vast marshland rich with oyster beds and fishing holes.

With no city magazine, Charleston, *Souse Cahlina* could cash in on some natural born skills perhaps, uh, new to the area.

Capitalization would be a cakewalk. We already had a writer and editor, and a crew cobbled itself together on a concept. Things rounded out on a partnership with a graphic artist, a printer and a salesman for the advertising. The product would be a thing of beauty and influence. Tim Littleton would drive a hundred miles up the coast to run the business side. Laid off and grateful for the quid pro quo, Tim confided that he was a 60s veteran at heart and loved wild stuff and had the know how to squeeze a dollar from a sumbitch. Alas, Tim had no squeeze. Worse yet, we met for breakfast.

Tim ordered the Lowcountry Marsh Wallow Supreme: three over easy, biscuits, grits 'n gravy, ham, links, sausage, toast and jelly. Juice and coffee were extra, but *what in a hail you fittin' a do, eatcher breakfast w'out some*? Tim didn't get so big for nothing, and he tore into the glop as I reviewed our needs. I tipped in at one thirty-five and got the usual: two over easy, grits and toast, hold the gravy and pig meat—and the juice and coffee; I had mine at home. Why not? We're trying to start a *bidness* here.

It's not much different, two over easy or three, but Tim got three because the extra egg was only ten cents more, and *you cain't be ignorin' the bargains like that in this day and age*. His breakfast ran six bucks and mine was two.

He never ate the third egg, and self-constraint is admirable; he was so fat, and everybody likes to see fat people cutting back. But he woofed his biscuits, two eggs and all his grits and pig meat and half his toast before rummaging his crumpled pack of Salem 100's for that first delicious puff of smoke right after eggs and grits and gravy. He inhaled big and turned our little space into a smoke out in menthol, what Salem called *a breath of springtime*.

Some people feel discomfort around fat people—not me. Tim was a friend in need and a partner. It got worse when he smoked his menthol 100 down by 50, then stabbed his third yolk with it, swirled it around to dead-out and dredged some grits 'n gravy residue for the lay down. I loved the action conceptually but couldn't stomach the ringside view.

We moved on to meet with the other partners to compare notes and develop ideas. I counted on Tim to keep us on course, but he nodded to every suggestion or demand on the table, and I doubted all those ideas could be good. I finally said, "Wait a minute."

Questioning the process became a personal transition, discovering the means by which we would throw off the yolk of the 50s. I mean yoke. This felt foreign to all experience, against the grain and clearly demonstrating that everything was not everything. Nor was it cool. We had a shot at making rent and groceries without manual labor and could not fuck it up on wrong moves—alas, one mo time. A proven radical took to business like Br'er Rabbit in a briar patch. Who knew? It wasn't a cop out. We hadn't made any real money and never would.

Besides that, magazine content went radical. Lively minds through history have felt repressed by stagnant values and fake morality. One department of the new magazine had the catchy title *Lowcountry Kitchen*, where doyennes of grace and hospitality shared precious family receipts, leading to paid advertising by the doyennes' husbands' businesses. Recipes were called receipts, a Huguenot colloquialism indicating original blood if not original thought. Yes, that department was a cop out to the regional delusion, but redemption came in April—get it? April? It was time for a joke, for chrissake! Unfortunately, nobody laughed at the featured receipt, Toadfish Manigault. The Manigault (man•ih•go) family was landed with 17th Century antecedents who Did. Not. Need. Yankee disrespect on a venerable institution. Toadfish were scorned—and left gasping on the dock as punishment for stealing bait and being ugly. Toadfish Manigault was a three-pounder on a bed of noodles presented by a disturbed young man with a curlicue moustache drawn on his face. The Manigault family did not buy an ad ever again. Blowfish bouillabaisse as a side dish didn't help.

Ah, well, the goof gods need offerings too. The business stayed afloat by sleight of hand and constant bailing. Eyebrows arched, but they rose on anything that hadn't sought approval.

Old Mom sent a clipping about a fat kid who went to the same high school. Burdened by intellectual self-awareness and a neurotic mother who'd divorced three times at around a million per, the kid got a job in New York. That was the news, and who could be surprised with all the breaks he'd had? I told her that life wasn't so bad in the catbird seat in a lovely coastal burg with good fishing, and I had natural business skill. Where did that come from?

"Oh, your father wasn't stupid."

It wasn't work but a spirit engaged, what the 60s had promised. Harking back to greatness of singular character, I bought a Norton

Commando, priced to sell with an Atlas front end. Seven years without a two-wheeler felt curable. But who would put an Atlas front end on a Commando?

A guy who wrecked his motorcycle and got a deal on an Atlas front end is who. How dumb and distracted of me; I didn't even ask about the goofy front end. Ah, well, it was Norton at last. Call it luck or faith in a muse confirmed. That Norton cruised up and down the Lowcountry coast and inland to the Red Hills, crisscrossing many miles to freedom restored. Reunited, we winged over marshland causeways like one more loon or mallard with a mind of our own.

Many people said they loved the city magazine because of what it could record, which was so important, lest we forget. Lip service was plentiful on beauty and execution. But a provincially sodden backwater will often muster pleasantries as an outlander sinks in the pluff mud. The magazine cost more than it made. I rode more miles, because the open road felt more like home, a place of solace in movement.

South Carolina is cracker country with a few twists. It's where Strom Thurmond mounted his presidential campaign as a Dixiecrat and mounted his…er…uh…Negro housekeeper too. History oozes out of South Carolina. A motorcycle is timeless, oblivious to society or history. It gave meaning to a soul in flight.

The magazine, like any holdover exhibit, ended. The little town settled back to how it was, which felt, alas, like it wasn't.

Many marriages ended naturally in the 70s, so it seems harsh to call them failed, especially when they only gave in to practicality. Starvation, foreclosure and waning prospects were the downside of *for better or worse*, and things got worser and worser. Marriage based on ideals and the love all around us among twenty-somethings did not often last to thirty something. Looking back, the fork in the road seemed inevitable for mates of such different approaches to life. The ending should have come sooner but like most endings got postponed in deference to improved conditions right around the corner.

The Norton went next, till it was down to two cans, cat food and cream 'o chicken, perfect for a writer and two cats.

A young man can get back up and jump back in, maybe not so convincingly as those guys who spring from their shoulders onto their feet, but new action waited just down the road as a matter of faith. And necessity.

Billy Prieshard was new in town and already dating former contributing writer and deb du jour Delia DeNerien hardly a month after she'd split up with her old boyfriend, an original redneck Republican. Billy was old hat, a traditional southern son but a might different on account of his fancy pants ways that he *shore as shit* didn't learn up in Myrtle Beach, where the Prieshards had lived and died these last few centuries. *I'm here to tell you they's something not right with that boy...*

Billy Prieshard wasn't to be trusted on account of being from up the road, which wasn't as bad as a Yankee but it Was. Not. Home. Nobody would leave home and come in somewheres else to fleece a few flatlanders but a carpetbagger or worse, a scalawag. Besides his apparent crimes against society, that godforsaken boy could not be trusted on political principle, in the emerging Republican tradition of distrust. Suspected of liberal ideas learned in the North, Billy Prieshard had gone and bought up some apartment buildings and sold the units as condominiums—what Dee's former boyfriend called condominials, to cast them in laughable light where they belonged. Why, who else but a scalawag sumbitch would take some apartments and sell them individually to separate buyers? Can you believe that shit? Condominiums were a radical new concept in South Carolina, with no grass nor bushes nor yard boys, none you'd need to care for anyway. But you would need to pay every month—*make at ever damn month*—for someone to take care of things. That was the catch. Topping off all that shit was the worst notion of all: this Billy fella made a heap o' dough in no time, and now Mister Moneybags was banging *our* Delia!

I couldn't make the next payment on the little house the estranged wife and I bought for twenty-five thousand by taking over payments with 5% down. But the bank didn't yet know of my situation, and with equity, an enterprising fellow had a month to borrow eight grand against the place on a dummy loan app, maybe ten grand, since those were the days of "banking relationships." If you knew a banker and a couple three jokes bearing down on pussy and/or football, you had a relationship. A relationship allowed the banking officer to approve the loan. The loan app was required like resumes were required, to demonstrate adaptive ability in a demanding society. Nobody checked.

I told Billy Prieshard I wanted to convert some condos like he did but on a smaller scale, because I only had eight grand to draw on. Maybe ten. Maybe I could line up fifteen in a pinch.

He said that could be the right amount to get going on a duplex or maybe even a fourplex, but he'd searched the entire town and could flat guarantee: there weren't none.

Fuck.

He said, "Look. I don't know what I'm talking about. I'm full o' shit most of the time. Okay? You go look for yourself. You find anything outa your range, you call me. We'll work something out."

That felt better. "What's your range?"

"I don't know." With the casual power shrug of an original bubba who'd been to town, he looked up as if to find his limit. "Maybe a million dollars."

He could have said a hundred zillion, which was about how much a million was back then. The region was crawling with rednecks like Dee's old boyfriend, with their outrageous conservative color and cocaine to balance the liquor—oh, and family values and a rebel yell as necessary. *Why, sheeyit.*

Billy Prieshard had that same twang, but he'd graduated Yale law school and was deemed dangerous because his law degree didn't show. Dee told me about his ticket to steal with a wink to keep it on the Q.T., because Billy didn't want people thinking he was uppity or tricky or taking advantage as a practicing member of the South Carolina Bar Association. Well, sir, it was a whole heap o' exotic shit they was packing into the heads of college boys back then, maybe some of it not so evil, but a Yale Law degree just felt wrong, what with him poking his nose into medium and low-priced real estate that way. Why, a man with a Yale law degree ought to aim a might higher. Shouldn't he? They thought Billy was tricky, what with his low approach and uppity manners, but no matter what anyone thought, Billy P was not your run of the mill redneck.

I found the Sans Souci Apartments that afternoon, for sale in the classifieds. The agent wanted to know who, what and *wherefrom* in a process known as qualifying—but the process felt like a stickler, so removed from the brotherhood so recently lived in another place that didn't seem so far away but was. Most importantly, the agent honed in on what he'd clearly established: that the *wherefrom* was not from around here.

Not so long ago that brand of exclusionary superiority would have been grounds for a demonstration. Times had changed, but with the will of a proven independent I responded to authority like a knee-jerk. The agent plainly heard an outlander on the line. He chuckled into the phone to indicate that some things could not be changed by any force of nature, and place of birth *was one o' them thangs*, meaning that the property would not be shown without clear demonstration of the means to buy the property.

Well, if a seller felt uncomfortable with money derived from, let's say, yonder, then a potential buyer could pursue other property or maybe contact the owner... "*Whoa, whoa, whoa bubba. Get offa yo high horse and get on down a my office and we talk.*"

The talking phase was meant to qualify the...er...uh...ability of...uh...you to...uh...put a deal of this magnitude together. The kid's name was Chester A. Arthur—*I shitchu not*—but it should have been Chester A. Riley by the time we got done. *What a revoltin' development this is.*

The Life of Riley was a gem of the 50s, what the 60s loved most for the amazing goofs.

That is, young Chester didn't have much to be proud of but his birthplace and the idiom he'd learned there. Chester knew the advantages of superiority and how to be superior in the scheme of things. Unfortunately for Chester, he had yet to romp with Br'er Rabbit in the briar patch. He may still be out there, by this time more seasoned in humility and judgment. Maybe not. Chester was old family, a youth ensconced in a time warp, meaning a King Street office way too big for anything but show. Chester wasn't only from around here, the Arthurs were 17th Century, ready for the wax museum. Huguenots and Tories peppered the place with family graves out back of the house from 16 ought 9 or 1714—or the Johnnie-come-latelies of only a century ago.

Young Chester A. Arthur sat in an old executive leather chair under an oversized coat of arms in the blue oxford cloth/button-down shirt/khaki pants/Weejuns uniform to demonstrate uniformity—or abject sameness. And a rep tie, because he was on the job. "How you do-een?" Beyond the rote greeting of the flatlands, young Chester awaited reverence, or at least deference. A dim bulb who couldn't read much by his own light, he asked condescending questions and provided nothing. Sitting back with a sigh he let the leather finish squeaking before he regretted have to decline to show the property on account of failure to demonstrate the wherewithal to…uh, you know…uh…bring a goddamn thing to closing. Outa escrow. You know what escrow is?

I went on down to the Men's Club I still belonged to, because it was only twenty-five bucks a month, because it was still in its original condition since around 1900. People liked their facilities in original condition in the sultry South. Original condition kept the dues low and gave practical value to the adage, too poor to paint, too proud to whitewash. The Club attracted its fair share of powerful men in town who wanted to relax without somebody hitting them up for favors or inside information. The Club was an afternoon stop where members played racquet sports or steamed, jawed and unwound—where the unspoken code relieved everybody of solicitation and need.

Truth be told, the old guys wallowed in the privacy and loved the recognition, when a young guy needed some inside skinny.

The Club didn't mind if I was a few months late on dues, because a young fellow's luck might change. Charleston was like that, showing the flipsides of ignorance and hospitality in short order. Every time I had cause to think it a mean place, I got corrected; it wasn't mean. It was only stupid in some people and only on occasion at that. Above all, it loved a sociable gathering, which wasn't *a'tall* like the love all around us but had the same warmth and glow. New Year's Eve, 1969 was a fur piece from the Club's annual dinner in a tent, where members anteed up three dollars for a pound of fresh boiled shrimp to peel and eat with cocktail sauce and a few beers and a rib-eye with ketchup and more shrimp if you still hungry and want another steak, fuck yeah, we got plenty. It wasn't the same but came from the same stuff, Southern hospitality and the love all around us.

I ran into Sonny Goldberg coming out of the steam room, just the guy I'd been looking for, because Sonny knew everything and everybody and everything everybody was up to. At sixty-two Sonny was a short, pudgy old man—no exercise, too much stress and fried chicken. Sonny used the Club for steam and solace from the ration of grief his father had dished out for years. Sonny's management of the family furniture company was plain damn careless. What good could come of a boy who plain damn won't listen? Sonny was still the boy. He'd gone through life with what Old Mom called all the breaks, and there he was, rich and suffering.

Sonny's father was eighty something, and Sonny never stopped asking what it was his father wanted. "I can't figure it out. We sell furniture. I do it wrong, because I don't do it his way. I bring in more money than he ever did." Sonny hated his father's daily rant, but he loved his father's survival, balancing stress and fried chicken with genetics. Sonny was proud of his management and sales skills too. Why, he had entire bedroom sets he'd sold three times—some of them priced right now to sell a fourth time for more money than the third time. He liked anybody who wasn't young and dumb and married with kids, unlike most of his clients. He shared his best opener on a regular basis and was proud of that too, because it could still close a deal to a newlywed couple surely as it did thirty years ago—or ten years ago, or last year: "You know, the bank says your credit isn't worth shit! And I say it is."

"Hey, Sonny. Who owns the Sans Souci Apartments?"

"I do. Why?"

"Why would you list it with such an ignorant schmendrik?"

Note the code word here, schmendrik, underscoring the secret conspiracy among Jews around the world, who let each other know in a single word that it's us on the inside and them what's out. Okay, it's the same behavior exploited by "local" guys in provincial burgs around the world. At least with us it's worldwide, and anybody can learn the jargon.

"I didn't list it. He wants me to list it. Why would I list it? He's advertising it. That's all. I told him he could advertise it if he wants to and bring me a buyer. He can earn a commission if he sells it. Why would I give him a commission otherwise?" Sonny didn't wonder why, but then he wondered, "Why? You want to buy it?"

Billy Prieshard remains unique for his Yale law degree and molasses drawl flowing sweetly over the teeth hanging innocently to his knees. Yes, Billy had the instinct for the quick and merciful kill, what some people called jugular, yet the odd counterpart to that formidable power was a heart that stands out with trust and goodwill. He listened to the summary disposition on the Sans Souci Apartments, turned to me and said, "Okay. We'll go thirds. Is that okay with you?"

A million questions flooded in, one for each dollar. Make no mistake, Billy Prieshard was no mystery tramp, but I stared into the vacuum of his eyes and said, "That sounds good."

A young man with no discernible means of support was asked to participate in a million dollar deal—and something echoed off the canyon walls. Maybe it was confidence or faith, either one learned best from the toughest teacher, Professor Hard Knocks. And yes, Bob Dylan encouraged a slow nod on a painfully repetitive lyric, because I had nothing and nothing to lose and felt invisible with a few secrets to conceal but still unmoored and loosely rolling as a rolling stone. How did it feel?

No doubt about it, feelings ran one decade to the next, but the times they were a changin'. In a phone call Billy Prieshard brought in a bank on a relationship of magnitude via the president, a former associate. So we set up escrow to close in a hundred fifty days concurrent with individual escrows on each unit to close the same day to individual buyers who didn't even yet know those units were for sale but would buy nevertheless—80% of them anyway—because they already lived there! All this in two minutes flat, three on the outside, roughshod to be sure but we had a hundred fifty fucking days to iron out the details and that's five months in any dialect. The bank also provided mortgage loans to those buyers at 8½%—this was 1979, when interest rates soared, eventually to 20% and higher—fairly imbuing us with characteristics similar to Robin fucking Hood, taking from the rich and giving to the poor.

How did we manage to pull off 8½%?

Easy. It was South Carolina!

We made a bank president our other one-third partner!

We wouldn't need any financing to buy the property, because we'd never own it, because concurrent escrow closing on the property and the individual units would happen in the same moment, squeezing scads of profit from the thin air!

Was it a cop out? Or had we broken on through to the other side? I suspected all new insight to the benefits of a regional concept called asshole bubbas? In favorable light the process rendered a young man ready for a lifetime of magnanimous giving.

Billy did the legal part. The banker's role was silent, what with the better part of valor and all that. And I handled sales—thirty units in sixty days. Oh, they were a good deal, and I was, in a cultural, revolutionary context once again, a natural. I had no money and couldn't believe these guys would just take me on, so I repeated my pledge to Billy to get a second mortgage on my house or better yet dummy up a loan application and—

"Stop."

Billy waved that one off, mumbling about cost benefit and enough risk where it was warranted without sticking our asses over the parapet for chump change. Then he covered my end. Few people in anyone's life are as generous and true as Billy. I used to wonder why he did that and years later realized that some people actually go through life without needing to screw anybody.

The canned cream o'chicken and cat food remaining in March went to eighty grand by December, and that was some dough in those days, mobilization dough, let's-get-this-life-started dough—dinner out with drinks *and* dessert.

Then came the tough question: would a free spirit with values intact and apparent narrative talent want to be a southern writer? Or would he best consider the rest of the world? A few southern writers shone with wit and insight though the truly greats seemed mostly dead, and those remaining sounded tediously similar to each other, leaning hard on idiom as a substitute for substance—like the accent in Charleston; it got thicker if the speaker wanted to emphasize inclusion or exclusion to those addressed. How else could the south be portrayed in narrative fiction without such caricature? Well, it could be portrayed as anywhere else could be portrayed, without the accent, the idiom and tedious repetition. What was wrong with that?

You'd still have the natural beauty, the country people and the wildlife teeming like few places in the world. Then again, most characters suffered from public education, and though a few rare intellects surfaced in the southland, nearly all yarns were burdened with idiom and accent. A narrative could consciously avoid bubba and cornpone, but why be in a place if only to avoid its character? Better to avoid the place if it still felt repetitious, tedious and predictable. Alternatives seemed less limited by pervasive sameness. Other places seemed more variable, formative and dynamic. It was a tough choice, with the southern place quickly becoming my place, opening its arms to a single man with some money, a man quickly becoming included.

Billy Prieshard and the banker offered another one-third interest in a new project with more reasonable potential. That would be an apartment complex not too far from the State Capitol in Columbia, South Carolina, twelve hundred units of abandoned HUD project housing—yes, right down in the heart of the projects. "What're you afraid of?" the banker asked. "You'll fit right in. Those people will *take* to you—don't get me wrong now. You're the best! You proved it. You think we'd do this project without you? Fuck no! You think we'd find another fella with your natural talents to send in there?"

That was the money talking. And I didn't take him wrong. I knew what he meant even if he didn't—that a white man in the 70s who judged people on compassion and manners had likely learned those things from the 60s. It was obvious, but a stranger in a strange land does not stop the action to explain what's blowing in the wind.

I felt that the banker would have no qualms about sending in any white boy in flip flops or a black salesman in a tuxedo if that person could squeeze the dollars from the project. I was the hustler they knew—I could shuffle the paper correctly and had passed the crash course in what not to say and to whom not to say it. I also believed that most of the project residents would indeed take to me and didn't dwell on the idea that it wouldn't take more than one of the project residents to stab or shoot me and kill the deal. I spent a night or two crunching the payout and figured it could well be the last non-artistic work a man would ever have to do.

Served on a platter front and center sat the golden opportunity only a fool would ignore. Here was damn near retirement in short order with no risk but the time required. My investment would be what the capitalist system calls sweat equity—except that the system vests no equity in sweat. You plain won't find a sweat-equity buy-in, but there it was. Bankers scoff at the notion, dismissing sweat equity as an oxymoron. Bankers are the first to insist that money talks. Bullshit walks. Yet my two main lawyer and banker bubbas offered a one-third interest in a multi-million dollar sellout with no money down. Damn. If that wasn't radical then I didn't know what for—an aspiring artist slipped time and again on easy slang. It put the goods at risk and was damn near impossible to avoid.

Never mind.

Quick and easy felt like a combo for success—along with honest value and minimal exposure. Yes, financing was marginally legal, possibly illegal, but the end result would be good for the buyers and us. We would go in with fire-rated sheetrock between each unit to get the places in legal conformance to the condominium building code, then paint up, fix up and get the hell out at 15% below market with below market financing available to buyers who could qualify for the loan or not qualify.

I loved those guys. They brought me in on a few million dollars of real estate with a few pages of options as the major up-front outlay that would get us into the deal. Actual cash down was less than the three of us would spend on a month of gas and groceries. Billy and the banker had no clue on market response but were willing to take the risk on our sales boy, who was me. My two main bubbas weren't so cynical on the right guy for the job relative to the sales issue. They loved me right back because we'd made solid dough together and could do it again on a more genteel scale, because I was perfect— because I didn't even wear shoes in the summertime! They couldn't get over it: thirty sales in sixty days in flip flops! They viewed my casual approach to *bidness* as the magic ingredient to several million more dollars.

Billy figured we'd clear ten to fifteen grand a unit, depending on momentum. Too much time meant too much exposure, so we might have to fire sale the last few. Who knew? But I should clear two or three grand a unit—wait a minute? Twelve hundred times two thousand? That's two million, four hundred thousand dollars!

"You gonna live there, bubba! Two years. Maybe three."

And I would have done it as a sentence without parole that wouldn't be so bad on account of the colorful adventures surely waiting. Talk about grist for the mill!

I declined.

Two to three years of prime fillet in a writer's career could not be sacrificed for money. And no, I did not want to be a southern writer, not even in the bona fide projects striving for gentrification.

They say nobody knows what might have been on the road not taken. I don't believe it, and I slap my knee on a peek down the south fork. *Sheeyit.*

Moreover, I had faced the cop out and moved on.

Westward Ho

JONI MITCHELL SANG of sitting in a park in Paris, France lamenting lost dreams but feeling so homesick for California she would even kiss a Sunset pig.

Heading down the road with the right tunes on the box has been a primary benefit to the spirit since cars began. It made sense of a migration in late youth—another migration, with the clock ticking. Paris seemed as far from South Carolina as crudités from corn pone. So did California, yet her siren song lured the whole show westward to new horizons, and California-bound with a couple of cats felt like old home week one more time, like getting back to where we once belonged. No generation generated music with such staying power; at ten years old the power tunes pumped like brand new, sometimes better.

Wait a minute—*Jojo left his home in bumfuck Carolina, for some California grass.* Well, hell, a westbound migration can take a quick look back with easy caricature and good riddance. Yet a tear rolled for those tidal marshlands and oyster roasts and down-home feeds with all the boys at the Club and the social warmth and so many fine women stopping by to say farewell. What the fuck you do-een, boy? You crazy?

Well, sir, you cain't very well leave a place hateful once't a place was good to you, though leave you sometimes must. No doubt about it, certain friends and aspects of the sunny south lingered in lovable recollection. The exclusionary code barring immigrants from true bubbahood would not be missed. The assessment was harsh, and so was its ring of truth. Do you really want to be a bubba?

California, on the other hand, waited to embrace another brother. Lazy went to laid back and the cool breeze felt rich with artistry.

Eighty miles south of San Francisco at the top of Monterey Bay sat a little beach town famous for surf and great weather.

Decades later, with twice as many people occupying the same spaces, on-ramp traffic would thicken dramatically, friends of friends and brothers in the bond would no longer be welcome to crash on the couch. Soccer moms would discover artistic endeavor as quaint pursuits, as busy parenting schedules would allow, and a bumper sticker would proclaim: *Not all those who wander are lost.* Things would get crowded, impersonal, injurious and unstable. Human population will double again before too long with new bumper stickers. But at the front end of the 80s the California coast glowed with options.

A refugee from anywhere could come home to California. South Carolina faded to the east, where many friends would remain content in a culture of decomposition, compulsive for history and paper mills poisoning the estuaries to create jobs for the people—not to be confused with power to the people, because the jobs were awful and the power and money went to the brokers. Hey, they'd never pull that shit in California. Southbound U.S. 1 at sunset on a misty moonrise felt like a reunion of sorts and a whole new life of other sorts. It was a Moonlight Mile, Mick Jagger one more time, but this time different. Self entertainment included lyrical adaptation, so Mick's refrain, *With a head full of snow*, changed to reflect a new world, a new mobility and a new reality. Isn't that what the maturing process and money are all about? *With a pocket full of dough*, and maybe just a tiny taste of toot folded safely in a bindle for easy access, because nobody really needed a head full of snow when a little bump every hour or so would keep things moving right along. Hey, it was the 80s. Besides, a little toot going down the road was a safety measure, preventing nod outs and helping perspective.

Paper mill mentality and desecration was a straw too many for a very tired camel. A marsh man could avoid the stinky areas and live happy. But only a corrupt, skewed place like South Carolina said, *Sho, come on down* so spent nuclear rods could ship in for burial at the Barnwell "reprocessing" facility. A passel o' folks had to be god-awful stupid to let their home get poisoned, or they cowed to employers scoring federal contracts in the billions on the Barnwell plant. Barnwell festered like a psychedelic downside in brown. From the Earth to the firmament it faded and tinged, dead.

Bummer.

The Barnwell line: *Shoot, it ain't but a degree or two is all it is— what them highbrow mucky mucks like to call thermal pollution—from all them hot nuke rods. Glowing in the dark is kind of nice, if you think about it. It weren't such a bad thing. Folks might ought to figgur how to get that glowy shit up 'ere to Myrtle Beach to light up 'em pee wee golf links. Now that'd be fun!*

How soon would the negative caricature and redneck persona go away? How long had it played in the background?

Santa Cruz caricature, on the flipside, defined California gothic, beyond liberal, past radical into pathological demands for fairness now, you fascist motherfucker. A rare benefit of gridlock and gentrification a few decades later would be confinement of the hairy street people to their proper *politikal* habitat under the bridge.

As *The Murder Capital of the World*, Santa Cruz was not statistically ahead of Houston or Detroit but led with singular flamboyance on blood and gore—and impressive garnish of gristle and bone. Homicide and carjacking were mundane next to West Coast grit. A jilted surfer snuck into his treacherous girlfriend's bedroom at night to behead the new boyfriend and stab the girlfriend and stick the head on a surfboard stuck in the yard. He went back upstairs for altitude on a jump out a window but killed another surfer on impact—a bystander who proved to be the father of the girlfriend's unborn child. Oh, the head was the girl's brother, *incestuous inflagrante*, honing revenge to a sweet double-edge.

California citrus and murder/suicide were the best, so juicy. The jilted surfer's suicide effort seemed sincere, but the cushioned fall only broke both legs. He had to stand trial, get convicted and begin a life sentence before successfully hanging himself.

Mother and child were doing fine, seen most mornings at the local coffee house, open-minded in their quest for a loving LTR, vegan, not over forty, non-smoking, bi-sexual OK.

An irate tenant compelled to demonstrate tenant's rights drowned the landlord in a toilet when the landlord came by to demand rent payment. It was only the tenth, which is what? Five days late? Which is bullshit, you rotten motherfucker, if you know about tenant's rights, and if you don't, you need a few laps in the toilet bowl, if you get my drift. The tenant put more social injustice to rights by setting the house next door on fire to cure the blaring TV, which, by the way, had pissed him off for way too long, and those fuckers needed to know just what kind of bullshit they'd gotten away with until they didn't. They didn't call it Canna Screws for nothing, and the place screamed with culture shock to arouse an aspiring writer. And it wasn't hot, as in sultry, humid and hot. And it didn't choke on bumper-to-bumper traffic except on weekends, and only guys of African descent could get laid on demand, but Caucasoids could occasionally score some secondhand leg. And nobody talked with a southern accent.

How good could it get? That first summer of the Brave New West celebrated priorities restored with a Super Glide showing only four thousand miles for only four grand. Nobody reeks revenge on poverty like a poor boy with a windfall. Harley Davidson had been out of reach since '68 when Harris Pollman got a Sportster and lit up the flames of desire in the hearts of all the other guys on campus—flames that would not die in some of those hearts. A nutcase and founding member of Jews for Jesus, Harris sounded like a brimstone kvetch when he preached for Jesus, yet he alone in the campus crowd could muster the seventeen hundred clams for a new Sportster. Of course his suburban Jewish parents gave him the dough. So what? He had the focus to spend it right. He never let anyone drive it, but he took me on back once, and the feeling stuck.

The jump in cubic centimeters and engine rumble felt huge. Great minds think alike, and so do middle class minds; in the 80s Harley Davidson came clean. The big V-Twin wasn't for greasers anymore but for old Triumph and BSA riders. Some tattooed toothless wonders still rode Harleys. They enhanced the "mystique." Harley Davidson reached out to the new guys who had money, the preppies and yuppies. The motorcycle wave that covered Europe in the 60s wanted to wake up from its workaday world.

"Hey," Pedro said. "Only a dollar a mile. Ha!" Notably thin and heavily inked with jailhouse doodles, Pedro said the odometer was broke, but he knew the motorcycle had four thousand on it, because he kept track.

"Hey, you know the ape hangers are long, so I pulled them back. You know." The ape hanger handlebars pulled down from altitude to waist level put my hands where my pistols would have been if I was a gunslinger. The context was not lost on Pedro, who drew imaginary pistols and fired two friendly rounds at my face then blew the smoke off each barrel tip. Ah, California and those wild Californians, working together to keep the show going on. "It feels, you know, different at first. But you get used to it. You'll see. I guarantee it."

The engine sounded good, and the motorcycle cut a lean, muscular profile, though a tad unusual in lavender. Why lavender? Because. Pedro got a good deal on the lavender, and nobody yet come by to give him no shit. Pedro was tough, and it seemed fairly evident that anybody on that motorcycle could be tough too.

Tall Paul and I shared a little toot one evening to gain perspective on life. Clarity came on a bottle of wine, another line or two for momentum, another bottle to take the edge off and a spliff for reverence. Reviewing life to date we agreed that it was largely the shits, except for the scootering parts. So he bought a Sportster in cherry red, not his choice but the color of the suitably priced unit.

I pointed out that cherry red and lavender looked like fruit punch. He suggested our club name: *Los Fruitas*. But that could indicate alternate sexual preference, which would make no difference in the wilderness, unless women came along. He modified, "Okay. *Los Machos Fruitas*."

AMF owned Harley Davidson through the 70s and added poor build quality to Harley's stone-ax engineering. The AMF models self-destructed like clockwork. Between Canna Screws and Idaho that Super Glide fell apart. Throttle cables and linkage failed in San Francisco, the brake rotors and pads went in Shasta, the clutch assembly in Bend and the transmission seals in Twin Falls. New components replaced failed components, and so on to both wheel hubs and tires in Boise, even with good tread, because failed wheel bearings caused the back tire to tilt off center and rub a fender bracket down to the sidewall cords.

Yet adventures endure in recollection of the high points. A sunrise piss is recalled as a bone trembling freeze—make that a frieze of unadulterated happiness, stoned again in the wilderness only twelve miles from coffee. Rolling down the road on a frosty morning can freeze your bones, numb your face and stiffen your joints. Breakfast on the Oregon plateau was dough balls in grim gravy. Forlorn people watched, wondering how two fellas could just walk in here and order up.

Small dark lumps floated beside the biscuits. "Looks like lizard chunks and peas," Paul said.

"Them ain't peas," the big woman said.

Those scenes linger with the foothills, mountain passes and broad sweeps alongside streams meandering through lush valleys. We pulled off one evening or another or yet another and again near a bank to pitch camp. Paul built the fire while I moseyed on down to the flow, fitting rod sections, stringing light monofilament line and tying off to a Mepps spinner. Casting across the stream six or ten times yielded a half-dozen pan-size trout.

People still ate the trout in the 80s. Nature had begun to fall apart and die, but the hard evidence didn't glare for a few more years, and that deep in the wilderness the trout seemed plentiful. The fire crackled. The hash pipe glowed. Pan fried trout and stream-chilled beer equaled perfection. As dusk thickened to twilight logs went on the fire till it flamed beside the burbling stream. The wilderness could renew perspective on growing complexity.

Firelight under big sky and a wealth of wilderness capped the milestones of recent months: migration from east coast to west, emergence from poverty to mobility and from youth to something else. The wilderness felt like home, and so did a new motorcycle. John Lennon had died the prior December. It was *all too much for me to take* too, the love that had shone all around us.

'69 to '81 felt like a crackle in the flames, a blip in time with a lingering essence. John Lennon said, "Life is long." And just as day follows night, the fire needed more wood and life would require more dough.

Moving north to the city by the bay made sense. People live in cities to make money. Country people don't take well to cities, but San Francisco was different. With a reasonably tuned motorcycle and a decent flat in the Upper Haight, a heterosexual guy could do well in San Francisco. The artistry at hand felt like a resource, so the scooter got a makeover in deep sea blue with voltage arcing the tank sides and fenders. A wrench in Canna Screws rebuilt the top end and went ahead on new jugs since she was peeled open. Sorry: a mechanic in Santa Cruz replaced the valves and went ahead on new pistons (the bottom end), since the engine was already open. What the fuck. Why not?

She growled sweetly. Harley Davidson tried to patent the sound but lost in court to the growling yellow peril and officially introduced the next corporate phase at Harley Davidson: looking foolish.

Meanwhile, I could ride across town and back to a North Beach curb for a lazy latte and girl watching easy as drifting into a backwater over a deep hole for lunkers. North Beach was as far from the Castro as Neptune from Uranus, and coy passers-by offered hope. A bumpkin could have fun in the city.

But too much fun in the city closed in on cold cloud cover, concrete, chronic hangover and the cocaine cringe, in which the body wanted more and rejected too much, defaulting to one mo' time. Then came the swinging dicks, so that a thin, healthy guy could not go to the grocery store without learning all about sexual objectivity. Maybe it was karmic. It felt creepy, possibly hateful; so it worked. Canna Screws was not warm and sultry and did not feel like home, but a house lot showed up for sale in the classifieds there and looked like good anchorage on a lee shore.

In the 80s a borrower could still draft a loan app and tax returns. Two stops, at the bank and the P.O., for blank forms, and a third at a CPA could align numbers. The banks were happy to lend, if the borrower could demonstrate no need and the ability to repay, and the loan apps could show comprehension of requirements. Fifty grand was a hefty construction loan in those days and got things well underway on a house that would go one-forty. Well, they all go over budget, and Canna Screws did call for extra artistry.

Something had to give, since a mortgage could not remain unpaid, and a man of no means was not king of the road. In that time of anxiety, bicycle riding felt meditative, a distraction of physical exertion, in which thoughts might sort out. One day I passed a twenty-two wheel cab and trailer in pearl burgundy with a chrome grill and red oval plaque: *Peterbilt*.

Native Americans and veterans of the 60s shared a weakness for beads and trinkets and color coming on in waves. The big rig sat in front of a house near a sign: FOR SALE. I leaned my bicycle on a bush and knocked on the door.

A hobbled man came out. Was the house for sale, or the rig? He said it'd come time to live in the house, and his rig had some miles but they didn't show because of the rubdown she got every night, the grease in her joints and fresh oil in her system and all manner of things that keep a rig young. "Why, she cost you pert' near fifty thousand dollars new. She worked good for me though, so all's I need is eleven. Eleven thousand dollars."

I didn't have eleven thousand dollars but felt I could get it and then pay it back fairly soon, what with my youth and vigor allowing extra hours on longer hauls. Endless highway stretched into the future—the road future. I knew that place. "I think I might…"

The seller squinted, "Nah! You don't want to be a long hauler. Why, you got your whole life ahead of you. What are you, twenty-three? Twenty-four maybe?"

"Thirty-four. I need to do something."

He looked every bit of seventy-five. "I'm sixty-two. I can't hardly find interest in life without a couple bennies and a quart o' joe. This rig'll break you, and you'll never get out of it till you're done for. Go on. Try something else. Not trucking. If it don't work, never you mind. Try something else again."

It felt like a kid getting chastised. I rode home to the new house I could cover for two more mortgage payments.

A visit to Hawaii seemed insupportable at the time, but it wasn't for warm weather, ocean frolic and scantily clad women. Kenny B had also survived our prolonged youth with recreational values intact. He too had grappled with practicality traction and urged the visit, to see if two nickels might rub together for twelve cents.

The truth was that the tiger would soon eat us if we didn't grab its tail. And over extended dreamy cocktails we agreed that the most gainful pursuit should include a yacht and a decent income. By chance, Kenny's friend Drug—make that Doug—was driving a charter boat loaded with tourists every day, each one representing a fifty dollar bill and a fair number of them representing the old, adventurous spirit as well. So we fed the delusion of greatness, this time in the tropics. Back at the bank—not the same bank but a new bank, new tax returns backed a new loan app for a sailing yacht just like the one we'd imagined ourselves owning. A neurosurgeon we knew socially wanted in on the yacht deal and agreed to stand behind the paper. Follow your dreams. They generally beat working.

Four months of an option to purchase the yacht ran a thousand dollars per month, but that money would be returned in cash at close of escrow, which occurred at ten minutes after five on the hundred twentieth day of the option period in a whirl away of mind, body and spirit and some solid new narrative coming right up.

The big problem with California was plain to see: fifty-six million Californians—few of them completely conformed to stereotype, but most dabbled in it. What was the last threat fled: idiom and repetition to the point of tedium?

Well, it hardly seemed to matter whether it was nuclear reprocessing and glowing in the dark or murder and mayhem scripted like a comic book. Exits were best with a flourish.

No sweat; change of scenery coming right up.

Steve Miller came on the radio, bidding farewell to friends at home and people trusted. He also needed further penetration into the world, where he *might get rich or might get busted*.

We didn't head out on a 707 but set sail out of Canna Screws Harbor into breaking seas and funky grays, wondering once again where and when and feeling busted already.

Sea Time

ZEN TEACHERS SAY age thirty-five delineates the two primary phases of life, the formative years and the person defined. Age thirty-five is the minimum advised for sitting *seishin*, meditation lasting three days or ten.

Sunrise on my thirty-fifth could not delineate sea from sky but pitched into gray scud on twenty knots gusting to forty under dark clouds bruised purple. Cross-seas banged heads as the harbor at Canna Screws shrank and sails went up a mile into Monterey Bay. With the engine cut the fifty-foot racing sloop *Whirlaway* fell off and heeled, bearing 240° south southwest, twenty-four hundred miles to go.

Many people declined the heavy-weather-at-sea phase of the Grand Tour and lived rich, full lives all the same, satisfied with loose reference to maritime scenes, like Stephen Still's fantasy lyric peppered with nautical phrases, like following seas and tradewinds, running downhill to Papeete on the outside, loving you and the *Southern Cross*, which was the name of the song. On the outside? Outside of what? Outside of the boat? Outside of the ocean? That was the problem when 60s rockers dabbled in imagery foreign to their experience; it came out silly or worse.

Southern Cross attempted the rolling rhythm of the best decade, and we did wear bell bottoms and loved to love each other in every way. But the lyric made a salty dog wonder: what the hell was he talking about?

Back on the real ocean, blustery, swirling skies and waves breaking over the bow were backdrop on a birthday boy moaning to inboard then rolling to port for the ho-heave over the rail. The four grand option money paid back in cash twelve hours before departure allowed a grand for groceries, two grand for beer and liquor and a grand for cocaine to celebrate, because failure to celebrate small victories could doom a life to no celebration at all.

A yacht in the tropics made sense as a reality of choice. So a momentary setback, with its puking, pain and hopeless odds, was only purgatory. Steve Miller capped it one more time with a biblical reminder that purgatory is prerequisite to heavenly ascension.

> *You got to go through hell before you*
> *Get to Heaven*

Of historical note is that cocaine got cool in the 70s—Johnny Carson asked Maurice Chevalier if WWI prisoners actually got cocaine from the guards. "*Mais oui*, but it was a different time, *avec esprit de corps*, and it was never more than one or two sniffs per day." By the 80s the toot defined us, drove us, thought for us and provided confidence beyond caffeine.

Doomsday would not be denied. You can't take illicit white powder to sea for practical reasons. It melts in the humidity—unless it's sealed tight in a humidor and left unopened. Fuck that. Besides practicality are many more reasons for going ahead and tooting up the rest of the toot. Many, many. You can get more at the far end. Tooting it up the night before was also addictive and destructive, but then failure accepted seemed better than failure's inevitability. Given proper perspective on timing, getting rid of the drug seemed most prudent in sustaining momentum.

In short order, two grifters arrived in the tropics, charm and spirit unvanquished, to meet a steady stream of tourists waiting for the adventure of a lifetime. Thirty grand a month in revenue felt great, and thirty-five in expenses didn't seem so bad. The tide would turn. Or could or should turn.

But it didn't turn, because it wasn't a real tide but another imperfect analogy, all ebb, down to survival mode in a backwash of monthly deficit, drugs and denial. Some women wanted to share the drugs and apparent prosperity. Circling below were insolvency, foreclosure and a federal marshal seeking a "stolen" yacht. The bank foreclosed, delineating the formative process from the situation defined. When you got nothing you got nothing to lose. Which could be the most frequently disproved lyric in music history.

Moving to an idyllic beach felt easy and anonymous. Charters could run so young couples could realize the romance. Free of pesky debits, a questionable future seemed easy as a marginal past.

Dreamlike and ephemeral, incognito life on a beach was fantasy fulfilled. Delivering day-sail adventure in a fool's paradise. Kenny asked when we would be arrested. I didn't know. We would hit the road with a judgment against earnings and make our way to retirement, which shouldn't take more than thirty years or so.

"Won't we go to jail first?"

A favorite pastime on campus was a layered goof called slo-mo football, which was just like real football—tackle football—but with no pads and stoned stupid. Pass plays reverted to real time briefly, but the game taught how much was possible with no time on the clock, if you went slo-mo.

We ran an ad for a yacht priced to sell—call it a steal, and the new owner was eased into payments with no lingering grudges. Okay, tapped into payments, but still. It was the ultimate hot mud sale. Just add water.

Kenny advised a legal career or banking for me. But banking is boring, maybe terminal, and no career is legal. Life circles are rarely concise as a good story, but that lap seemed tidy enough. On another pass through the doors of perception, a shipwreck in Hawaii felt lucky.

Any port is snug after a storm, and a familiar port was even better. Betty Boop came on from out of the blue. Our psychic horizons melded in a Hawaii coffee shop for me, on a Texas shrink's sofa for her.

She'd moved to Boston in '71 as a married grad student and got her master's degree in English literature. That degree and eight dollars could get her a cup of coffee in any of your better resort hotels, but she did enjoy the intellectual discourse. Her new Ivy-League husband called the marriage perfect, though perfection was relative to his campaign for the PhD. Betty was an academic wife, which is similar to political wifery with equal measures of tedious small talk and hopeless good cheer—and with limits on certain topics to keep the husband's profile perfect. As an up-and-comer on a fast track to tenure, the husband's instinct for literary meaning and campus politics endeared him to senior faculty. His mentor, Professor Pontius Polyneseus Pough, the Charles Grey Gildquist Chair for Elizabethan Prose, struck a pose of wisdom for the ages. The grad students spoke of genetic descent from the masters, and though some took the genetic reference as a joke, others did not.

Prof Pough would bang Betty twice on each visit after regular office hours on Tuesdays and Thursdays for three months at her insistence. This from the Boop's mouth. She'd been so alone, so beside herself with the new husband's preoccupation and total distraction from everything but the PhD and academic potential with regard to agonizing analysis of the most boring verse on Earth. She felt abandoned and stifled. Make no mistake: Betty was horny, which was not a fault but a clear and present maintenance issue accruing to any husband with a third-grade education or the equivalent in common sense thereof.

In time, on a carefully laid trail of slips, subtext and blatant clues, she felt sure hubby was wise to the hanky-panky, as intended. He said nothing, leaving her no recourse but to keep banging Pough, a chore in itself, she said, given his effusions of self-esteem and his tiresome failure at getting it up. The latter problem sounded like an attempt to discount the exchange as real sex, in which the hot and steamy is a function of mutually consenting adults. I would not ask how she cured his equivocation. Didn't she say twice on each visit?

Finally, she left a note from Pough referencing romantic innuendo lying on the kitchen table. Hubby found it and kept it. The note praised Betty's skills as equal in a global context to Pough's own literary insights. Well, it was painful for hubby, she'd hoped. But she'd forced the issue, demanding that he stand like a man to re-declare his love and challenge Pough to a duel or a game of whist or something. He didn't. He began helping her cover her careless clues. He remained true to academic potential. He seemed grateful for her support in the cause.

Betty finally told him point blank that she was banging the head prof twice on Tuesdays and Thursdays. Each.

How did hubby take the frontal verbal? He made a beeline to Professor Pough's office to apologize for any misunderstanding.

I got the tale in '85 on the phone. Betty and I hadn't spoken for years, till the day of our psychic reunion, a phenomenon extraordinary only to those with routine lives, which, they say, last a long time, which is great if you like routine. Surrounded by chitchat and 2% double macchiatos, hold the foam, hold the cinnamon but one light-medium shake of the dark chocolate sprinkles, and make that a grandé, I did not think of Betty.

Staring into a motherfucking cup of black coffee felt perfect for soaking up sensations: no wind, no waves, no sun, no spray, no tourist questions and no impending consequence.

Movement in the periphery vanished on a glance. The aerie faerie crowd will tell you that spirits, nymphs, gnomes, leprechauns, *menehunes* and many elfin creatures frolic in the periphery. A cloud drifted by, a talk bubble like the lyrical array of Led Zeppelin II on New Year's Eve of '69 on late lift off. We'd been warned of acid flashback—hallucination or reality warp could revisit any time. Polite media profiled flashback as a hazard for the duration of life, but the experienced saw flashback as a bonus, like a trailer of a great movie showing the best bits.

Maybe the coffee shop talk bubble drifting out front was a flashback. After spin-cycle at sea and life, the flashback felt easy. It said:

Betty Boop.

The words wobbled into focus with bumps and wrinkles, perhaps a warning of what svelte coeds come to—but such a warning would only concern a sexist, soulless man.

I loved her.

I looked away.

I looked back, and it was gone. What a relief. I feared surface crazing and rigging failure. It reappeared, floating over the crowd:

Betty Boop.

So I wondered as men do, where she is now. Betty Boop stood out on many levels. She'd chosen me as the recipient of her bounty. She'd treated me like the man I could only hope to be.

I had errands and chores, but early that evening I tracked her down and made the call.

It was thirteen years since we last spoke, or fifteen, and caller I.D. was still years into the future. When she picked up the phone I said, "Hey. What are you doing?"

"I can't believe you called."

"Why shouldn't an old friend call?"

"You should call. You should have called years ago. No. Really. It's okay that you didn't. But I was talking about you today. I don't mean casually. I talked about you for an hour."

"About me?"

"To my shrink."

"Is that good?"

"Well, no, it hasn't been good. But it was good today."

I'd heard that she divorced the first husband. A year or two later she'd begun dating Randy Mutton, a slovenly boy who'd ignored those challenges that can get a kid down. Late-blooming acne and surface shyness only hid the young dynamo inside. She hadn't known Randy in our college days, though he'd admired her from afar as inaccessible and way too perfect—just as I had. Randy's heart-thumping crush began the first time he saw Betty on my arm.

But Randy M and Betty B as an item? Wha!

Randy had lived in a fraternity house where I waited tables in exchange for meals. The fraternity's theme of gross humor focused on bodily function. Top rung of the value system there was anything scatological, disgusting, unfortunate, impolite, indelicate, embarrassing and in your face. The bathrooms had no walls around the toilets, so the boys farted and shit in traffic, perhaps to better ditch their inhibitions. Fifteen years before the movie the place was Animal House. Any given night could trigger the food fight of the Century. The pledges cleaned up, and the dining room stayed on simmer with many eyes roaming for the first toss or flick.

The place went mum when Betty Boop slipped through the back door to wend her way through a few tables and whisper in my ear. The boys could not fathom a creature so far from gross. When she left, one brother speculated that her shit must taste like marshmallows.

Another brother concurred that he would like to suck air through her asshole.

Randy Mutton stared in awe and wonder.

A popular guy in the brotherhood, Randy was known for his generous nature. An event captured his essence, proving a truth that was, to Randy, self-evident: that pussy is great and should be shared with friends. That college town was known for its high school girls and their yen for college boys. I'd seen one such girl around town, shopping with her mother, getting it right on the dress, the hat, the shoes. Calling her snooty would be unfair, but she would not look at longhairs in purple vests and bell-bottoms.

I saw Randy one day in the parking lot where I shared an apartment with two other guys. He huddled with five other guys, as if calling a play. I went over, and Randy pulled me into the circle. "Okay, okay. She's ready. I told her six but she won't notice if it's seven. Okay. We'll horsengoggle. Okay?"

Randy had met the same girl and asked for sex for himself and his brothers, because, after all, they were good guys who could use a break. She'd agreed, in need of a break herself, and waited in an apartment. Horsengoggle pre-dated rock-paper-scissors in determining order. Participants recited in unison *ein, schvei, drei, horsengoggle!* On the last note we thrust one to five fingers into the center space. With all fingers tallied, the total was counted off around the circle. The last number went first.

I got first. I told the high school girl I was engaged to be married and bound by faithfulness but would surely appreciate the, you know, special relief. She sighed and said I was engaged to a very lucky girl. Gee, to have a guy who would be that faithful.

Randy went fifth, so he had time to walk over to the vending machine to get the girl a Coke, since she'd want something bubbly after so much mayo, and he was a service-oriented guy.

It's only a strange story till it fast forwards a dozen years or so, when Randy Mutton wooed and won Betty Boop. Sick and tired of menial jobs, reaching the age of routine or risk, he made his move. His friends laughed. Randy laughed too; he cut such a funny picture at his wheeled stand with stainless bins and Sterno cans to heat his hotdogs and buns behind a bank of squeeze bottles out front: mustard, ketchup and relish. The awning read:

Hotdogs $2.

Business was spotty, so he altered the awning:

De Luxe Kosher Hotdogs $2.

With a slight bump in sales, he tweaked the awning again:

Kosher dogs like you get at the ball park $2.50.

Sensing progress he evolved to:

Mutton Dogs De Luxe Ball Park Kosher FOOOOOT LONG!
$4.

He got a steamer for the buns and added beans for two dollars more. He went to the three-tier bean upgrade on another sign that dangled from the awning on metal rings:

Fartless Beans $2. Fartful Beans $3.
Sudden Death Beans $5.

When Sudden Death Beans made the local paper, Randy went to a new awning with a starburst:

$10 Sudden Death Combo De Luxe includes Cola of Choice.

People approached murmuring yeah, this is the place. So Randy built another stand, and then another.

Mutton Dog stands peppering the greater Houston area and then the region led to the Annual Mutton Dog Sudden Death Fart Off. A significant segment of the Lone Star State laughing and farting out loud proved that Randy Mutton's time in the Gamma

Alpha Gamma house had yielded the self-made man profiled in the Sunday Chronicle—that would be the Houston Chronicle. Beside the story were photos of Mr. Mutton, his lovely wife Betty and their infant son Max.

All this came on the phone many years after last speaking with Betty, her voice faltering on this tale of success. Randy had it made, she said, raking in scads o' dough. All he had to do was not mess it up. That was easy for her to say. How many years can a guy hustle hotdogs and beans and not wonder about the great, wide world? Anyway, he started mumbling a mantra when Subway came along and put a dent in the street-side market. *Fuck! Why didn't I franchise? Fuck! Damn! I could have franchised. Fuck!*

Randy had made his million dollars in a few years but suffered a barrage of self-inflicted regret—it could have been millions and maybe millions more. He probably hung himself when Quiznos came along, but that was a decade later.

Meanwhile, his amazing strategy for staying ahead of the curve was to build a bar dedicated to sports fans, what is now called a sports bar. This was the leading edge, and Randy Mutton got it right, almost. His place was carpeted and nice, in respect to sports fans, who are not a bunch of loudmouth louts but have feelings and sensitivities too, who appreciate recognition as fans.

But they didn't want carpet or nice. They wanted to yell *You fuckin' has-been bum!* They wanted to drop fries on the floor and mash them in without feeling guilty. They wanted a barn with big TVs. Randy's living room sports bar failed. He'd gone in with cash, because he had it. The place never caught on. He spent weeks in denial, laying off the entire staff and drinking in the bar alone with twelve TVs tuned to different sporting events. He could re-hire the staff when the crowd showed up, which it surely would, once it remembered the great good times.

The cleaning crew arrived one evening, and Randy struck up a friendship with a maid, a short, squat woman of forty-five who agreed that they both needed a break. They became an item, so Randy moved out two weeks after the birth of his and Betty's second child. He told her he was in love.

Betty was thirty-seven and still a knockout.

We were old enough by then to know that life can get very strange, but few of us could sort the strangeness or make much sense of it. Betty had post-partum difficulties with her new baby, because things had gone so wrong. She couldn't hold the baby without crying. She became distraught, feeling like a two-time loser at marriage—her, Betty Boop, the pussycat queen, the sexual object who made every passing male in her entire adult life ogle and drool.

Her obstetrician had seen it before and referred her to a shrink, who asked how these events made her feel. "I told him I'd fucked a bunch of guys. So what? Most women do. Maybe it was different for me, because so many guys came on to me. I don't think I fucked nearly as many guys in proportion to the number of guys who came on to me. You know? But it was mostly just pussy for them. Maybe not with Glenn. He was the pussy on that one. Ha!"

Glenn was the first husband who conquered the PhD and is renowned to this day for his juxtaposition of late 19th Century syntax with post-modern meter and/or rhythm. But it was mostly pussy with all the rest. They craved it, had to have it, wanted more of it and could not get enough till they rolled over and snored. Pitiful fuckers. I listened to her woeful, loveless tale, guilty as one more cockhound asleep on the lawn, till she said, "Except for you."

"*Moi?*"

"It's been so miserable, trying to sort through things, and this shrink keeps pushing my buttons. He asked me to reconsider the guys I'd been with to see if maybe someone or something other than sex comes through. Like affection and intellectual bonding. I didn't even need a minute. It was you. Only you."

Gulp. "So…we're still in love?"

She laughed, a hardy, healthy laugh, what a young fellow must learn to encourage in women prone to anxiety depression. "Yes. When are you coming to see me?"

A man was never too beaten to ponder a Boop weekend. The tiger's tale had been released, but dreams still imploded when the tiger lunged. She would be the antidote; next stop Texas.

Betty seemed emotionally and financially stable in the suburbs with a tiresome boyfriend who was way too analytical—

What?

She'd invited me, an old beau of no income, to travel five thousand miles to visit her and her boyfriend? No, silly. Interest in the boyfriend had died and so would the liaison, soon. It was just…nothing. She would tell him that day, the day of my arrival. Don't worry—the boyfriend would not be around, and her kids were young enough to fall asleep by eight.

We'd changed physically, grown out of self-conscious youth and beauty. My hair had thinned. I had skin damage from the sun and a scar slanting across my forehead where God whipped me with a running backstay in heavy weather to chastise my sins. She said it wasn't noticeable in low light and hiked her shirt to show breasts of two different sizes. "What can I say? They wanted the right side." I assumed they were the children.

Most notable was the comfort we shared, the open affection and bonding she'd recalled in her time of crisis. We snuggled on the sofa to share more. She said I should sleep in the basement till she gave the boyfriend the news. We shouldn't hurt him.

Because he really was a great guy. She simply couldn't stand to be around him anymore; he was so boring she could scream, and the sex was way off. "He eats me for forty-five minutes. Where the fuck is that at? That's not foreplay. I got chapped lips—wait! You'll love this!" She scooted to the edge of the couch and turned to me to better animate her point, her immersion in the world of diapers, babies and domestic routine. "I was on the phone with my friend Cookie, telling her how I have to get eaten for forty-five minutes. She was so envious, but I told her it wasn't what it was cracked up to be, because I had chapped lips. I had Suzy Q on my lap—you know how parents think their children can't hear. Well, Suzy Q says, 'Mommy, am I gonna get chapped lips from I eat too much?' Ha! Don't you love it?"

I laughed on cue, ignoring her free flowing imagery as we harked back to the good old days. We dallied on the prelims and Betty led me by the hand to the basement where we swooped to old home week in our world of discovery newly spiced with experience. Betty seemed happy, loved and appreciated. She said it was best, messing up the guest bed like that, so the soon-to-be-ex boyfriend could see that I was sleeping downstairs. Then we had tea.

Anticlimax can be comfortable in the suburbs. The charade to hide our middle-age liaison would make no difference to anyone. Her affliction had been sex with no affection. The shrink drew it out. Randy Mutton worshipped her, fucked her a few thousand times and then left her—the love went away, or maybe it never was. She moped, saddened by the shortfall. I consoled her with a reminder that love's irony was not hers alone to bear.

Embraced again by beauty and fantasy fulfillment, we renewed the bond. She broke up with the boyfriend a few days after I left, though he must have known. Betty and I could not be an item, and she must have known that too, yet her post-coital happiness got wildly emotional, recalling Betty of no spaghetti and certainly no acid. Then again, she'd achieved a rare interlude on our brief time together, which amounted to a cock-a-doodle-do over love everlasting. Never mind that it would last forever because of the chronic distance between us. It made us both more secure with ourselves.

We stayed in touch till I had a layover in Dallas two years later. It was still a decade before cell phones, and a few hundred miles proximity warranted a call. "Hey. What are you doing?"

"Who is this?" She'd recognized my voice in the past, and likely recognized it again.

A man behind her reiterated, "Who is it?"

"It's me. Your one true love. I'm in Dallas."

"Uh… It's not a good time. You can't come to visit. Okay?"

"I said Dallas. I can't come to visit. I called to say hello and ask how you're doing."

"It's not a good time. I'm very busy."

"Who is it?" asked the mellifluous voice nearby, its benign curiosity telling the tale. Among Betty's many effusions had been a confession that came at the tail end of our visit. She'd asked if I remembered a certain fellow. We'd been friends years ago, and this fellow had also been pals with Randy Mutton?

Sure, I remembered the guy.

"I fucked him."

Maybe it was good for her, but it sounded like something else. She got curiouser and curiouser; it happened on a Christmas visit to her parents who lived in the same town. He couldn't get it up until he could, because she helped him as only she could—"Do you have any idea how many guys have told me that I'm the very best?"

I hadn't dwelt on it because I had an idea how many guys, and avoiding her stats and ratings seemed more convenient. "I got him up. But then he couldn't keep it up." She sighed, maybe at the replay. Then she laughed. "What a mess."

Was the mess figurative or literal? Was it him, her or the gooey aftermath? "Why did you do him?"

She didn't hesitate. "I thought I'd give him a thrill. He was so depressed all the time. It was miserable—oh, God! Do you remember Dick Dunning?" Yes, I remembered Dick. He too was Randy's pal. He and I got arrested in Florida when—never mind. She'd done him later that same week. She laughed; she and Dick were inevitable, they were such good friends for so many years, and when Randy left, well… Boy, no problem keeping it up on *that* guy, which really was what she needed after the disaster with the limp noodle guy. Oh, and Keith Schaeffer. And Ricky Berman…

"Busy week."

"No. Not the same week. Please…"

"Rick Berman?" Rick Berman wasn't friends with Randy Mutton—he was opposite, conservative to a yawn, a serious student focused on a dental career. "You dated Rick Berman?"

"Not dated. We just, you know, hung out one night. I got to tell you, that guy is the worst fuck on the face of the earth. God! So demanding, and for what? Six seconds of bang, bang, bang, grunt, snort and out." She laughed again at the ridiculous package Rick Berman had presented.

"Why?"

She sighed again in a set piece. "I don't know. Give him a thrill." She dented my continuing affection through eight or ten guys, till she came to the denouement, the be-all, end-all of Betty's affliction, transforming my fondness to enduring sympathy. She'd been horny, "really horny," much worse than usual, and she couldn't relax or think of who to call. So she called a babysitter—a babysitter! At ten o'clock at night! Well, a woman has to do what a woman has to do. To think that she would have gone "out" without getting a sitter would be unacceptable. And irresponsible.

With the sitter secure in front of the TV Betty headed out just anywhere and wound up near the airport at a hotel with a lounge and a bar, empty except for a guy who agreed to buy her a drink. He also agreed to fill the gap in her love life up in his room and repeat as necessary. "Hey, he was a twerp, a salesman in a cheap suit. You'd think he'd never been laid. I know he never had what I gave him— especially not from his wife. Oh, man, he starts calling me, and then he found out where I live and started parking across the street. He stayed there three days, till I called the cops. I had to get a restraining order. Man."

I didn't ask why; she'd made the why of her adventures apparent: because.

Also apparent on that last call from Dallas was that her new man would stick around as long as her past didn't come sniffing the bushes for more. Maybe he'd said as much or she sensed it, so she was curt, not rude, really, considering the circumstance. And there we were, hardly a decade out from fifty with communion behind us.

Betty Boop defaulted to basic need. That night she needed long-term romance. Good for her, sacrificing an old flame to keep her new man. Was Betty teaching me a lesson in love lost with her marriages and a cavalcade of buckaroos eager for the blue ribbon thrill ride?

I don't think so. If it was convenient, she would have invited me to Houston for another round of friendship. I wouldn't have gone, because a man and a dog will judge a journey's distance by the reward at the end. More tea and crumpets seemed like water and dog biscuits by then. I called to see how she was doing and found out.

Very well, thank you. Please don't call again.

The high points in life are passionate. Friendships fade. People go away. Or they become somebody else, or things change internally, which all amounts to the same thing. Betty Boop faded to patterns and the national anthem. We went full circle and then some. Terminal from the outset, as many couples prove to be, we gave each other what we could.

Forty is young enough for vigor, old enough for true friendship. A man learns that women grant favors like the Easter Bunny hides eggs, with plenty for every kid to find his fair share. The wildly experimental world of the 60s settled out by the 90s.

A new woman moved in, and hardly a year later came a blessed event, a new two-wheeler.

Around the Clubhouse Turn

MOST PEOPLE DON'T die one day. Failures accumulate: teeth, kidneys, gall bladder, appendix, uterus, ovaries, prostate, joints, pancreas, colon, gums, heart, lungs, skin—like a fire sale, everything must go. A man can feel wrung out at thirty-five if he's sunburned, windbent, beer-funked, broke and indebted. One day in the charter trade, a fat man came up the stern ladder in apparent pulmonary complexity. He was twenty-something and breathing hard.

"Are you in trouble?" I asked.

"No," replied his diamond-studded wife. "He's not used to so much exercise." He'd snorkeled seven minutes. At a hundred forty pounds with no body fat I sometimes swam an open ocean mile just to blow off steam, so I was wealthy next to the guy ten years younger who couldn't even see his peepee. But at the grocery store he could fill a cart with anything he wanted—two carts—and I couldn't, until I could. Hungry people generally live longer, but hungry isn't happy, and pangs become chronic. Or maybe a growing appetite was the first symptom of crazy youth fading away.

At a social event, an interviewer asked George Burns at ninety-seven if he was glad to be there. Sure it was a setup, a good one. George Burns twirled his cigar. "At my age you're glad to be any-where." He lived to a hundred, but how much had he seen pass away as he still quipped with the best of them? Inventory tends to shrink on friends, abilities and what will last. What's the compensation?

Laying it over in a sweep and farther over into a curve connects the world to the self, matches speed with angle, balances centrifugal force keeping the bike up and centripetal force holding it to the road. Thoughts are gyroscopic, mortality and acceleration engage in sweet symbiosis, up and out on a gentle twist, goosing reality to seventy-five at four grand.

Into the straightaway the cosmic/mechanical interface clarifies life. Memory fragments tumble with simple labels: youth, aging and the time in between and maybe what's left and how much. Painfully obvious to aging persons is the complexity of maintenance, till it's easy to speculate on what component will fail and take you out.

The 90s opened on a new Sturgis. Harley had a Sturgis in '83 to debut the Kevlar belt as secondary drive—the belt that turns the back wheel, in this case replacing the chain. No Sturgis followed till '91. It looked like a Sportster or Super Glide with external shocks, and like a Sturgis, black and orange with the big engine. It prototyped the Dyna series, attempting agility in a heavy cruiser.

The shop owner stepped up and said, "You want it. I see your checkbook in your pocket. What you came here to do is get excited. You could write a check and ride it home. Like you want to."

What a nudge, not even aware of the big fat fault in his Mr. Smarty Pants idea. "Oh yeah? What would I do with my car?"

He laughed. "Leave it here. Park in my spot. I'll move mine across the street." He shrugged. "Have your girlfriend drive you down later for your car. You got a girlfriend, don't you?"

Yes, I had my checkbook and a girlfriend. He said his wife just had a baby, and he was getting high again but without drugs, on sleep deprivation. He seemed haggard. "A baby? How old are you?"

"Fifty-one."

"So when the kid is thirteen, you'll be sixty-four."

"Yeah. So what? How old are you?"

It was a lazy, sunny Saturday with nothing on deck. An easy check could liberate things from inertia. And yes, I wanted it. But I played it cautious. "I'll drive it down the street and see if I like it."

"Fine. First write me a check so I can be getting the paperwork together. You don't like it; we tear everything up. Okay?"

"You're pretty good."

"Yeah, I am. But you're good too. This ain't rocket science. You got it written all over you."

The Sturgis sat high but ran well. Seventy-four cubic inches was overkill on an island that ran out of road in short order. That rig logged mostly sundown trips to the grocery on a road that wended along a volcano slope and headed to the grail at last. Hanging on to scooter grips after gripping a phone all day felt refreshing, at times game changing. Straddling two wheels instead of a bucking business bronco brought the old spirit home. War cries in the wind expressed gratitude. Two years and three thousand miles to the grocery store later was enough. Tropical countryside was nice, but the road was brief and repetitive.

A friend who introduced me to meditation years before had a landscape company, so I hired him for my new place. One day on the way to lunch he advised in his minimal way that I'd done well and should never sell. What an odd thing to say. I'd just built it and moved in—a house aloft on two acres of lush garden in a place called Haiku. Well, it's nice to arrive at a place not so different from youthful values; arrival came sudden as a surprise after forty years of wandering. A magical home in the country, income, a great woman, good prospects—could it be another setup, too good to trust?

"Everything changes. Be aware."

"You mean beware?"

"No. I mean be aware. Take nothing for granted."

"That doesn't sound relaxing."

"Maybe you relax too much."

"I doubt it."

And that was that, except for wondering what the fuck.

The business partner was bankrupt when we met. As a would-be mover and shaker he wasn't afraid to gamble, like many low achievement people. That sounds harsh, and he really didn't seem low achievement. He'd driven a taxi and pimped a bit on the side, as your Honolulu taxi driver will do by necessity, to make ends meet till things pick up. And things invariably picked up, notwithstanding a masters degree in business administration. His graduate degree was not from a State U, but it wasn't Ivy League either, which may have accounted for his intermittent common sense. My business partner could generate cash flow easy as low pressure makes for breezes. He just lost it all, every time. Well, I could fix that; just watch. Impressively inured to insult, he laughed at my rough critique on his losing situation. As friends in need, we would partner his business smarts on merchandising, personnel, payroll, legal docs and tax returns with my street level smarts and raw talent on advertising.

Between '89 and '95 the business paid no taxes. Federal tax is based on net income. Hawaii tax is 10% of the net and 4% of the gross, along with payroll tax and withholding taxes. Not filing is worse than not paying; the statute of limitations begins with filing. In August of '95 the State Tax Division called to say, "Ey. You know what? You no pay your tax."

The partner explained, "I've been meaning to tell you about that." He'd been meaning since '88, when we'd last filed.

Why does the Grand Tour stop in scenic overview of business failure? Because failure or marginal success came naturally for so many years with no fault or shame, because of nothing to lose. But losing on a bunt, on an easy lay up or an end run through a hole can indicate flawed fundamentals. Or maybe things can go more wrong with something to lose.

As cosmic veterans with know-how we saw ourselves as raconteurs, time travelers, spacewalkers—as veterans of the Age of Aquarius, we knew right from wrong and how to avoid the reaper. With proven skills in the ground game and the air game we took the lead. Indifference became strength and we won on daring, wit and contentment. Comrades in the goof could do no wrong...

Until rough weather loomed on a camping trip to Montana, where psychic phenomenon signaled the downfall, dead ahead. Beginning at a camping emporium in Missoula with a few grand in knives, binocs, sleeping bags, cook kits and on and on, it felt grandiose, another goof in retail therapy with a vengeance on what we'd missed. Stuff sailed into the giant cart—exotic toys for the partner's kids—wait a minute. They weren't there, and such obtuse spending seemed wasteful, no matter what we'd missed. He scoffed. "What? We don't have the money?" So I shrugged and tossed a camp latte maker onto the pile. He shook his head. "Man. Loosen up a little bit, wouldja?"

Okay, maybe he was right.

He read a book high on the bluff in a canvas chair as I cast a Mepps spinner across the stream—across the years for the old magic. Sunlight on little wave faces shimmered in a steady breeze. Reeling, tugging, waiting could simulate an injured fish, but the stream felt empty; the world had changed. Trout don't like cloudy water. The flow was lifeless in the crisp Montana air. Wind waves lapped the shore as gusts wafted in sudden exhalation, and in a minute I buckled with terrible sadness.

Welling out of nowhere, sobs heaved under a burden of grief. Setting the rod aside I knelt and wept. The partner soon stood there. "Hey. What's wrong?" I couldn't say—it wasn't the day or the moment or the shape life had taken or its potential. But the love all around us caved in.

He laughed. "What the fuck, man?"

With wits finally restored and eyes wiped I stood, shrugging it off and casting again. But fishing was over and just as well; it was time to head up the road and make camp where black bear roamed but no griz. The store clerk had recommended a special place.

Sundown was quick with hundred fifty foot conifers casting the clearing into shadow. We ate and drank well, with fillets and a few bottles of fah fah de blah blah cabernet in the two hundred dollar range. Why not? Did we not *deserve* the very best? Who would better celebrate us than us? The evening felt unique, and fine vintage wine could raise fine rhetoric.

The partner opened on a few things that must change, like attitude. I took no offense; we were blitzed and had a happy history of candor. He honed in to money management. We lacked trust. We ignored the skill and intention of others. We were woefully doubtful. Doubt is so cynical, and frankly, it's negative. And we must stop the paranoia—people were talking; no need to mention names. Above all we must show faith in humanity rather than questioning petty expenditures. They might seem lavish on the surface, but they actually affirmed long-range wisdom, what we might call vision, if we could ditch the attitude.

He'd been insolvent and had gone to bankrupt on a beach shop specializing in silk dresses in an opulent setting, back when four hundred grand was some real money. Normal floor tile ran a buck a foot installed—or you could spend four bucks for the Cypress Mint Collection imported from Italy, and he did. Plus a buck a square to install, but what could he do, not install? And a buck and a half on freight, but that didn't count, if you…

What was the attraction to partnership with a financial delusional? The guy could turn a half-starved calf into a cash cow. That he showed symptoms of mad cow disease had seemed curable. It wasn't. No matter how much he generated, he spent more. He kept a checkbook ledger with a negative balance and wrote more checks, bad checks. He said, "No, I'm not."

"You have brackets around this figure." The balance: <$1,800>. "You're writing a check for thirty-two hundred. That takes the balance to negative five grand. *Capiche?*"

"Yeah. So?"

"So it's a bad check."

"No it's *not*! It's not a bad check unless it bounces. The checks above it won't clear for seven days. Or nine! We'll cover it."

"What if it rains?" That question had brought the first lecture on attitude. Twenty years later investment bankers would money-manage economic collapse on that same approach. The partner, sadly, got no millions for his vision, not one.

It rained. A few checks bounced, requiring phone calls and happy explanations on true intent and resolution from a Master of Business Administration. As a major in leg and reefer I then required that all dollars written into any check would be considered spent. It sounded like a theorem, graduate level.

Once spent, those dollars could not be spent again.

He called me amazing with money and laughed that it must be those Jewish genes.

As a recreation director for a major resort hotel he'd learned a thing or two about service. Still early in our liaison, when I viewed fifty dollars as potential inventory, we pulled into a hotel, where he tipped the parking valet fifty dollars. As I stared in shock, sputtering what the fuck, he said, "Trust me on this one. Watch me get their attention. This is gonna be fun."

That is, he'd seen wealthy people tip heavily on arrival at a posh hotel, causing murmurs from valet to bell to fine dining, setting up gold-star service down the line for a fifty or hundred dollar tip from the man—what he most wanted to be. I remained skeptical through checkout with nary a twitch in service. Had I missed something in our return on investment? He mumbled about attitude and loosening up then too, explaining that sometimes returns are deferred, like when a parking valet would remember the man from last year. Word gets out quickly that the man is back.

Oh, brother. But it was good, with the wine and reefer loosening us up on a camping trip. It was wilderness time, still the best time, time to relax and to point out that my cynical view had spawned a dynamic media campaign.

"That's fine. I wouldn't change that for anything. But who do you think can live with your distrust every day?"

"Distrust?"

"You distrust my judgment."

"Ah. Well, my ex-wife couldn't live with it either."

"No, and I don't blame her."

"You never met her."

"I can imagine. Oh, man, I can imagine!"

The breeze had increased into twilight and was stiff by nightfall, nature's bluster preempting that of the partner. I brewed espressos and stoked the pipe, lighting it with great effort in the wind. Another vintage wine for vintage fellows would come next.

He began again on trust, business, worldview and women, using his new girlfriend as a shining example of "what two people can have together." He was married with seven children. The new girlfriend was a manikin, posed and mute. She provided the great calming salve that cleared his head for better business.

Janel at forty-two had never married. The partner was amazed that a woman so stacked could remain unmarried. "Did you hear what I said? She's never been married! Can you believe it? And we just met! Just like that! Like it was meant to be!"

Meant to be or simply was—either/or seemed incidental to a common drive: screwing early and often just like the free spirits used to do. Janel didn't like so much screwing but didn't mind—it meant so much to him. He loved his little bird for her sacrifice and stupendous rack swinging to and fro. "They're not just huge, they stick out. They could poke you in the eye! Ha!" He loved playing with them and talking about them when they weren't around. He equated her marital status with virginity, casually dismissing three long-term boyfriends in the four- to eight-year range, though all three relationships had led to the same familiarity and contempt as marriages. All her long-term relationships ended on the same realization that life is long and should be better.

Not a pretty woman, Janel turned heads with her practiced profile. She could lure men with her wares, and she knew it. So she wasn't surprised when she hooked the partner on fool's bait.

He couldn't get enough and wanted to prove his love. One day they passed a shop window with a nifty little sundress at seven hundred clams, not nearly as much as an evening dress. She wanted an evening dress but glanced at the sundress. He said, "Let's get it," like they would share it, which they would, when you thought about it. Seeing her in it would make him happy.

The cute little shift with plunging neckline and supple support for separation, lift and spread on the dazzling cleavage went on the company card, as in business-related. Six eyes watched the transaction, two jaundiced, two beaming in joy and two resigned to marginal return. I was a ripple on their lovely pond. Janel knew what a good man provides beyond basics—any grunt could come up with basics. She wanted the flourish, the whimsical and fantastic, not all the time but whenever she wanted it.

Between that spontaneous act of love with a sun dress at seven bills and the best camping gear money could buy on a blustery night threatening eruption, many thousands more dollars supported the partner's love and largesse for his new woman and the world. Surely they would love him back. He had discovered colloidal silver, a purifying mineral as costly as its name implies. Ten bucks an ounce isn't so bad, when a four-ounce bottle lasts a few weeks. But it got bad by the case at twelve hundred bucks.

In a positive light, a case earned an additional discount. Besides that, the partner's office staff could absorb cases of the amazing new product, so it was win/win all over again—his specialty. That would be the office of his side business, reselling healthcare products. Colloidal silver could be part of inventory, with adequate testing and results confirming improved health as another win/win by-product.

Then came gold teeth. The nine staffers of the side business each had three to five mercury amalgam fillings removed and replaced with gold crowns, gold inlays and/or gold overlays, also charged to the company card—my company. Other embezzlements would surface with a whine, "I was gonna tell you!"

But alas, the hammer fell.

The love all around us had warped. The partner could not tell the difference between love and a pathological need for love. Was that bad, being guilty of excessive goodness? Who could pay taxes with so many better uses for the money at hand? He stole everything he gave away, like Robin Hood, except nobody was rich or poor; the victims were duped, the beneficiaries willing.

In the legal scramble ahead he was made to admit duplicity; he'd promised to bring university-level smarts to the partnership but provided stupidity. "You bought gold teeth for people I don't know?"

"You can know them anytime. They're good people, in spite of your attitude. Do you know how important dental health is?"

"Do you know how important livelihood is? The company is insolvent. You will render fifty people unemployed." But that came later, a long way from free- spirit concerns for solvency and employment.

Back in Montana on a blustery night, the wind howled. Treetops whipped and crashed. Massive limbs plummeted to Earth with dramatic impact. A camp chair stupor and exciting visual fare warranted another pipe and another swig and kept me seated.

The partner glared at this perfect example of attitude with limbs crashing around us. He gained momentum, proclaiming danger. "We could be killed here!"

"Go hide in the car. You accuse me of distrust, cynicism and no faith. Look at you. You're scared. You have no faith that the motherfucking universe will protect you from falling limbs. That's hypocritical. That's attitude. So shut the fuck up."

A limb crashed into the fire and the camp latte maker to highlight the great windstorm story. Sleeping in the car seemed best, and by morning the spirits were becalmed. A stoned, drunken tirade was what the doors of perception had led to, and untidy devolutions were easily dismissed with prosperity upon us. Once again we had not copped out but deferred to the developing process.

Two weeks later I could not meditate. Years of morning meditation had connected things, till they disconnected. I visited a psychic—an imposition because of the energy required for what I requested. But something was amiss. Fidgets haunted the stillness. I told her of the creek-side episode, though the trip seemed good otherwise.

Carol asked about recent confrontation. My grandmother died, displeased with my disrespect for her turd of a son, Old Mom's brother. Carol put a limp hand in the air, went snake-eyed and then went inside. Twitching like a sleeping dog, she soon came out. "It's not your grandmother. The Montana incident was real. You were standing on the spot where your family was killed."

"My family?"

"Your Indian family. You were there. You saw it. You felt it. But I can't tell if… I'm getting something in business. What's going wrong in business?"

"Business couldn't be better. I walked away from a shitty lease deal on the Big Island, but that was a good thing." She went back in for a long stay, five or seven minutes, and came out spent.

"It's hard to see, but I still get business and numbers."

Ten days later the tax office called. In the next few months and the first sixty grand of legal defense, we dodged a criminal charge and copped to seven misdemeanors, one for each corporation. The partner had proven his genius twenty years before Wall Street worked the same scam, borrowing from one corp to pay another in a shell game too slick for the human eye to follow. Appearance and substance merged. Was copping to pleas the same as copping out?

The Feds were easy—come in from the cold, pay the tax and gain amnesty.

The State wanted blood. The house got leveraged in three days flat, because the State doesn't want indebted property. With a huge mortgage in place, the house looked like a flawed gem. I rented it out, then sold or packed everything from a life so swell it seemed like a setup but didn't have to be if I could have been aware. I moved with my girlfriend to Seattle. The partner became ex- like the ex-wife, no longer subject to ambient attitude.

The partner does not linger but serves as disclaimer to the love all around us. No generation is invincibly moral. The rough time felt spiritually genetic, descended from peoples who died well, with a war cry—my people. The old tribe would have been proud, and so was the current family.

Philip Roth called Native Americans the original *goyem*, but he wrote of urbane characters, constrained and self-obsessed. Philip Roth, "man of letters," was not a man of action. I sensed something else in native peoples, a warrior spirit linking generations on trails of tears, and those warriors are *mishpocha* to me.

It felt like full circle from war resistance to war cry, and the love settled again all around us.

Asymmetry as an Indication of Life

WORD WAS OUT on a guy building Norton Commando replicas with improvements: disc brakes, a bigger engine and better tranny. I punched it up but alas, the Commando had gone muscular and looked more retro classic than comfortable.

I punched up BSA and got some diehard guys wrenching tappets on ancient Beezers. I hit Triumph for the warm and fuzzy feel—and found that Triumph was back. Triumph morphed years ago to a clenched fist engine on a twisted pretzel chassis with a riding profile that looked prostate-exam-ready.

But ownership had changed at the Triumph company, and the crotch-rocket line got pre-empted. The classics were back, born again in the first rule of retail: don't forget what got you here. The Bonneville was back in a replica nearly identical to the original, with disc brakes and a new engine up from 650cc to 865cc.

You see an old friend after decades and recall the old times and how it was and…God…the life that will not be lived again. Unless… Nah, the new Bonny rode too high. The classic bench seat seemed soulful, but a rider would stop more air than a truck grill. And who wants a high center of gravity?

Nobody is who, but under New Cruisers, Speedmaster claimed Bonneville genetics with a longer wheel base, lower seat and center of gravity, forward foot controls and stock stuff that would run thousands on a Harley Davidson—like a 180 back tire with no compromise on a skinny belt because this wheel was chain driven—the superior secondary drive. Double discs up front, a tach and a discreet oil cooler between the double down tubes suggested the raw appeal of a matchbox full of kief at a Pamplona campground in 1969 and felt, uh…correct.

Eighty-seven hundred? My last Road King went forty grand and wanted to fold up in the curves. Yes, that was forty thousand dollars on an addiction to the V-twin fantasy.

Never mind. Idle fantasy had been good, but another motorcycle would not be good. I went down to the Harley place to see the new Wide Glide, descended from the Sturgis. It seemed straightforward but the Harley Davidson cost twice as much, and that was BC— before corrections. The correct windshield was four hundred more and the official Harley Davidson windshield mounting brackets were more than that. Then came the Harley Davidson windshield quick release mounting bracket levers for another hundred or two hundred or four-fifty. The Harley Davidson saddlebags were nine hundred, plus another two hundred for the rear turn signal relocation kit, because the rear turn signals had to move so the saddlebags would fit. The tachometer was another five hundred plus installation, but Harley Davidson riders are supposed to get along without a tachometer by listening to the pipes—audible pipes would run another five to seven hundred.

At eighteen to twenty-one grand, depending on dealer surcharge over MSRP, the rig had admirable low-end torque on the bigger power plant but still wanted to fold in the curves. The sales guy held back on an explanation or defense or any response at all, as if familiar with the deal-killers. But it wasn't a deal. It was a mugging. Worse yet: "This thing has no taillight."

"Oh, that. You don't need one."

"I don't need one?"

"Yeah. I mean no. Harley Davidson figured it out. You don't really need a taillight."

"What about the guys who got creamed from the rear. I bet I can get a taillight."

"Yes! They got a kit. Two, three hundred is all."

"Plus the labor to tie it into the wiring harness."

"Well, sure, you got to tie in. How you gonna get power?"

"You just run it back from the battery?"

"No. You take it through the fuse box, because, you know."

"Yeah. What's installation on the taillight?"

"Uh. I'm not sure. Let's walk back to service and find out."

"I'm out of time right now."

"You save two hundred on the turn signal relocation kit if you get the taillight kit."

It was over, because instinct overrides appetite, or you just keep getting fucked.

In Honolulu soon after, I stopped at the Triumph dealer. Holy moly, the Triumph Speedmaster could track. Look left; it went left, no bulldogging, coercing, hoping or hoisting. Or folding at the swing arm. So this was engineering, what the motorcycle geeks kept talking about.

In coming weeks I thought the Harley salesman would call to *give me a taillight*. This is the rationale of an addict.

But it didn't matter, because it was over.

Motorcycle of the Year went to the Triumph Speedmaster, for engineering, balance, quality and value—beating out Honda, Kawasaki, Ducati, Yamaha, BMW and the rest.

The business also tracked well, but the gallbladder inflamed as annoying emails announced that year's Fall Smoker, the gathering of guys for the annual debauchery tour of the Pacific Northwest.

I hadn't gone in seven years and would not go again. The guys embraced online, reuniting in unspeakable joy. Liberated at last from what we'd fought clear of decades ago—home, wife and kids—they would hit the road one more time, stopping a mile up to burn a fatty and remember when. Some nicotine would enhance the best feeling in the world. Non-smokers smoked. Smokers smoked more. The weed bag shrank like a puddle in Death Valley in a scene so repetitive and tiresome that it felt like vengeance but not redemption. The Fall Smoker was tragic and comic, a random group of blue-collar grunts and white-collar wannabe road warriors riding into the wilderness with liquor, reefer, bad behavior and pussy jokes in delusional pursuit. Old stories were told and retold for the benefit of newcomers. Stories involving road dogs of the female variety were a source of validation, as if we were unique among men, and these very miles were like history in the making.

In the year of Whoredog, two elderly women wended through a crowded bar to sit near us. They'd read the odds and picked the winners. One of us engaged one of them and made her laugh. She loved his jokes. In no time it was the wee hours and he asked would she please suck on his weewee. She declined. He begged, *come on, you gotta help me out with this thing*. She declined more firmly, "No way in hell I'm gonna suck your dick, motherfucker. Now back off!" She demurred, however, that a girl might change her mind for four bills. That would be four hundred dollars, U.S.

The story emerged a few hours later that our guy got a hand job for twenty-five bucks on a compelling case based on the exchange rate—Canadian dollars were so worthless—and the sorry nature of a handjob compared to a blowjob. He asked for sympathy. And understanding.

She scoffed, but she did get the stuff out like a jackhammer on a sewer main. Hell, she could have killed him on a blowjob, unless she took her dentures out. Ha! The story died on the toughest question: "Was it daylight yet?" The dour breakfast crowd moaned.

Yes, sunrise illuminated a desperate man and a practical woman with a madly pulled pecker between them. Haggard faces, beer bellies and slurs framed the romance.

Pathetic, yet it paled next to the second guy, a fellow short on stature who could barely reach the pedals, who rode a rented Harley-Davidson with no motorcycle experience or social conditioning, dangerous in curves, in the passing lane and in public. Full throttle on straightaways showed his skill. The swarthy little fellow was somebody's guest, because of potential sales contacts or something.

The second woman fell in with the little guy. They chatted. He moved close to her. They made out—tongue thrusters. Harry Woo scooted back, leaned forward and puked between his legs. Coming up flush he said it wasn't them; he'd smoked a cigarette, his first cigarette ever; it had seemed so right.

The scene was off, as in off-kilter, a distortion that fit the misadventure, the extreme heat and cold, a road fund facilitating drunkenness in a weft and warp on nature and culture. By morning the little guy strolled the parking lot hand in hand with his date.

She'd given him a terrific discount, and he wasn't even from Canada. After farewells and promises to do it again, some time, he swaggered triumphantly into the dining room to announce, "I got my road name." Nobody looked up from his eggs. "I'm gonna be Sparky."

"No. We got a Sparky. You're Whoredog." The dour breakfast crowd laughed.

Whoredog smiled, frowned, smiled again, frowned again and twisted to full throttle on a final smile, as if to force the beat upwards. That night, a few hundred miles down the road a cafe owner happily engaged our group of hail-fellows drinking top drawer liquor, when into a lull barreled the little man: "You know, I get a taste for pussy when I'm on the road. You know where I can get some pussy around here? I had some last night, and there's nothing worse than a little taste to make you crazy for some more." Humanity bemoaned itself in excruciating silence.

Since it was Elko, Nevada, the little man got served just up the street. We waited in the bar, where his date emerged in flimsy negligee and moved lightly for such a heavy, worn woman. With practiced mystique she drifted to the beat of a different violinist. The dour drinking crowd moaned. In an artistic striptease she playfully revealed her rebuilt torso and multiple stab wounds. She scanned above and beyond the fray, perhaps seeking greater appreciation of her skills from the more sophisticated men in the bleachers. But there weren't no bleachers. Whisking a frilly scarf from her lower self, she looked startled and then demure, till an acerbic fellow belched and called out, "That thing looks like a carwash mitt!"

The evening's entertainment ended on a huff. Whoredog sauntered out swinging his arms wide like President George W. Bush, and in a victorious baritone ordered the king of beers.

That was a highlight of the year of Whoredog. Sitting out was easy. What was to miss? I sat out for years and would sit again in a rare actual feeling of win/win. I called a Triumph dealer outside Seattle. He had two in stock but this was not happening.

For starters, daily mileage ranged three fifty to four fifty.

Posing macho is one thing; teasing death with bad judgment is another. Acuities diminish in the cold. Joints stiffen. You get cold and lose your shit. Hands go numb. Core heat drops to the verge of hypothermia. The trembles feel like bad bearings. Approximation loosens up. The odds on rider mishap swing dramatically to favor the house on long, cold miles. Numbness moves south from the ass, till a foot couldn't feel the ground if it had to. Depth perception and reaction time follow in short order, till the laws of physics enforce the death sentence.

They say freezing is a painless death; drowsy goes to sleep. How bad could that be? But on a motorcycle the crash would wake you just in time for the pain. Nobody has the riding chops they had in '69 or '81, and every trip had its near-death encounters or, in road talk, close calls. They became part of the bullshit spume, as if getting a load off a chest could displace the lingering fear. A common close call was shooting the gap, passing Pa Kettle over the double yellow into oncoming traffic in time to avoid the cream, but even on a shortfall you could always squeeze in there. You might get tagged by a mirror, or thwacked with an air pocket if the oncoming was a truck.

Ha! Man! Fuck!

Stupid, stupid, and everyone knew it, especially those who nearly left it out on the road. Drifts and short calls, close shaves and miscalls made us smart enough to doubt the margins even as they shrank. Road wisdom leads to patience. A rider can lay back, but the near-death tally never goes to zero.

But then other traffic comes on frightfully fast and feels like impact may be unavoidable: decrepitude, assisted living, death by boredom. Difficult thoughts accompany the aging process. It's natural, just as a traveler wonders how much farther, and what comes next. Nobody wants to dwell on the end or what waits yonder. Why not pass in a Barcalounger instead of French kissing a Mack truck at eighty?

Was I afraid of the Smoker? May be. But only a fool would mount up for a long haul without knowing what might kill him. Fear has always seemed like a first component of courage—but close calls paled next to angina, which is not where babies come from but what takes Daddy away. What came next was not the big one but gallbladder inflammation. A big, greasy stone jammed the bile duct at intervals, like a truck parked on the rib cage and backing onto the sternum to offload hot oil—beep, beep, beep. A stuck gallstone feels like a coronary thrombosis, because the gallbladder is next to the heart and pumps bile that can't get out, because the stone is in the way. On the bright side, a man *in the pink* should remain vital, with the gallbladder removed.

"There's really nothing to it," the doctor said. "Unless we get in there and find the thing attached to your liver. Then we have to open things up and cut it off. It must come out."

Most people survive a nothing to it surgery. U.S. Congressman and generally good guy Jack Murtha was vital but did not survive. His inflamed gallbladder got infected—infection is tough. He may have resisted surgery as many do, because gallbladder attacks come and go. And surgery can kill you. Jack was a Vietnam veteran, seventy-seven already.

Given a time and season to every purpose at a breakneck pace, life can lock up its rear wheel on reflection. Mind follows body sooner or later in a lose/lose process—unless you let go, have faith and give peace a chance.

Now where were we: motorcycles, whoredom, time and relative value? Yes, and money—George the broker in synchronous convergence called for quarterly assessment, opening as usual on the The Materialist's Golden Rule: "The one thing you don't want to do is outlive your money." Except that this quarter seemed different, with so much time spent harking back to youth that had seemed eternal not so long ago.

"But I do."

"Oh, man," he moaned, like I wasn't getting the picture. "Listen: old age doesn't mix well with poverty."

"I get the picture, George. If I end up broke you think I should drop dead and be grateful. Fuck that, George. What I don't want to outlive is my vigor." *In the pink* had become my mantra.

George didn't want to condescend but explained age and money. "Your vigor will fade. With money you'll have the best medical care."

"You mean I can live like a lump as long as my bankroll holds up?"

"Yes! And you can live well, even as a lump."

"George. People around the world have no money and aren't ready to die because of it. Some people value spirit more than money. In some cultures, comfort is set aside to better seek spiritual light." George sighed over irrelevance to strategic financial assessment.

"I think you know what I mean," he said.

"I'm afraid your meaning may not be my meaning. I hope you learn the difference before or after your money runs out. But fuck all the death talk, George. Make me some money." So we got down to oodles of moolah at last as the best distraction.

Strategic financial assessment felt like a hairpin turn near the pass. George shuffled mutual funds with forgettable names, each one a letter or syllable different from the others. George sold a shitload of some and bought a shitload of others and in no time the numbers rolled like an electric meter with the AC on High Cool and the windows open. But gains felt like nothing, because you must sell the little blips to realize the gain. Short of a sale, positions merely improve. Was I in the position?

By the next quarter, positions weakened. George wailed, "Stay in!" I frankly didn't care. I could stay in and watch my position improve or deteriorate and feel nothing either way. The numbers rose and fell with numbing failure to change anything, to feel better or worse or in the least consequential. And he could not say how these numbers representing an idea of money could rise and fall and feel so ungodly different from the buck fifty an hour I turned on hash slinging and pearl diving forty-five years ago. Those dollars had dynamic value, spendable on the celebration of life with a hard-driving downbeat on a blood surging rhythm and a gang of friends discovering the world and ourselves.

How can things change so much and then poof, be gone? People stay hungry for meaning and lasting value.

A surgery coming up would require anesthesia, which shuts down the five physical senses, except for pulse and breath. The edge of death seemed a decent vantage point from which to look into the abyss. The character of the void seemed obvious, but it seemed a good time to look. Near-death experience commonly occurs above the scene, often with friends and family gathered below in loving company, encouraging the near-deather to descend back to the body to live a while longer.

The elevated view suggested a new sensory function engaged in passing. The unconscious person could have imagined the scene from above and then remembered the scene, maybe. A spirit has no eyes in the conventional sense but it might see by other sense. Dolphins "see" with sonar, proving non-ocular vision. Why not humans?

"Is out-of-body experience possible under general anesthesia?" I asked the anesthetist while rolling into the operating room, a harshly lit chamber with no windows and many instruments. Bacteria must have been discouraged by the freezing cold. I was.

The anesthetist murmured directions to the nurses then instructed me to transfer myself from the gurney to the table. The table, colder still, was narrow enough to fit between shoulder blades. A nurse covered me with a quilt that felt fresh from a hot drier. "Thank you," I said. She smiled warmly.

Another guy leaned over my face from the top for that odd appearance of talking upside down. "Here's the part you'll love…"

Wait a minute. Is he the anesthetist? "Do you think a spirit can ride a motorcycle? I mean sense riding a motorcycle?"

Fuck. It was the same as dead, and I wasn't ready. Well, you don't gain insight in giant steps. I should have known. Dylan Thomas woke in the night with *the answer* but forgot by morning. So he put a piece of paper and a pen on the nightstand, and when the answer came again the next night, he wrote it down. Jubilant, he went back to sleep with the answer secure, and in the morning read: *Green cheese.*

Spirits can ride motorcycles. Spiritual senses align for a feeling that is greater than the sum of its parts. The act of riding engages spirits. Unique dimensions overlap—feelings test a theory, and the data proves that time and money unspent are forfeit forevermore.

Could the theory be worthless as a gallbladder? Or could it tap into mobility in a limitless universe?

Gallbladders are not worthless. Some must come out, but the dog will keep hers as long as she can.

What occurs to a spirit in life is the same as what occurs to that spirit after, call it an old familiar movement. That which is known is the best base for jumping off the edge of the tangible world into what is not known. Or riding off.

Motorcycle Resolved

FUCK, I DIDN'T know. And who cared anyway?

Who needed that heady, depressing shit with a motorcycle trip to plan?

Well, it was easy, dismissing Harley Davidson for Triumph. But it was time to move on—or get back. Less was more with half the weight at half the price and twice the performance.

Freedom from embarrassment felt like a bonus—who wouldn't want away from a dog 'n pony circus played out by a fat-gut wanna-be crowd and a bunch of V-neck *poseurs*? The transition felt uplifting, lean and mean as a skinny kid scrambling for the whole wide world out of split-level confinement. The suburbs are comfortable and Harleys are fun, primitive and heavy with poor build quality and a silly scene. Freedom from the lifestyle, the merchandizing and the imagery felt like a hard won victory, and there we were again.

Surviving surgery hones the appetite for a ride. Cold, wet weather seemed less threatening post-op.

I cancelled again on seeing the itinerary. The road captain called to urge, "Come on, man!" The tedium came back in numbing clarity.

"No. Are you crazy? Four-fifty a day? That's torture."

"Most days are only three-fifty. You can do that."

"I can ease a broomstick up my ass too. We've done three-fifty plenty. And four-fifty. It hurts. It's far enough to guarantee a mountain pass—or three mountain passes. It hurts in nice weather. In cold and rain it's torture. Not once, ever, was it fun or enjoyable."

"That was miles. This is kilometers."

"This is kilometers?"

"Yeah, man. Come on!"

"Oh."

Let's see: point six times three-fifty is two-ten. Four-fifty would be two-seventy. Hmm. That might do, with a comfort quotient extrapolating from two hundred fifty miles requiring x energy to three fifty at 2x, more or less, depending on weather, curvature and delays. And age. Four-fifty would run $2x^2$. "You're saying the daily mileage—that's mileage, as in miles—will run two-ten to two-fifty?"

"Yes? You can do this!"

"Maybe. Let me think… Why kilometers?"

"British Columbia, man. BC bud!"

Pipes, bags and a windshield came in under a grand—what Harley Davidson wanted eighteen hundred for, not counting the taillight and installation.

Perception wobbled for another week of pro and con—on the one hand, but on the other hand. I studied the map for easy outs and shortcuts home, till things solidified on another phone call.

"Hey, what are you doing?"

"Oh, hey. I'm just sitting here. What are you doing?"

"Do you remember driving me to the airport and giving me five hundred dollars to use for emergency?"

"Yeah. You used that money to buy that *thing*."

"What thing?"

"That motorcycle."

"Very good. You're not senile. Do you realize what time it is?"

"You mean here or there?"

"That was forty years ago."

"No it wasn't."

"Yes it was. I need another five hundred."

"You're not."

"I think I am."

"You said you were done with that."

"I thought I was, like you thought you were done after your second marriage."

"That was different."

"How?"

"I'm not playing games here."

"Oh. Well, anyway. I'm going again."

"I wish you wouldn't."

"Of course you do. You wish I was at your place, sitting on the couch watching TV and eating two-handed. Playing it safe."

"What's wrong with that?"

"It would be more dangerous than a motorcycle trip."

"I don't know how you can say that."

"Because I would have hung myself by now."

She laughed. Old mom had turned ninety-one—a hundred fifty-two in kilometers—but she could still parry and thrust. "You said you weren't going. It's dangerous, and in case you haven't noticed, you're not as young as you used to be."

"Yes I am. You're older. Not me."

"Have it your way."

"Thank you. I think I will."

Besides wit, old mom still had instinct; waning youth wasn't the half of it. I feared—or rather anticipated—lower energy reserves than in the past, along with muscle spasm between the shoulder blades, cramping in the hips and bloating in the gut.

On the other hand, with age and seasoning came insight to herbs and supplements. Not reefer—I knew enough to shun the reefer until inside a fifty-mile radius of the destination, and even then keeping intake to one hit. Okay, maybe two. But no more than two hits and most definitely not four. That would be crazy, no matter how wild the times got or how high the sky seemed.

What a laugh it was, not so many years ago, when consensus ruled that road smoke would be limited to working gauge and the Aztec Ceremonial shit would wait till the last fifty miles. What a reasonable concept, rendering out-of-body experiences that may have been near-death in their own right. Hands worked clutch, brake and throttle with no input from telemetry, keeping things between the ditches with intricate timing in the purple haze, as if they had a mind of their own, along with the feets working the shifter and the back brakes.

The working gauge rule was another sentiment of denial—we weren't even fifty and felt young. Fuck. But free will and motivation converge in youth to a point. Then comes the blessed infusions of road wisdom and most clear alignment of values—then begins the divergence, in which body follows mind only on a slower tempo.

The herbologist recommended electrolyte drops to maintain optimal energy and avoid mineral depletion. Dehydration is a challenge on any outing, but plain water won't restore minerals and salts. One drop of electrolyte elixir per ounce of water preserves equilibrium. Energy is also enhanced with red ginseng, two caps daily. Ibuprofen eases cramping and a muscle relaxant inhibits spasm, but the muscle drug was only for nighttime ingestion. Daytime could bring the ditches into hazardous focus. Finally, a digestive enzyme with meals keeps the dukey chute lively, so the meat and French fries wouldn't stack up.

A plastic tub in the garage opened like a tomb on old leathers, mildewed but supple, soon aired and cleaned. Foul weather gear, gloves, gussets, boots, scarves and stuff from years in the saddle rose from the folds to wake up and embrace the rider one more time, maybe with a tad too much emotion—tighter in the waist and looser in the shoulders.

The fuck?

The question is rhetorical but suggested yet another alteration in reality. Old enough for elderly discount at the movies, on buses and in some museums, I viewed age as seasoning. The old days weren't so long ago—I don't mean the old, old days, but the recent, old days. Not even two decades ago I rode my first Road King around the state of Washington casually as some people head to town for groceries. The North Cascade Loop ran a hundred sixty-five miles over the mountains to Winthrop for lunch with the Canucks, who rode down from Lake Cristina about the same distance. The Loop gave us rain out of Seattle easing to partly cloudy near Arlington, and up to sunshine on the pass with sweltering heat on the far side. After lunch with friends, the Loop went on around, home by dusk.

Another run across the North Cascades would be a first step back. I forgot the twenty-mile freeway scream up from Everett to Arlington, but it wasn't so bad and not too loud with the Harley-Davidsons in back. The country road to the mountain remained free of development, and a biker bar on the outskirts of nowhere looked laughable. Many times we backed to that curb and bowlegged in for beer, low-rent ambience and the sheer raw camaraderie of men bonding on common values, like hunky cams, loud pipes, low-end torque, custom paint, pussy jokes and jukebox tunes.

Years later it seemed parochial and quaint, like a scene in binoculars viewed from the front. The massive power station at the foot of the pass still buzzed. Third-gear curves along the mountain felt easier, not so jerky and freer of close calls. Long straightaways through the forest felt shorter. Maybe it was the better ride, balanced and lighter, no bulldogging required. Maybe it was less dope, fewer stops, lower speed, and time passing more evenly on fewer thrusts. Or maybe it was more scenery and less scene.

What about the Triumph? Like all things anticipated, it was more and less. Flawless fit and finish, superb handling and responsive tracking made a blink as good as a nod. Taking five hundred pounds through the curves instead of nine hundred made for joy instead of work. At sixty it wanted seventy and leaned into eighty. Ninety came on a perfect sweep along the Salmon River in Idaho. Twenty miles of it connects White Bird to Riggins Hot Springs, so a hundred was easy with an inch of throttle to go. But a hundred was plenty and helped round the cogs, tame the gear dogs and ease things in. Decelerating from a hundred, eighty-five felt eerily slow. Did I already feel that, forty years ago?

So far so good, but judgment would come at motorcycle Mecca: Lolo Pass, a hundred twenty miles connecting western Montana to eastern Idaho. Lolo is revered. After Labor Day, Lolo is empty. A road sign on the Montana end states the rider's prayer:

S
Winding Road Next 120 Miles

Lolo Pass is engineered to curve through nature's grandeur on a spiritual banking that embraces every rider. Warm, crisp air and rustling trees or rain and mists; all connect the rider to the place. All components flow through Lolo. The road follows a river and feels like life.

Spirits linger at Lolo, beckoning and receiving till goose bumps rise from head to toe. Spontaneous war cries rise at Lolo, where we ride again together, warrior brothers of the ages. We die in a wave of civilization and cry out for what was and yet could be.

The blood-and-guts Harley Davidson guys made fun of the Speedmaster, calling it a Mixmaster or a good ride for a crack addict. But blood-and-guts was a show, a shallow rumble of tall tales in the drunken half-light of a smoky reverie. Most tales were of past Smokers, told and confirmed by liars who were there. Short of road tales, any macho bullshit would do.

I rode casually around seventy-five, but that seemed hurried. Sixty-five felt right. The Canadians grew up with a dollar discounted to seventy-six cents, often less—and a ninety day riding season. None went to college. But they'd had no war to dodge, so things evened out, more or less. They spent money in two columns: liquor and reefer on the one hand, chrome and cubic inches on the other. Many went to jumbo jugs, a hundred ten cubes to the pair. Nearly all had chrome pegs or chrome floorboards or chrome floorboard inserts, chrome passenger pegs and pushrod sleeves, chrome grips and header bolt covers. Chrome and muscle were a motif for the Canadians, and they parked their rides in a casual array of chrome muscle in any parking lot to take a break and break out the B.C. bud and mix up the cocktails—in glasses with ice, in a catalogue shot for a lifestyle market—a shot surely censored by Harley Davidson.

Cocktails in the parking lot were nice at the end of a ride. Most guys wanted to shower or lie down or check their messages or call the kids. Not these guys—hanging in the parking lot was like lingering on the road, kind of going that extra mile on a pic a nic for alcoholics. Drinking, smoking, leaning on their rides, remembering binges and wild pussy, these guys could hang and shoot the shit for hours. The road bond was bliss with no work today or tomorrow. It couldn't get much better, except maybe in a few hours when they could get really fucked up and find some trouble to get into and maybe get laid. Road romance was rare, but the old stories got dusted and buffed, stretched and swollen. Hope sprung eternal, even in Canada. Besides, what can you do, *ey*? Go to bed?

They lived at maximum macho, looking down their noses when we agreed to hit a few bars. We walked; they rode. Around the corner, down a block and down twelve steps to the bar, they rode. We quit by midnight. They hit every motherfucking stop till the last light went out, night after night. When a female went along for one ride or another, they would crowd around, move in, press for new limits in the sexual anarchy universe, as new yarns would spin. But the women had also aged and in time they too turned in early or died off or laughed out loud. New honeys replaced the old, but what would any honey want with a gang of drunk and crusty old guys?

Events occur in threes. A few years prior we'd met Kevin, a likeable, self-possessed guy, or so it seemed. Kevin had seven earrings on one ear, eleven on the other and tattoos like a NASCAR racer, with crawlies up the neck and out a bushy eyebrow and Maori patterns across the chrome dome. His biker duds were sleeveless in leather or denim, and shirtless. Last, but in no way motherfucking least, the ride: a hardcore Softail in gold-sparkle green with massive chrome and a double-stack calliope carburetor like a milk bucket with jets on the end to force feed the power plant down to monster megaphone pipes that could drown out a steel foundry. The package may have been a setup on a change of pace; Kevin was so soft-spoken and well-mannered. Maybe the package was to balance the softness. Speculation came later.

The night of our gathering, Smoker Eve, Kevin drank in the lead, bonding till daybreak. Not to worry, ninety minutes of sleep would be plenty for three hundred fifty miles of desert, mountain pass and high plateau—if a man was a biker and a Canadian, *ey*. He only needed a quick stop at a drugstore for some of that stay awake shit, a half bottle or so oughta do it.

Bug-eyed and twitchy, Kevin rode well enough for forty-five minutes out of town to the first sweeps that soon tightened, rising to the pass. A few guys had an eye on him, but when his head wobbled, his loud laugh let them know: didn't mean shit, not if a man was… yadda yadda.

By the sweeps everyone was deep inside and outside; this is what we came for. Blue sky, sunbeams, charged air, a thousand moving parts coherent as a babbling brook converged on a greater flow. We climbed to the third sweep, where Kevin eased over to the shoulder and a sand drift, till his wheels broke loose. He went down flailing, bouncing, skidding, breaking ribs, puncturing a lung, trashing his ride and hanging things up for the three hours it took to get the ambulance and flatbed in, and Kevin and his motorcycle out.

Kevin never came back. His neighbor, Gino Marcione, had invited him on the ride and after his low-speed crash caused by sleep deprivation and a NoDoz OD, Kevin fell out with Gino. Why? Gino said, "Fuck if I know why. Guy must be a prick or something."

And that was the end of that, till a few years down the road on an understated sweep at low-speed just after lunch, when Gino drifted off the shoulder and went down. I saw Gino two years later and asked what happened. "Fuck if I know. Fucking road just...fucking disappeared." Gino was succinct on a tender subject he'd cogitated many times, pressing for the why with the most difficult follow-up: could it happen again? Gino was the second guy.

Anyone with a few miles or a hundred thousand knows it can end in a blink. With a few seasons in all conditions you think you can avoid it—or avoid the avoidable at any rate. But you know the rule of the road: shit happens. You take a calculated risk by first calculating the risk. Details in stories of crashes usually involve at least one of four factors: youth, speed, liquor and urban traffic. Car creaming is a major threat and can happen anywhere, often in the left-turn lane, while you wait.

The boys didn't scoff at safety but did not want to appear overly concerned. They would rant and rave about the blind bitch who came in for the kill. Safety stops allowed for sharing thoughts on road hazards to keep everyone alert and stoned.

What? A bunch of guys on motorcycles are supposed to stand around with no dope? That wouldn't be likely. But a seasoned rider processes stimulants better than an unseasoned rider. It goes to second nature. The calculated risk is weighed against the jackpot payout of joy in movement. With acceptable odds, you make the bet. These and other thoughts and joints pass round the safety stop.

Riding is solitary, no camp songs or talk. You can pull alongside and yell, but meaningful dialogue is with the self. A rider on back, often a wife, may complain about the cold and the leaning, but the seasoned rider will not have a passenger on a long haul. You remember things while riding, things to share at the next safety stop, like the time so-and-so got shit-faced and saw this woman at the bar. Turns out she's a nun, one of those civilian clothes nuns, and he asks if she wants to...

So many miles, stories, meals and joints make for kinship. Common experience is a bond on beauty and bad weather, on close calls, long hauls, buffalo in the road, a bear on a bluff, elk on a hill. Big trucks blow retreads at high speed with lethal shrapnel. The boys know this but still pass, each taking a turn with faith in the road gods, downshifting, goosing to the power arc and shooting the gap in gratitude for money well spent on bigger cams and jugs. The other boys see. They feel and know.

I didn't press Gino on details. Sudden impact can erase short-term memory. Or maybe he still sorted his odds on survival. He may have known why he crashed, but riders keep rider error to themselves, in another solitary place.

The Senior Discount

BULLDOGGING THE BEAST hard over could not prevent the wheels from easing over the double yellow, because every curve reaches a point of no return, especially a curve that runs deep and laughs at all your miles and seasoning and road wisdom. Don't mean shit, bound for pavement, crunch time.

A collapsing curve can convict the defendant on a violation of the laws of physics. Enforcement is strict and harsh. The big difference between four wheels and two is between steering and leaning. Steering is fundamental, leaning intuitive. Another big difference should be obvious but can require learning: that four wheels can stop from high speed in a straight line. Two wheels can't, or won't. Ditching speed quickly can save a rider; sudden braking can challenge a rider's health. Engine braking is vital. Throttling down in anticipation of need will reduce speed internally rather than at the friction points. But the squirrelly stuff sets in if you go too slow so far over into a curve. You'll lay it down without the umph to the back wheel, so you goose to hold the line, but you need to pull things back inside the double yellow. You bear down on the bars even as you scrape pavement, even as you know that things just don't aim to work out this time.

With an SUV oncoming and bearing down, life/death decisions transcend logic and rationale. The passionate moment defers to instinct, striving for minimal loss, deferring to life and limb, even in the severely depressed, which I wasn't. In defense of rider skill— my skill—I will say that the error did not occur on my Triumph but on a ride that will remain unnamed, a heavy cruiser weighing nearly nine hundred pounds with a V-twin engine. It could have been a Harley clone. All the Japanese manufacturers were building to the

V-twin market, and two guys rode them, one a Yamaha, the other a Kawasaki. So maybe I traded with one of them. What difference could a tank emblem make?

It's common to trade for a stretch, especially on unique new scooters so different from the norm.

Jerry from Kelowna rode the extreme opposite of my Triumph, a heavier shade of heavy with gross power. We'd struck a friendship, talking about livelihood and what a man must do. Jerry called himself a jackoff all trades, cobbling a few bucks here and there, turning back. His odometer aptitude had earned good money for years, beginning with his first motorcycle.

After a hundred thousand clicks he buffed that old motorcycle till it shone. But with all those clicks showing, the trade-in value was still low. Easy enough, he took apart the odo through the traps and lockouts on mileage wind-down—deconstructing down to the little solder points on gossamer-thin foil, sealing layers of mechanism. It was surgical, penetrating to the nerve center to take years off the life of his very used scoot. At a different dealer he traded for twice the first offer. "Hell, even if a guy had to spend the money to put in new jugs he'd still have a great ride."

The first mark of a true thief is his ready rationale. Jerry's resume was peppered with logic, reason and good deals, really, through years of ever more challenging odometers. Hardly circumspect, he got a reputation, and customers came from miles around. "Fuck. Two, three hundred bucks, I'd wind 'em back a hundred grand. It doesn't matter—if a car or a motorcycle is a piece o' shit, it'll show anyway. I did a couple junkers but then decided not to do that anymore. If a car is in good shape, the mileage doesn't matter. I never fucked anybody. They were all good cars. Ran great."

I couldn't really trust Jerry, and his circus wagon of a ride ran like a semi with rocket thrusters. It looked frightening in curves—a fear that proved correct. But I gave him the nod when he wondered aloud just how crazy it would feel to ride something half as big with the same power to weight ratio. Pride is not a virtue.

Heads turned for my response, as if Jerry had offered alternate sexual relations. The wry eye of the Canuck contingent followed the volley. "What? You guys think Jerry wants an anal romance? You got the V-twin addiction. Your nuts are sagging halfway to your knees, and all you can come up with is bigger engines."

Har har. What a laugh. So Jerry and I would trade for a stretch. For me it was a whack off the tee on hugeness at a hundred-ten horsepower. It all came back in a curve or two, the weight, the folding, the bulldogging. Like anything, you adapt to make it easier, give a little more here, hold in some there. I didn't get cocky but that didn't matter; I went into a tight one, misjudged by a freckle on a gnat's ass on the hundred-ten horses and went over my head. No biggy, I'd just, er, oh...

A seasoned rider survives by application of basics, like braking. Front and rear brakes must apply together, but the back brake can be lethal. Bicycle riders fear front braking—stopping the front wheel of a twenty-two pound machine at speed can throw a rider over the handlebars. But a motorcycle is hundreds of pounds, and it's the back brake that can eject a rider in a phenomenon called high-siding. If the back wheel locks in braking, the tire skids. If the brake is released in that skid, the rig will spring the other way like a boulder from a catapult. High-siding must be avoided.

But drastic conditions call for drastic measures. I stomped to lock the rear wheel. Into the skids I pop-released, springing back to vertical and then some, which meant laying it down the other way. What an immortal moment, actually planning best conditions for a lay down. But the cliff wall to the inside did seem the lesser of two evils. Nobody talks about a controlled high side—I made it up on the split second, savoring the admiration of peers over a cold one only an hour up the road. At least I wouldn't eat a gob full of grill. But too far over, low enough to go under the oncoming SUV, this move looked bound for greasy mangle. Ha! Except that the boneshaker between my legs wouldn't fit under there. Well, maybe it would fit with enough momentum.

Another critical skill is push steering, whereby a motorcycle does not align with the rider into a curve but is pushed into the curve via the low end of the handlebars. Push steering separates the posture of the rider, which remains more vertical, from that of the machine, which is pushed down into the curve. Push steering can feel like steering in the wrong direction, pressing the bars to the left in a hard right curve. Given the hang of it, push steering can get a rider through far tighter curves at speed than body alignment steering. The vast majority of riders in non-fatal motorcycle crashes never heard of push steering.

I knew all about it.

Jerry stands out for a crowning achievement: he didn't wreck my Triumph. I drove his rig over a cliff. It's amazing, what fits into a fleeting moment, and how two moments forty years apart were as one. Time slows down, making plenty of room for regrets, hopes and dreams, with a niggling caveat that nothing will stop this action from going down.

The first such warp came in 1970, doing a hundred ten on a Daytona 500, the twin carb Triumph, slightly smaller than the Bonneville. You can't help catching slower traffic at that speed. Okay, you keep your wits. Pass like you should. But a truck threw a pebble that grew into a rock and then a boulder till a megalithic asteroid was screaming toward Earth. It passed in a flash on a push to the opposite side as the truck flashed pass. I tried a harder push forty years later to get around an SUV but not to the inside because of the rocky cliff. It seems irresponsible for anyone to go one ten on a scooter doing LSD, even in 1970. But a young man can take psychedelics better than an aging rider can pull rabbits out of his ass on an intentional high side with a goose and a push. Now that was radical. And so it went, over the falls.

Shit. Motherfuck.

I must have shucked clear, deferring again to instinct. Bouncing down the slag until the old bones came to a stop in two piles: one a clutter of stone axes in chrome, the other a road warrior in denial.

Then came the days and weeks slowing to hours and moments with far less passion. Tic. Toc.

Recovery time can be productive and free of Pollyanna optimism. It can seek a better mode of consciousness. Would I make the same effort at self improvement if I were up and about, tempted by daily life and its blandly satisfying distraction? The attending physician's nametag says Tsadik below the Hebrew letter called tsadik, צ, used for the ts sound. Tsadik is also a Hebrew word for persons of spiritual renown. How did I know that? Well, in fact I didn't know that, but then I did.

Tsadik watched me blink and said: intermittent coma.

I take long naps in conformance to diagnosis. He may be wrong. My naps can be dreamy. I also doubt his skepticism on complete recovery. Physician, cover your ass. Isn't that what they teach you in med school?

Many agree that the puzzle parts may soon fit together. They chat like I'm not there, and when my wife does the wifely thing—not *the* wifely thing; come on—of bending from the opposite side of the bed to murmur lovely thoughts on improvement and eternal love, the doctor cops a tit shot, like I can't see what he's doing. Why would she come to the hospital in a loose blouse with no bra? Oh, you don't have to be dead to be forgotten.

But I can't complain for lack of visitors. They're comforting, even if a nuisance otherwise. The trouble is, I can't tell coma from coherence. Self-tests help, but I'm clever enough to cheat and pass. That is, how could Betty Boop know of my accident and condition? How low are the odds that she called or found out? Why would she come see me? Well, I knew why, after all. It was the love all around us, maybe just the love in and out of us, but that counts.

Betty was living in Utah but not as a Mormon, and not with a Mormon, at least not with a practicing Mormon. Not by a long shot. Her new man saw the light on that situation years ago. Besides, what was she supposed to do, share him with a few wives? If anything, she'd need a few husbands to soak up all the love she had to spare.

Ha! I think maybe I should be a Mormon. You know what I mean? I think you do.

I did.

Betty apologized for visiting Hawaii a few years back and not calling. She wanted to call. What harm in old friends saying hello? But her date was so insanely jealous that she couldn't call.

I honestly think he'd never had what I showed him, and that made him insanely jealous, because he inferred that every one of my men had got the same treatment. The last thing he wanted was for me to call you. You know what I mean? Next thing you know I'd be telling him we were going to grab some lunch, just you and me.

Jealous? Just you and me? We got it on forty years ago. Besides, all your men did get the same treatment.

I know. It was a long time ago, but it sure feels like yesterday. Okay, like last week. Ha! And no, bubby, they didn't all get the same treatment. Give yourself some credit. Okay? Gee, it's good to hear your voice.

Can you hear my voice?

Why shouldn't I hear your voice? They say you have a great chance to recover. I'll come back and see you then. Okay?

I'm married. Didn't you meet Rachel on the way in? Where did she go?

No, I didn't meet her. But I got an eyeful of her. How do I know where she went? Maybe she couldn't stand up to the competition. Maybe she's copping a quickie with the doctor. He's a hunk. Now I could show him a treatment or two. You know what I mean? Hey, I'm joking. I don't mean we're going to get hot and heavy, you and me. That's for sure. But we can get lunch, can't we? Remember when we used to get lunch?

I cannot remember lunch with Betty Boop, ever. She often took a taxi to the house near bedtime as a surprise and crawled in alongside just for fun. Or was it forty-five years ago? Maybe she wanted to see who else she might find there, so she could yell at me, because we weren't getting married, so it was then or never on rough love with a possible ménage. But I digress. We had no lunch or frolic anytime other than dark. She was engaged with appearances to maintain. She had me confused with somebody else. It happens.

Especially with Betty, she was so promiscuous. Then again, people tell stories of great times among friends—of when we all laughed and had such fun, and I can't access a single frame. They look at me like I'm nuts. Maybe I am, but those stories are nearly always pointless and forgettable, so maybe I did forget. Good for me. But lunch with Betty? Never. It was late night academia, period. The end.

You used to get so mad that a deli in the Midwest would have the chutzpa to sell cheese blintzes that tasted like day-old dreck. That's what you said. You swore up and down that your mother's were so much better. I got the cheese blintzes every time, just to get a rise out of you—that wasn't too hard to do, if you know what I mean. I think you know what I mean. I thought they were delish.

Betty Boop had great skills, chief among them a charm and fluid beauty classically framed and leading post-haste to everyman's fantasy. She begged the question: is this actually happening to me? Well, of course it was, because life is full of extremes, good and bad. We know this truth to be self-evident, but a young man still feels blessed, as it were.

I wanted to nestle and caress my private Boop while we waited recovery. It didn't take long back then, but she made it weird with a little routine. On an exhale and a burp, like a gouty patrician after a feast, she'd lick her chops and say *that was delish*. She made a serene moment awkward with emphasis on her unusual tastes.

I never heard of a deli in the Midwest serving cheese blintzes. My mother made them once and they were okay, if you like crepes with cheesy stuff inside and sour cream on top. I don't.

After four or five decades I can't imagine Betty bending to the task again—then again, most people don't forget how. We'd curved a bit in the spine and were both a tad rounded in the shoulders, so she wouldn't have as far to go. Everybody gives in to gravity and gains weight. Everyone dries out—skin, hair, humor—but tender ministrations don't change, and you can't see rheumy eyes in the dark.

Oh, Betty, you are the greatest...

Wait a minute. That didn't happen. I'm in a hospital room. It's near dawn, judging by the slim light in the window that can't outshine the inflammation of this place. My nurse is attractive in her way, though not like Betty Boop—black hair gone to charcoal with dark eyes, olive skin and a figure more blatantly curved. Her nametag says Marisol, like the flame in Spain. It couldn't be, or seems unlikely. Marisol?

"Yes."

Are you from Spain?

"Yes." She's not surprised that I would guess Spain instead of Mexico. My pulse rises from seventy-eight to ninety-two, because she's pulled back my blanket and sheet as a mechanic might lift a hood on a vintage vehicle. With a washcloth she wipes the residue of Betty's visit, which obviously did not happen but just as obviously was different than a dream. I wonder if this dark-skinned nurse named Marisol is a dream, and I know she's not. She cleans my parts and must have put alcohol on the rag; so cold. Who could sleep through Betty Boop? Why would I dream that?

Are you from Pamplona?

She rinses the rag to finish the task, impressed by a debilitated man's profusion. Not as young as he used to be, but he's no dud on spermatozoa output. Surely she knows that some systems persist oppressively. Nurses are resigned to difficult truth. I wish she knew how much her care means to me. I wish she'd slow down and show more tenderness. Who could have foreseen that our glowing innocence creekside so far away and long ago would come to this?

Where were you? I waited for you by the creek. An hour I waited. I missed you. Do you remember when we met?

"Breakfast. You like oatmeal? It is good for you. You must eat. Then you get well. I will help you."

Isn't it odd, that the memories lasting longest are those of the caregivers? I didn't know decades ago that she was a caregiver. It couldn't have worked with Marisol and me, but I loved her.

And in a blinding realization I knew that it could have worked. The fuck. It did work, was working. Look at her. She cradles my head and spoons oatmeal into the mouth hole, loving me right back. I know that I will honor and obey her, till death do us part. See her catch the dribble and scrape it back up and into the hopper?

We often and easily imagined old age in the 60s, because a wizened self comes to mind on psychedelics—the alternate plane extrapolates freely on hidden data, granting perceptions otherwise unattainable. Probability goes to 100% on whatever you like. You can be Uncle Wiggly walking a crooked mile. Storybook imagery is as accessible as refracted light sparkling though a prism. It wasn't real, yet it survives that time.

The boomers graduated. The boomers got married, divorced and remarried. Some had grandchildren, and all learned to love the senior discount and would not mind bankrupting Social Security. Fuck you; we paid.

Marisol goes from the chin wipe to the rollover and ass wipe with the same wet rag. At least she got the order right. Was it a fresh rag? Well, the task is done. We adapt. What was once embarrassing becomes routine. But not Marisol; she's one in a million. Then again, most of them were great, given half a chance. A young fellow can forget to give a chance. Not to worry. They're here, waiting their turns. Now they'll get a chance to be great.

Who am I kidding? Maybe they won't take the chance. Would they come to make fun? Please. Maybe after my nap would be best. Or would that be after my nap within a nap, in a few hours or days or a week or two?

Denial is common in dreamtime. The subconscious grasps at a better truth. Dreamers pull out of a nosedive to level off and fly. A poor boy finds money in a pot with a rainbow sticking out. A dream can repair life, so that life can open and be good forever. So life can accept what will come, and be happy, no matter what.

My father and Flojo the cat stood before a coffin to sum things up. Empty and full are phases of the same transition. *Caterpillar sheds his skin to find the butterfly within.* That's a song. I know it. *First there is a mountain, then there is no mountain, then there is.*

The most compelling transition is bodily failure. Dr. King said, *Free at last. Free at last.* But it's a process.

A dreamtime stiffy is not the dependable stiffy of youth. Coma is also called a persistent vegetative state, but vegetables don't get stiffies. A man's first response to death is often the piss, shit and stiffy series. What's the diff between sleep and coma? Either one could be an attempt at bladder control, but a coma stiffy would have no romantic component—Boop came to me! I sleep, therefore I am.

What month is this?

Old Dad came around when Flojo died to take her along. He'd never mentioned cats when I was a kid. What got into him? Any shrink would tell you it was in me—but we share a common nature.

A seasoned dreamer develops control—pulling out of a fall, quelling the monster with a fade out. And stay out! My script is also a work in progress. To whit:

Here come Rianne, Rayanne and Rianan. Their buxom shape and graying visage may be a stereotype, and so is their singular warmth and fortitude. Who the hell is Rianan? She's from a Fleetwood Mack lyric with some odd syllables for a chorus. Okay, she has an aging cosmic vibe.

Hey, Rock 'n Roll. You look great, but don't lie to me. No smoke up the ass. Do you remember when I was skinny?

> *Oh, Juanita, oh, Juanita*
> *Oh, Juanita I call your name*

Gee, it's great to see you. It's good to know you care. I was just realizing how lovable the caregivers come to be...

Where are you going? Don't say your needs were met, that you must be... Wait...

Last night's ride was different—I say last night; it could have been between brunch and siesta or Thanksgiving and Chanukah. Tsadik speculates on REM behavior disorder, a more precise name for sleep-walking, or physically acting out on a dream script.

Marisol pressed, "How he can ride a motorcycle in a hospital? Is crazy."

"That's just it," murmured Tsadik. "He can't!" The verdict is final, even in the face of overwhelming evidence that I can.

Tread marks on the walls? Sheetrock gouged in the corners where I laid it over to get around? All night I rode, many laps around the room, a side run down the hall, a jaunt through the burn unit and radiology, up the stairs to the ICU and up again to the children's trauma unit, where the tykes watched, longing to join in.

It feels like the fix is on.

I need a nap, coming right up.

A little voice calls, *Sleep, my friend.*

It fades beneath the snoring of the fellow I've become.

Time Has Come Today

THE CHAMBERS BROTHERS said it best:

Mmuhh... Mmmmuuuuhhhh!

We laughed out loud. We'd hardly anticipated that Chambers Brothers' gut moan could be both prelude to a rock classic and our wakening moments in decades to come. Nothing new there: aging people wake up slow. Drudgery and fatigue take more time as I sit up forty and fifty years later, taking inventory on aches, daze, hangover and too much meat hanging up in the lower G.I. like tampons in a P-trap.

Damn.

Why did I do that?

I'll tell you why: it's because a rib-eye medium rare is tough to turn down after a long day in the saddle and a mountain pass to pucker the butthole on any rider on any scooter of any size. Turn down? Hell, it made perfect sense, like sundown at the end of a day. A sizzling rib-eye seemed fuckinay righteous after the sweeps and twisties at the heart of the Bitterroot range, the scent of it blending with heart-thumping vistas and a searing stretch of interstate over the top and down the backside at 11% grade. That's four lanes posted at seventy with brake failure warning signs every half mile giving distance to the next runaway bailout—gravel beds and drifts to bog a big rig to a dead stop without rolling it over, maybe.

The uphill rigs chugged about thirty, requiring the breakneck speeds downhill to make up for lost time and put these bennies to use—get outta my fuckin' way! The eight-mile drop to the flats was a white-knuck motherfucker with headers and fluky gusts that felt much different than French kids with pillows. Bouncers grabbed your lapels, shook you up and shoved you out the door if you came up on a big rig too close or you didn't. The slow lane averaged about seventy but got thick with traffic, and the passing lane ran eighty to one oh five.

Of course the slow lane wasn't too thick, and anybody could hang out with Ma 'n Pa Kettle, trudging along, covering miles slow and steady. I took a break with them for a minute or two, till it got too slow—till the younger guys pealed around a curve too far out front to ever catch.

Finally rolling in to Tony's ranch at the hot springs, kicking the stand out and leaning a ticking rig over felt like a pattern. Day's end and relief was a feeling of well-being, looking forward to a joint and a hot soak and a few beers and feasting with friends, road brothers in a daily reunion of the wholly alive. Hmm. Didn't die. Well done.

I would get through this and set motorcycling aside just like Old Mom predicted on the way to the airport that sad day long ago—set it aside with gratitude, all things considered.

I didn't want to drag my sorry ass off the thing, so I reached for composure, coordination and a lively step, like a man in the morning on a walk in the basil. Making the ranch and easing in and showering out and pounding enough beer, ibuprofen and reefer to trade one buzz for another and calm the wobbles made sense with a sizzling piece of red meat and a puddle of ketchup front and center—not something a man dove into by choice but rather fell into by sheer, raw momentum no less than gravity accumulated on that long stretch down. Top that with some sipping grade tequila to take the edges off just as so many edges had been beautifully honed, and available insights didn't only include the meaning of life but tapped into some impressive pleasure centers too, from which additional profound meaning could be drawn. That would be meaning on the spiritual plane beyond rationale or logic or the well-worn 20% of the human brain most often used—in most cases carelessly. That feeling was rare and needed savoring and development. It went beyond omniscience or presumption.

In those golden moments of perspective—those moments earned by whatever time was necessary to hone those edges—a person could see and know. Whatever was questioned could be known, not so much by way of an answer that seemed to fit in the conventional sense but by transcendence. We had arrived. That was not to say that it didn't mean shit, but as a matter of fact in that time and place…

It felt odd to realize that I'd come on that trip against better judgment, in denial, to use the popular jargon. But it felt right, because unique perspective often carries a price. I came in order to be in that place of knowing a thing or two, because I wanted to feel again like I'd done the right thing. A day up on two wheels for a few hundred blazing miles, a crazy mountain pass and a friendly race along the river topping us out at a hundred-five seemed fair. Monks meditate for days on end to gain similar states of consciousness—or at least consciousness as elusive and hard to come by. That was the long and short of it. That was why I came.

For all I know, which seems like so much and nothing at all, I came for an old feeling—one of those feelings that must change as the physical being changes, yet with age the appreciation is so much greater. You come to realize that knowing a thing often begins with immersion in that thing, and it's been a life of immersion.

Good flavor, good feeling and good company made it a rare evening to savor. Well, we survived, and every man among us knew without speaking it that the odds on surviving day six had lengthened severely over day one. We'd loosened the bindings and added sail in a freshening breeze. That's why I imbibed with no constraint, because I could, because the day was done, the miles run with no crashes or skids, and a swerve or two or near miss in the passing lane can shake up a beginner who doesn't understand the meaning of marginal clearance or the difference between high speed wobbles and incremental wind sheer, but we understood.

I promise that I won't ride like that again.

It was Central Idaho on a morning steeped in slows with pain coming on in headers, fluky gusts and pangs, like yesterday. Oh, God. Some guys time their longest pisses to know when a world record is being set. I wondered if I should have begun timing the interval between rolling the legs over the side and standing up. Should I have begun then? I wondered if setting that measure aside indicated an improving attitude.

What would be the point, other than recording another decline? Now where's that?

At.

I knew how to untangle the Gordian knot of inertia: slowly, one strand at a time. I also knew which strands came first but I needed a minute to sort them. I moved the first strand, rising and stepping to the sink to brush the teeth, but I stopped over the sink to wonder what the hell I could be thinking with a bladder so full it had kept me uncomfortable all the way through the prime filet of the entire night's slumber, five to seven. That was the first strand, the order of the thing, and I got it tangled.

The lizard drained for what was surely a world record piss as I wondered where was my watch to make it official. That had to be four minutes. But I was only fooling myself. Old guys piss longer because of reduced pressure and flow, because of the swelling prostate gland that impinges on the ureter, and no matter how many times the doctor sticks his thumb up your ass and squeezes, it will swell. Tequila, beer, red meat? Fuck.

Hey, when does a guy know he's in trouble? When he feels both the doctor's hands on his shoulders during the prostate exam. Joel stared, obviously wishing nobody would tell him that joke again. Joel is my doctor. He's only thirty-eight.

Back in Idaho I was getting a memo from the interior that seemed like a certain thumbs up on a turn and squat, and I couldn't help but wonder if my rib eye had been knocking cotton during my prime filet. And to what, Mother Nature, do I owe this honor?

I thought it was only a fart, and I'd be better off waiting on coffee, about a half pound of fresh fruit, a couple over easy, toast and some Tater Tots—hey, we were on the road, where you eat what's available— to establish adequate back pressure to jettison the entire load, because you don't really get a decent second chance, on the go with all those layers to peel off. Well, hell, things would be much easier today. But I went ahead with some tap water and a stool softener, single dose, to better manage the process and minimize collateral damage—as if the old dukey chute was a vintage unit itself, in need of meticulous care. Then again, there weren't no *as ifs* about it, and the exhilarating return is often as great—vintage cars and motorcycles, old assholes. What's the diff? Talk about a symptom of the aging process; you know you're getting old when getting lucky means success on a major dump. Pay attention. Don't squeeze. But don't linger.

I didn't crash. I only dreamed of crashing. I couldn't tell the difference anymore. Maybe I didn't want to. The fuck was that? Well, I knew what it was. It wasn't a subconscious fear of crashing. It was a subconscious fear of trading motorcycles with a crazy Canuck for a stretch and then crashing.

Marisol. Rayanne. Rianne. Betty Boop.

Of the whole bunch Betty's the only one I'd be able to find. She's way past sixty. I could call her. That would be fun—tell her I was still on two wheels in the wilderness, and I took a dump this morning to make an elderly motorcyclist proud. Wait—not proud. I didn't feel pride in my big dumps. It was purer than that. Pride is a vanity after all. It was more like happiness, because empty bowels meant another day of riding unencumbered. Hallelujah, I thought.

Let's see, I had the vitamins and mineral drops, the anti-inflammatories, the ginseng and the well-being tonic. It wasn't like rolling a wake-up before turning in, but ready to rock 'n roll is relative to output and need. And I was ready. Except that I had to call Rachel to let her know I didn't die yesterday. I should have called last night. I forgot. Fortified and suited up—boots, chaps and sun-screen—I carried my jacket, neck gusset, skull cap, gloves and shades down the hall and figured I wasn't so over the hill, first up, first out.

Down the stairs I wondered if I was still dreaming in the entry foyer. I stopped in the kitchen door to watch Kirk pour coffee, light a smoke, load his pipe and set it aside. He popped the aspirin bottle and shook four into his hand, down the hatch with a black coffee chaser. He fired the pipe. Canada sells codeine aspirin over the counter, underscoring national reason and mercy. He held a long hit from the pipe, savoring it till losing to a nasty cough. He covered with a drag of nicotine and another jolt of coffee, exhaling, relieved.

Kirk was in his skivvies and a t-shirt and looked ready for an oxygen tent and transfusion but not ready to ride. Stepping through the screen door he grasped a deck post to brace himself while hunching over and reaching deep on a formidable morning gob. He dug in, worked it up to ready and lobbed it in a lazy arc out to the dirt. He turned back when I poured my own cup and popped three special aspirins. I complimented his form through the arc and landing. He looked stupid and asked, "What?"

"Your gob. It held together."

"Oh, yeah. Thanks. I been working on it." We stood apart in morning postures of slovenly consciousness, reaching for wakefulness, and the embarrassment was mine to bear. I'd also forgotten that it was a lay day, the interlude most anticipated in the annual ride, the day of rest and recuperation. Kirk smiled, seeing that my forgetfulness was a symptom of age that well outpaced his symptoms of abuse, at least on one level. Kirk is fifteen years younger than me. He eyed me up and down and asked the universal question, "What the fuck?" He had tactfully avoided direct focus on my senility.

"I forgot," I said, feeling as ridiculous in riding gear as I ever felt dreaming of being the only guy naked in the hot tub. "What are you doing up so early?"

"Just enjoying the morning," he said, lighting the pipe again and passing it.

"What the fuck," I allowed, erasing more memory or maybe jogging it, then slipping out of my chaps and heading back up for my shorts and flops. I called Rachel, which was best after coffee, really. She wanted to know how it was, so I told her about the long descent and stiff breezes like pillows at full force and the long groove arrived upon at last on long miles and long days of perfect weather and sweeps engineered to perfection.

She was hardly taken. I know how boring it is to hear of other people's dreams, so I kept it simple, relating the strangest dream that seemed to take days and nights with that unbelievable feeling of being real.

"Then it was believable."

"Yes, it was." I didn't request that she refrain from busting my balls first thing on dream description semantics but let it slide, over and out on a summary of strange settings and people from the past and mostly on her, Rachel, comforting me in my spiritual wanderings.

"Me? Comforting your spiritual wanderings? That's a first."

"But it's not. Surely you see your influence."

"I'll try harder." She paused for drama—make that melodrama. "Wait! I think I'm seeing it."

"It's a lay day. What a relief."

"I can imagine. You won't believe this, but I miss you."

"That's believable too." And so on, take care; it won't be long now. Oh, baby.

Well, hell, it was nearly seven forty-five, and the boys were stirring. Tony was born into ranching and couldn't get over how grown men could sleep past daybreak. But he tolerated bad habits, and though he was only forty-four he understood the aches and pains of the road.

By that time Kirk was rattling pans, laying on the bacon, breaking eggs and stacking toast.

Tony said a massage therapist and a chiropractor were willing to come out to treat anyone in need, but he had to know who wanted what, so they'd know if the trip was worth their while. The ranch was a good half hour down a river road that started a half hour out from town.

Mixed in with the moans and groans was the laughter of prisoners informed of liberation; hell, yes, every man among us wanted the crunch and the rub. A Canuck asked how much this was going to cost, wary of being over charged, but he was shouted down, so he said he'd never been to a chiropractor and wanted to know how long the benefits would last.

So I told him he wouldn't hurt as much till his next visit in a few days. I remembered and told the others, "I went to this chiropractor once, and he gave me this questionnaire, and the first question was: *When was the last time you felt really good?* I put: New Year's Eve, 1969."

The others sipped their coffee. Some lit smokes. Some waited for the punch line, as you sometimes must do when elderly people need a minute to sort things out and remember the point intended. I shrugged. "I took some acid. I had a top hat then, and it was snowing. I guess you had to be there."

Acknowledgements

SPECIAL THANKS TO the music makers, the musicians, lyricists, poets and all who captured the age and then some—who gave voice to an idea as old as the ages but long since forgotten, until the 60s. Noted herein:

Sly and the Family Stone, The Beatles, Donovan, Joni Mitchell, Buddy Miles, Mike Bloomfield, Electric Flag, The Chambers Brothers, The Byrds, The Rascals, Creedence Clearwater Revival, Frank Zappa, Janis Joplin, Big Brother & the Holding Company, Jimi Hendrix, Captain Beefheart, Country Joe & the Fish, Joe Cocker, Mad Dogs & Englishmen, the Rolling Stones, Buffalo Springfield, America, Steely Dan, Quicksilver Messenger Service, The Moody Blues, Little Richard, Steppenwolf, Led Zeppelin, David Bowie, Bob Dylan

And the movies: *Full Metal Jacket, The Deer Hunter, Good Morning Viet Nam, Platoon, Born on the Fourth of July* and many more, including the benchmark of reasoned insanity, *Apocalypse Now.*